HOLOCAUST

Key Words in Jewish Studies

Series Editors
Deborah Dash Moore, University of Michigan
MacDonald Moore, Vassar College
Andrew Bush, Vassar College

I. Andrew Bush, *Jewish Studies*
II. Barbara E. Mann, *Space and Place in Jewish Studies*
III. Olga Litvak, *Haskalah: The Romantic Movement in Judaism*
IV. Jonathan Boyarin, *Jewish Families*
V. Jeffrey Shandler, *Shtetl*
VI. Noam Pianko, *Jewish Peoplehood: An American Innovation*
VII. Deborah E. Lipstadt, *Holocaust: An American Understanding*

HOLOCAUST

An American Understanding

DEBORAH E. LIPSTADT

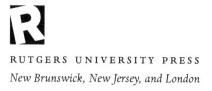

RUTGERS UNIVERSITY PRESS
New Brunswick, New Jersey, and London

Library of Congress Cataloging-in-Publication Data

Lipstadt, Deborah E., author.
    Holocaust : an American understanding / Deborah E. Lipstadt.
        pages cm. — (Key words in Jewish studies ; volume 7)
    Includes bibliographical references and index.
    ISBN 978–0–8135–6477–7 (hardcover : alk. paper)—ISBN 978–0–8135–6476–0 (pbk. : alk.
paper)—ISBN 978–0–8135–6478–4 (e-book (web pdf))—ISBN 978–0–8135–7369–4
(e-book (epub))
    1. Holocaust, Jewish (1939–1945)—Foreign public opinion, American.   2. Public
opinion—United States.   3. Holocaust, Jewish (1939–1945)—Historiography. I. Title.
    D804.45.U55L57   2016
    940.53′18—dc23

                                                                                    2015035675

A British Cataloging-in-Publication record for this book is available from the British Library.

Visit our website: http://rutgerspress.rutgers.edu

Manufactured in the United States of America

To the memory of two dear friends
whose lives were cut short far too early
Debbie L. Friedman (1951–2011)
and
Amelia Eryn Samet Kornfeld (1948–2011)
And you shall continue to be a blessing in my life
and the lives of so many others

Contents

Foreword by Andrew Bush, Deborah Dash Moore,
and MacDonald Moore   ix
Acknowledgments   xi

Introduction   1

1   Terms of Debate   6
   Finding a Name to Define a Horror   6
   Laying the Foundation: The Visionary Role of
   Philip Friedman   13
   Creating a Field of Study: Raul Hilberg   17
   Survivors in America: An Uncomfortable
   Encounter   25
   "Holocaust" in American Popular Culture,
   1947–1962   31

2   State of the Question   46
   The Eichmann Trial and the Arendt Debate   46
   "Holocaust": Shedding Light on America's
   Shortcomings   57
   A Post-Holocaust Protest Generation Creates Its
   Memories   61
   Faith in the Wake of Auschwitz: Shifting
   Theologies   64
   The Baby Boom Protesters   71
   From the Mideast to Moscow: Holocaust Redux?   76
   Survivors: From DPs to Witnesses   82
   Severed Alliances   86
   The Holocaust and the Small Screen   93
   America and the Holocaust:
   Playing the Blame Game   95
   The White House: Whose Holocaust?   98
   The Kremlin versus Wiesel:
   Identifying the Victims   105

3   In a New Key   109
   Counting the Victims, Skewing the Numbers   109
   An Obsession with the Holocaust?
   A Jewish Critique   113

The Bitburg Affair:
The "Watergate of Symbolism"   117
Memory Booms as the World Forgets   124
Assaults on the Holocaust: Normalization,
Denial, and Trivialization   129
The Uniqueness Battle   132
Impassioned Attacks   137
Competitive Genocides?
The Holocaust versus All Others   147
Scaring the People: On How Not to Proceed   151

Notes   155
Index   195

Foreword

The Rutgers book series Key Words in Jewish Studies seeks to introduce students and scholars alike to vigorous developments in the field by exploring its terms. These words and phrases reference important concepts, issues, practices, events, and circumstances. But terms also refer to standards, even to preconditions; they patrol the boundaries of the field of Jewish studies. This series aims to transform outsiders into insiders and let insiders gain new perspectives on usages, some of which shift even as we apply them.

Key words mutate through repetition, suppression, amplification, and competitive sharing. Jewish studies finds itself attending to such processes in the context of an academic milieu where terms are frequently repurposed. Diaspora offers an example of an ancient word, one with a specific Jewish resonance, which has traveled into new regions and usage. Such terms migrate from the religious milieu of Jewish learning to the secular environment of universities, from Jewish community discussion to arenas of academic discourse, from political debates to intellectual arguments and back again. As these key words travel, they acquire additional meanings even as they occasionally shed long-established connotations. On occasion, key words can become so politicized that they serve as accusations. The sociopolitical concept of assimilation, for example, when turned into a term—assimilationist—describing an advocate of the process among Jews, became an epithet hurled by political opponents struggling for the mantle of authority in Jewish communities.

When approached dispassionately, key words provide analytical leverage to expand debate in Jewish studies. Some key words will be familiar from long use, and yet they may have gained new valences, attracting or repelling other terms in contemporary discussion. But there are prominent terms in Jewish culture whose key lies in a particular understanding of prior usage. Terms of the past may bolster claims to continuity in the present while newly minted language sometimes disguises deep connections reaching back into history. Attention must be paid as well to the transmigration of key words among Jewish languages—especially Hebrew, Yiddish, and Ladino—and among languages used by Jews, knitting connections even while highlighting distinctions.

An exploration of the current state of Jewish studies through its key words highlights some interconnections often only glimpsed and holds out the prospect of a reorganization of Jewish knowledge. Key words act as magnets and attract a nexus of ideas and arguments as well as related terms into their orbits. This series plunges into several of these intersecting constellations, providing a path from past to present.

The volumes in the series share a common organization. They open with a first section, Terms of Debate, which defines the key word as it developed over the course of Jewish history. Allied concepts and traditional terms appear here as well. The second section, State of the Question, analyzes contemporary debates in scholarship and popular venues, especially for those key words that have crossed over into popular culture. The final section, In a New Key, explicitly addresses contemporary culture and future possibilities for understanding the key word.

To decipher key words is to learn the varied languages of Jewish studies at points of intersection between academic disciplines and wider spheres of culture. The series, then, does not seek to consolidate and narrow a particular critical lexicon. Its purpose is to question, not to canonize, and to invite readers to sample the debate and ferment of an exciting field of study.

Andrew Bush
Deborah Dash Moore
MacDonald Moore
Series Co-Editors

Acknowledgments

Much of this work was written while I was in residence as a senior faculty fellow at Emory University's Bill and Carol Fox Center for Humanistic Inquiry. I am exceptionally grateful to all those who were at the CHI—fellows, graduate students, and the exceptional staff—who made the act of "doing scholarship" such an exciting, productive, and supportive enterprise. Martine "Tina" W. Brownley and Keith Anthony together with Amy Ebril and Colette Barlow did everything possible to make my stay there a comfortable one. They succeeded beyond measure.

To my Emory colleagues in both the Tam Institute for Jewish Studies and the Religion Department, I extend my thanks for their support and interest. Mary Jo Duncanson was an island of calm and helped me keep track of critical accounts and funds. Danielle C. Pitrone tracked footnotes and sources and saved me countless hours. Lilly M. Faust did important bibliographic research.

To the editors of this series, Andrew Bush, Mac Moore, and Deborah Dash Moore, my deep gratitude for their guidance and insights. I owe particular thanks to Deborah Dash Moore, who during the final stages of this project was a steadfast conversation partner and who endured with great good cheer my myriad ideas and queries. Marlie Wasserman and her team at Rutgers University Press were supportive and encouraging during the book's writing stage and amazingly efficient during the production stage. I am grateful. Eric Schramm's copyediting was elegant and precise.

Though writing and research are a solitary endeavors, most books, particularly one such as this that addresses contemporary culture and experience, are enhanced immeasurably by bright, thoughtful, and inquisitive conversation partners. I had many of the very best. Some of them had no idea that they were providing me with invaluable information and observations when they recalled their personal experiences "encountering" the Holocaust. Grace Cohen Grossman, Sara Bloomfield, Erica Brown, Elka Abrahamson, David Engel, Jonathan Rosen, Leslie Harris, Tim Snyder, Michael Marrus, Peter Joseph, Anthony Julius, Sander Gilman, Michael Berenbaum, Eric Goldstein, Mel Konner, and Wendy Lower.

I wish to thank all those who so graciously agreed to be interviewed by me, including Robert J. Lifton, Peter Balakian, Christopher Browning,

John Roth, Bob Ericksen, Alice Eckardt, Karl Schleunes, Father John Pawlikowski, Carol Rittner, Hubert Locke, Mary Boys, Victoria Barnett, Doris Bergen, and Peggy Olbrecht. Particular thanks goes to Peter Hayes, who pointed out certain lacunae to me when he read the penultimate draft of this book. Sometimes the obvious is so easily missed. And so it was in this case. His comments made this a better work.

My family and friends—large and small—were a wonderful support system during the writing of this book. I have been blessed with special friends in every stage of my life. Two of them died far too early and within a few weeks of each other. No words can summarize what they meant to me. It is therefore with great love and loss that I dedicate this book to them.

Deborah E. Lipstadt
Hartsfield Airport, August 16, 2015

HOLOCAUST

Introduction

In 1945 at the Nuremberg trials in Germany, the word Holocaust was not used.

In 1960 NBC televised the stage production of *Peter Pan* with Mary Martin and Cyril Ritchard. In Act V, as Captain Hook contemplated his plan to make the children walk the plank, he proclaimed with nefarious glee: "A holocaust of children, there is something grand in the idea." There is no record of anyone registering a complaint.

In 1968 the Library of Congress (LOC) added the category "Holocaust. Jewish" to its list of classifications. The classification was assigned to "works on the genocide of European Jews during World War II."

In 1978, when NBC aired its blockbuster miniseries on the destruction of European Jewry by Germany during World War II, it called the show *Holocaust* with no explanatory subtitle, such as *The Destruction of European Jewry*.[1]

In 2011 there were over seventy-five museums and memorials throughout the world with the word "Holocaust" in their name. In the first decade of the twenty-first century well over 900 books were published that had the word in their title. In the twenty years since opening, the United States Holocaust Memorial Museum (USHMM) has welcomed twenty million visitors, making it one of the top tourist attractions in Washington, D.C.

"HOLOCAUST." This is the word most frequently used to describe the murder of Jews by Germans during World War II. Today the word is so firmly and directly linked to the Final Solution, the attempt by Nazi Germany to annihilate European Jewry, that when it is used in another context it is generally modified in order to differentiate it from the Holocaust. When abortion opponents want to conjure up images of dead babies, they speak of the "abortion holocaust." When the animal rights group PETA conducts a campaign about the treatment of farm animals, they call it a "Holocaust on Your Plate." When scholars of slavery want to stress the horrific impact of that institution on African Americans, they refer to the "Black Holocaust."[2] When those concerned about nuclear annihilation want to alert the public, they speak of a "nuclear Holocaust." A Ph.D. student writing a dissertation on the mass killings by the Khmer Rouge in Cambodia entitles it "The Asian Holocaust." When Chinese writers, some of whom have but limited knowledge of the history of the

Holocaust, want to stress the horrors they endured during the Cultural Revolution, they name it "the ten-year holocaust." A Texas graduate student analyzing the tragedies of the Texas dust bowl writes of "the agricultural holocaust."[3]

In contrast, when the word stands without modifier—United States Holocaust Memorial Museum, Holocaust Memorial Day—there is no question as to its meaning. It is so closely linked to the Nazis' attempt to wipe out every Jew within their reach that it requires no specificity. This is true even within discussion of the Nazi Holocaust itself. A recent *New York Times* article reported on the dedication in Berlin of a memorial to "Roma Holocaust Victims." The article noted that the dedication was attended by Roma and Sinti victims of the Nazis' racial purge and "Holocaust survivors."[4]

But it was not always so. The historian Raul Hilberg, who more than any other person helped shape the field of Holocaust studies, observed that "in the beginning there was no Holocaust."[5] There was neither a word nor a field of study. There were few public memorials and barely the language with which to discuss it outside the circles of those most closely connected to the event. Yet the topic was not totally absent from American life. For the first two decades after the end of the war, the Holocaust, as we now call it, was certainly discussed and commemorated, as Hasia Diner has demonstrated.[6] Surprisingly, American popular culture addressed the topic far more than we might imagine, certainly more than political leaders, academics, and even theologians, including rabbis. A few television shows considered the topic.[7] The topic was dealt with in bestselling books and in critically acclaimed and popular movies.

Yet, while the topic was not absent from the American scene, things were quite different from the contemporary situation. There were no memorials on public land. There was no commemoration in the Capitol Rotunda, a ceremony that has taken place yearly since 1978. And there certainly was no use of the proper noun "Holocaust" to describe it. Nathan Glazer in *American Judaism,* one of the earliest scholarly surveys of post–World War II American Jewish life, remarked in 1959 that the Holocaust "had remarkably slight effects on the inner life of American Jewry."[8] The absence in the first couple of decades after the war of a direct impact on what Glazer calls "the inner life" of American Jews may have been more natural and logical than some critics are willing to recognize. It can take a while to integrate personal and communal trauma.

There were instances of opposition to public commemoration and study, sometimes in surprising places. In New York City, home to more Jews as well as more survivors than any other city in the country, repeated attempts by local survivor groups to build a memorial on public land were unsuccessful. In 1947, when the site for one of the proposed but never to-be-built memorials was "dedicated," 15,000 people attended the ceremony. But nothing further happened. Other attempts followed. There were multifaceted reasons for these failures. Many Jewish community leaders, though officially in support of a memorial, believed that communal funds should be used to help needy survivors both in America and in Israel.[9] The most significant obstacle was lack of support from outside the Jewish community. Government officials were decidedly ambivalent about the project. Proponents of the proposal believed that if they could win over New Yorkers at large, that is, non-Jews, they might stand a better chance of gaining a governmental imprimatur. Consequently, they framed the proposed memorial as something that was not "just" about Jews. Rabbi David de Sola Pool, the venerated leader of the oldest Orthodox synagogue in New York, insisted in a letter to the *New York Times* that the monument was not "a strictly Jewish memorial." While it commemorated the six million victims, it also represented all who thought "Nazism repugnant and odious."[10] But even the rabbi's attempt to cast this as a universal effort that would speak to all Americans was to no avail. None of the politicians involved, including those who thought the effort worthy, actively supported it. There simply was no political advantage in doing so. In the early 1960s, when Holocaust survivors tried again, they too failed. Even Jewish community leaders offered only tepid support while New York officials were in outright opposition. They contended that the public parks were "places of enjoyment" and, consequently, not the proper venue to expose people to "one of the most dreadful chapters of human history." Memorials about "distressing and horrifying" events did not belong in New York City parks. When reporters pointed out to one of these officials that New York's parks were already home to monuments that depicted violent events, she justified her opposition by noting that these monuments were limited to moments in "American history." In this instance the Holocaust may have been an event, as James Young observes, of some Americans' history but, according to New York City officials, it was not of "American history."[11]

One of the last arenas to embrace the topic as legitimate for conversation and exploration was academia. Over two decades after the war there were still no university-level courses on the Holocaust. Virtually no graduate students were conducting research on the topic. This may have been a more natural course of events than many people recognize. For a topic to become part of the academic arena one needs research, reading materials, and faculty willing to tackle the topic. (We should note that it took a number of decades for serious nonpolemical courses on Vietnam to become part of the academic agenda.) What is more striking is that a place such as Yeshiva University, America's premier institution of Jewish higher learning, was quite ambivalent about teaching the topic. When Rabbi Irving Greenberg tried to introduce a course on the subject he ran into obstacles from the school. Inexplicably the dean insisted that the course be given the nonspecific title "Totalitarianism and Ideology."[12]

While there was commemoration in the 1950s and 1960s, there is no doubt that it does not compare in any manner to the situation today. As noted, one of the most visited sites in Washington, D.C., is the United States Holocaust Memorial Museum. Located adjacent to the National Mall, it is a federal institution built with the active support of four presidential administrations and countless members of Congress. Every year a Holocaust Memorial Day commemoration is held in the Capitol Rotunda in Washington, arguably one of Washington's most sacred venues and the place where presidents and other select Americans have laid in state. There are city and state memorials throughout the country. College courses on the topic are common in American universities.

How did this happen? There are those who would like to believe that it was all due to the machinations of the Jewish community. Succumbing to a view, probably unconsciously so, that contains traces of antisemitic stereotypes, they insinuate that Jews were able to orchestrate this great attention to the topic. Somehow they were able to ramp up interest among all segments of the American public and they did so for their own limited goals. I shall argue that this view is shortsighted, false, and fails to take into consideration broader developments in both American society at large and in the more narrow confines of the American Jewish community. These authors take an unnuanced view of that which did exist in the 1950s and 1960s and argue that there was no attention to the topic during that era. They do so, it seems, in order to point to the avalanche of remembrance that exists today. There may have been no use of the word Holocaust. There may have been no museums on public lands or university courses. But the topic was not absent from the American scene.

Ultimately, I shall also argue that the evolution of America's "remembrance" of the Holocaust tells us as much and sometimes more about America and the broader contours of American culture and society than it does about the event itself. We shall trace how in the United States the strands of memory, evidence, testimony, and history eventually became not just a narrative with its own distinctive form, but a potent symbol, one with enough power to prompt American presidents to take military as well as political action.[13] We shall ask how a singular genocidal effort waged against one ethnic qua religious group became something to be commemorated in the Capitol Rotunda, America's most prominent public square. How might we explain the fact that the event "lives" for generations that were never directly connected to it, and that it did not "live" in the same proportions for the parents and grandparents who were chronologically far closer to the event?

Because this is a study of the emergence of the Holocaust narrative in American cultural, scholarly, and popular spheres, we shall ask: What did and does this event mean to Americans? How did Americans contextualize it within the orbit of their own history? Few scholarly fields have developed with more rapidity and vigor than this one. A field that was virtually nonexistent but three decades ago is now intellectually vibrant. What does this scholarly evolution tell us, not just about the history it explores, but about the age in which scholars conducted these explorations?

1 Terms of Debate

Finding a Name to Define a Horror

In the immediate aftermath of the war, the search was not for a name but simply for language to describe what had happened. Those who had survived the annihilations perpetrated by the Third Reich struggled to find a vocabulary to describe what had been done to them. The memoirs and articles survivors penned and the interviews they gave during the first years after the war suggest that what they primarily wanted was not a name for this tragedy, but a means to make it comprehensible to those who had not been there. Even as they tried to comprehend what had happened to them, they also sought somehow to get the world—both the Jewish and larger world—to care about it. Many survivors were convinced that "no one who has not had any personal experience of a German concentration camp can possibly have the remotest conception of concentration camp life."[1] Even the newsreels, taken in the days immediately after "liberation," did not, some survivors observed, fulfill the task. In December 1945 Buchenwald survivor Jorge Semprun complained that the newsreel images of the liberated camps failed to give viewers the tools "to decipher them [and] to situate them not only in a historical context but within a continuity of emotions." Consequently, "they delivered only confused scraps of meaning." Ultimately, survivors worried not about epistemology or etymology. They had little concern about the implications of one term or another. The challenge, as a young man observed in 1946, was that "one can never tell enough and present things how they really were."[2] Of course, those who suffered the ultimate fate— death—could not share their experiences. David Boder, one of the first American social scientists to interview survivors systematically and record their experiences, made this point explicitly when he entitled his book *I Did Not Interview the Dead.*[3]

Even "survivors"—a term that did not yet exist in relation to those who emerged from the camps—were not sure how or what to call themselves or what had happened to them. One survivor, Nellie Bandy, who wanted to secure refuge with the U.S. Army after the war ended, went to a checkpoint where she asked an American soldier to be allowed into the camp. He asked, "Well who are you?" She did not say, "A Holocaust survivor" or even "A Jewish survivor of the death camps," both of which might have helped her get what she wanted. None of those names existed for her—or any other survivor—at that time. They lacked the nomenclature to describe what had been done to them. Instead, she concocted a category: "I'm a French political prisoner." The guard checked with his superiors and returned to inform her that he had no instructions for political prisoners.[4]

Even those who had access to the broadest array of evidence found it hard to fully comprehend the extent of the tragedy. Telford Taylor, a reserve colonel in army intelligence, was privy during the war to the most secret German communiqués and other forms of information, many of which contained details about the annihilation of European Jewry. Yet he insisted that he was not really aware of the Holocaust until after the war, when he began to review documents in preparation for his service as chief counsel for the Nuremberg tribunals.[5] Nonetheless, the prosecutorial team subsumed this German attempt to wipe out the Jewish people on the European continent and beyond under the general category of "crimes against humanity" because they did not grasp, or did not want to grasp, that it was something different in scale and scope. When the camps were opened, American journalists, who accompanied the troops, and the publishers and editors who visited at the insistence of General Dwight D. Eisenhower, tended to describe the inmates they encountered as members of an array of ethnic, religious, and political groups—Jews just one among them. Today, an action that was hardly noticed or understood in the immediate aftermath of the war has been transformed and "redefined" as a traumatic event—both symbolic and real—for a broad array of humankind.[6]

Even some intellectuals, many of whom had lost much of their immediate family in the Final Solution, found themselves at a loss as how to describe this event they believed was a singular evil, something separate and apart from the general devastation wrought by the Germans during World War II. Columbia professor of Jewish history Salo Baron mused in the aftermath of the war that the generation which endured this trauma could not "divorce itself from its own painful recollections." For them, writing the history of this "turbulent" episode was very difficult in the extreme.[7] Around the same time Gershom Scholem, a distinguished professor at Hebrew University, someone who left Germany before the Nazi period but whose brother was murdered by the Nazis, made a similar observation: "We are still incapable—due to short distance in time between us and those events—to understand its significance . . . [and] to grasp it in the intellectual and scientific sense. . . . I don't believe that we, the generation who lived through this experience . . . are already capable today of drawing conclusions."[8] That does not mean, as is often assumed, that the topic was ignored. In 1945, in their first issue, the editors of *Commentary* magazine wrote, "Jews . . . live with this fact: 4,750,000 of 6,000,000 Jews of Europe have been murdered. Not killed in battle, not massacred in hot blood, but slaughtered like cattle, subjected to every physical indignity—processed. Yes, cruel tyrants did this; they have been hurled down; they will be punished, perhaps."[9]

Even though no one was looking for a name, it was inevitable that, given the scope of the tragedy, one would emerge. It did so in an organic fashion, that is, no person, leader, or organization decided that "Holocaust" was the name to be used. There were no votes, no board meetings, no campaigns, and no discussions of which word conveyed a particular meaning. It took close to two decades for the Holocaust to become "the Holocaust." Initially, there was an array of other names that were in use. Yiddish speakers tended to speak of the *khurbn,* utter destruction. Deeply rooted in Jewish history, literature, and culture, this word entered the Jewish lexicon as the name for the destruction of the First and Second Temples in Jerusalem.[10] To denote the extraordinary scope of the tragedy, many Yiddish speakers took to calling it *der lester khurbn,* the last or ultimate destruction, or *der dritter khurbn,* the third destruction.[11] Though *khurbn* comes from the Hebrew "to destroy," it had been "Yiddishized" in its pronunciation.[12] For both religious and secular Ashkenazi Jews, particularly those with roots in Eastern Europe, where so much of the killing took place, this was both a natural and appropriate name for this tragedy. *Khurbn* situated it within the context of Jewish history and left no doubt, for those conversant with Jewish tradition, as to its significance. From the victims' perspective it was a deadly accurate term. Their world had been destroyed and those who managed to return home in its wake recognized that it could never be resurrected. The scope of their loss was graphically demonstrated by the recollections of Baron, the first person to hold a chair in Jewish history at an American university. When he testified at the trial of Adolf Eichmann in 1961 he recalled two trips he made to Tarnów, his Polish hometown, after having immigrated to the United States. In 1937, he found a population of twenty thousand Jews, "outstanding institutions, a synagogue that had existed there for about 600 years, and so on." When he returned in 1958, there were twenty Jews of whom "only a few . . . were natives of Tarnów."[13]

Zionists, particularly those already living in Palestine, were committed to the revival of Hebrew as a modern, everyday language, and had a troubled relationship with Yiddish, which they eschewed as the language of the diaspora. It epitomized for them the world of the medieval European "ghetto Jew," a world that they were anxious to escape and which, in their eyes, represented all that they, as "new" Jews, were not. They worked the soil. They had freed themselves from the shackles of their Gentile persecutors. They saw themselves as the diametric opposite of diaspora or "ghetto" Jewry. When attacked, they, the "new" Jews, fought back. (This rather skewed perception of history was rooted more in ideology than historical fact.) The Zionists' contempt for Yiddish and its culture began in the late nineteenth century and was still extant well after the establishment of Israel. At the Eichmann trial (1961), when the representatives of Yiddish newspapers from throughout the diaspora asked that a daily trial summary be prepared in Yiddish, as it was in numerous other languages, a representative of the Israeli Press Office berated them and told them to go learn Hebrew. (A compromise was eventually reached.)[14]

Hebrew-speaking Jews gravitated to a purely Hebrew term. They used *Shoah*, a biblical word meaning complete destruction or devastation.[15] While secular Zionists ardently rejected anything that smacked of religion, they considered the Bible a direct link between the Jewish people and the land of Israel. Therefore the word *Shoah* could appeal to both religious and nonreligious Jews. Even before the killings began, Hebrew speakers used *Shoah* to describe the Nazi persecution of the Jews. In 1937 Moshe Sharett, then head of the Jewish Agency's Political Department, the unofficial equivalent of the Palestinian Jewish community's foreign office, described what was happening in Germany as a *Shoah*. In 1939, shortly before the outbreak of World War II, Zionist leader David Ben-Gurion predicted that a war would "visit upon us a Shoah."[16] In 1940 the Jerusalem-based United Aid Committee for the Jews of Poland published a booklet, *Shoat Yehudei Polin* (the *Shoah* of the Jews of Poland), which detailed the terrible treatment meted out by Germans to Jews during the first years of the war. Those who used this term were neither speaking in a theological register nor predicting the far more terrible treatment that would ensue. What they knew about the fate of their families and coreligionists was bad enough for them to describe it as a *Shoah*. Not surprisingly, the reliance on *Shoah* increased in late 1942 when the Allies confirmed news of annihilation and not just persecution.[17] English speakers, including those in America, used an array of other words, among them "catastrophe," "destruction," "mass murder," "the six million," and "Hitler times."[18] Sometimes, in those very early years, they used "holocaust," but in lowercase and with a modifier attached. As Chaim Weizmann, the president of the World Zionist Organization, wrote to an American rabbi in December 1942, shortly after the Allies confirmed that the Germans were murdering the Jews of Europe and that two million Jews were already dead: "You are meeting at a time of great tragedy for our people. In our . . . deep sense of mourning for those who have fallen . . . we must steel our hearts to go on with our work . . . that perhaps a better day will come for those who will survive *this* holocaust" (emphasis added).[19]

A few months after the war, a Jewish commentator expressed his contempt for those who might try to rebuild Jewish life in Europe: "What sheer folly to attempt to rebuild any kind of Jewish life [in Europe] *after the holocaust of the last twelve years!*" (emphasis added). This practice continued after the war. The official English translation of the Israeli Declaration of Independence (1948) referred to both the "catastrophe which befell the Jewish people" and the "the *Nazi* holocaust."[20] By 1949 the word had come into usage among English speakers working in postwar Europe. Forty years after the war, Franklin Littell, one of the earliest Christian theologians to write and teach about the Holocaust, was surprised when he learned from a scholar who was reviewing Littell's papers that in an August 1949 newsletter that he had circulated while an officer in American Military Government in Germany, he was "using the word freely." Littell speculated that he had "picked up" the term from various organizations and Jewish chaplains who were working with displaced persons, as the survivors were increasingly called.[21]

But at this point it was hardly the universal choice of all English speakers. In his opening remarks at a 1949 conference in New York dedicated to the annihilation of the Jews, Salo Baron, who convened the meeting, possibly translating the term *khurbn*, made frequent referral to the "great Catastrophe."[22] In 1955 the fledgling Yad Vashem, Israel's national memorial to the Holocaust, chose "Disaster" and announced that the study of the annihilation of the Jews would be divided up: "The Approach of the Disaster, 1920–1933," "The Beginnings of the Disaster, 1933–1939," and so forth. Two years later, in 1957, when it published the first edition of its research journal, Yad Vashem had migrated to using the word favored by Baron: "Catastrophe." The editors, reflecting the Israeli tendency at the time to balance the killings with resistance, entitled the journal *Yad Vashem Studies: On the European Jewish Catastrophe and Resistance.* Toward the end of the 1950s some scholars started capitalizing "Holocaust." A number of the papers presented at the 1957 World Jewish Congress included it in their titles. The first mention of the word in conjunction with murder of the Jews in the *New York Times* seems to have been in 1959.[23] By this point Yad Vashem was regularly using "Holocaust." This was probably not the result of any deliberation or discussion. In all likelihood it reflected the choice of translators who may well have been inclined to use a word that was increasingly becoming the synonym for this tragedy. Perhaps, some observers have posited, that it was the translators or editors who chose "Holocaust" because Yad Vashem's official name, the Study Center of *Shoah u'Gevurah,* sounded better in translation as the alliterated "Holocaust and Heroism" rather than as "Catastrophe and Heroism."[24]

In light of the ubiquitous nature of this word in our time, and given the inexorable link between it and the murder of one-third of world Jewry, it is noteworthy that "Holocaust" has Greek—rather than Jewish—linguistic roots. There are Jewish languages from which a name could have been chosen. Hebrew, the language in which Jews have prayed, studied, and communicated for millennia, would certainly have been an appropriate source. So, too, Yiddish and Judeo-Spanish (Ladino), the languages spoken by a major portion of the victims. Moreover, Jewish history has had its marked share of tragedies. Consequently, these Jewish languages already have an array of synonyms available, some of which possess deep-seated roots in Jewish history and tradition. Nonetheless, a Greek word has come to describe the event that virtually destroyed European Jewry. But its origin in a foreign language is not the only thing that has caused some commentators to take note. *Holokaustom* (*holos* 'whole' + *kaustos* 'burnt') means an offering totally consumed by fire. The earliest known usage of the word was by the Greek historian Xenophon of Athens to refer to pagan sacrifices.[25] About a hundred years later the Septuagint, the Greek translation of the Hebrew Scriptures, rendered the word *olah,* the sacrifice the Israelites were ordered to offer (Numbers 28:11) on the New Moon, as *"holocaustos."*[26] In contrast to the other sacrificial offerings, most of which were eaten either by those who brought them or by the priests and Levites, the *olah* was completely burned on the altar. *Olah* is derived from the Hebrew root meaning "go up." The sacrifice literally went up in smoke, as did those murdered by the Nazis.

Does the use of this Greek word in reference to the Nazi annihilation of the Jews suggest that the victims were "sacrifices" who were offered up on an altar? Such a notion runs contrary to basic Jewish doctrine, which eschews any notion of human sacrifice. Furthermore, it could be interpreted as absolving the murderers' guilt and suggesting that the Germans and their accomplices were simply acting as "instruments of the Almighty" by carrying out the divine will. Moreover, depicting Jews as "offerings" implies a Christian theological perspective on the tragedy. According to Christian supersessionist theology, Judaism had been superseded—rendered obsolete—by Christianity. This theological construct posits that, after the rise of Christianity, Jews who insisted on remaining Jews were clinging to an "anachronistic" religion. Over the course of millennia many Christian antisemites justified their actions against Jews by arguing that they were punishing the Jews for their obstinacy and compelling them to see the light of Christianity.[27] All these suggestions about the secondary meaning of the word and the notion that the victims were sacrifices have been rendered moot today because the vast majority of the people who use the term have no idea of its original meaning.

In all likelihood those—both in the scholarly world and outside it—who used this word did not do so because of its theological connotations. Rather, they probably chose it because it was frequently used to denote tragedies, conflagrations, and other mishaps. In common parlance it had long lost the theological connotations it once had, particularly in relation to biblical translations. In 1928 a *New York Times* article about a building that was a firetrap noted that a city official "Fears a Holocaust."[28] In 1934 an article relaying Stalin's perception of the European situation proclaimed that the Soviet ruler was sure the "World [was] Preparing Another Holocaust."[29] In 1936 members of Brooklyn's Junior League gathered to hear a talk on "The Spanish Holocaust."[30] The *New York Times* was not, of course, the only paper to use the term. The *Washington Post,* writing about a major fire in Minnesota, announced "500 Die in Holocaust."[31] Jewish commentators also utilized it to refer to tragedies that had befallen the Jews. In a preface to the English translation of a book about recent events in Jewish history, Rabbi George Kohut, who had been educated in American public schools and at Columbia University, wrote about the Russian pogroms of the early twentieth century: "In one Russian town, . . . an eyewitness informs us, there was a holocaust of Jewish souls."[32] But the word was used for more than just tragedies. The *Los Angeles Times* described an Olympic medal Dutch boxer as "The Holland Holocaust."[33] Even after World War II the word was used in a more lighthearted fashion. In the *Palestine Post,* which would after 1948 become the *Jerusalem Post,* an article on women and housework observed that some clumsy housewives break china and glasses and engage in a "holocaust of housework."[34] Clearly this was a multifaceted word.

By the late 1950s "Holocaust" was increasingly being used in conjunction with the murder of the Jews, but it still did not yet have the singular connotation it has today. That was made abundantly clear when in 1959 Paul Benzaquin published a book about the tragic Cocoanut Grove fire in Boston that took the lives of four hundred people. It was entitled *Holocaust!* Such examples help to explain why there were apparently no complaints lodged against Captain Hook's joyful anticipation of "a holocaust of children." The change in denotation came in the 1960s as a result of a number of unrelated developments, including an international kidnapping, a subsequent Nazi war crime trial, a major scholarly debate about that trial, and speeches given by a little-known journalist and writer who, though he would eventually win the Nobel Prize, initially earned much of his living as a Yiddish journalist and an itinerant lecturer in the North American Jewish community. By the end of the decade the word had become firmly associated with the Third Reich's murder of the Jews.

Even more central to our inquiry than the choice of this particular word is why it took two decades or more from the end of the war for a name to be ascribed to this genocidal event. We form understandings of the past by melding a series of incidents together into a coherent whole and giving it a name. Such was the case with the Protestant Reformation, the Industrial Revolution, the Great Depression, and, ultimately and far more tragically, the Holocaust. By the beginning of the 1960s a name had been ascribed to this genocidal event.[35] But that was only a step. There were many others that had to be taken before one could say that a field of study had emerged in America and that those outside the scholarly realm, that is, the public at large, possessed even the most general concept of what it meant.

Laying the Foundation: The Visionary Role of Philip Friedman

When one of the great historians of the Jewish people, Simon Dubnow, was being deported from the Riga ghetto he reportedly exhorted those Jews who were standing nearby: *"Shreibt und farshreibt* [write and record]." Dubnow's eloquent exhortation may have been superfluous. Even while under the yoke of Nazi oppression Jews were already writing and recording their experiences. In the Kovno ghetto (Kaunas, Lithuania) Jews meticulously documented how they lived and how they died. In Terezin (Czechoslovakia) inmates hid an array of paintings, drawings, diaries, photographs, and documents, all of which depicted scenes of everyday life. After the war those artifacts that were unearthed constituted potent evidence of the victims' resolve not to disappear from the world without leaving evidence of what they had endured. In the Warsaw ghetto, the historian Emanuel Ringelblum created Oyneg Shabbes, a group dedicated to documenting all aspects of ghetto life. Its comprehensive archive, two-thirds of which was retrieved after the war, included reports on cultural activities, children's games, soup kitchens, relations among different groups of Jews, postal delivery, the crucial role women played in sustaining their families, and the ghetto's vast educational system.[36]

After the war survivors, motivated by the conviction that without evidence of the catastrophe the world at large would never fathom the scope of their experience, increased the pace of documentation. Recalling how their Nazi guards taunted them by saying, "Even if you survive no one will believe what you tell them," survivors seemed intent on proving the guards wrong. But they had more immediate motivations as well. They wished to amass a record that could be used to bring their tormentors to justice. Within days of liberation, some camp survivors began to assemble testimony and evidence against their captors.[37] But many former prisoners harbored yet one more goal. "We [wanted] . . . a monument to our fathers, mothers, our brothers, and sisters. We wanted to perpetuate the memory of our massacred parents, our siblings, our children, and our fallen heroes."[38] In the years following the war these efforts, mainly undertaken by survivors, increased exponentially. It was as if these documentarians—amateur and professional—had internalized Dubnow's plaintive cry: write and record.

The Jewish research institute YIVO, founded in Vilna in 1925 but moved to New York in 1940, was also deeply involved in documenting the tragedy even while it was underway. After the war this inclination to document increased exponentially. In December 1945 survivors in the American zone in Germany created the Central Historical Commission. Within three years it had established a network of fifty active local committees based in DP (displaced person) camps in Germany and collected 2,550 personal testimonies.[39] Historians and academics, survivors themselves, convened scholarly conferences. The focus of many of these early gatherings was on methodology. These early researchers understood that the topic with which they were dealing was so large, composed of so many disparate elements, unprecedented in many respects, and ultimately so heartbreaking that they needed a particular methodology to try to make sense of it. In 1947, only two years after the end of the war, Isaac Schneerson, a brother of the Lubavitcher Rebbe, organized a conference in Paris to discuss the "study of the Catastrophe." The attendees attempted, with little result, to coordinate the activities of the disparate groups involved in this effort. In 1949, the Conference on Jewish Relations, an arm of the New School for Social Research, convened a conference on the topic. Participants included Professor Salo Baron, the philosopher Hannah Arendt, and historian Philip Friedman, all of whom had been directly touched to one degree or another by the Holocaust. By 1950 conferences on the methodological problems facing researchers had been held in Paris, New York, Warsaw, and Jerusalem.

But these efforts to document what had happened faced an uphill battle. When the European war ended in May 1945 Jewish woes were subsumed in the horrors that had been inflicted on virtually all Europeans. Millions had been killed. Millions more were homeless or displaced. As the historian Peter Hayes rightly observes, "Amidst seemingly endless devastation and suffering, many people simply could not recognize the distinctiveness of the Nazi onslaught against the Jews."[40]

One man who did recognize the distinctive quality of what had happened was Philip Friedman. He would emerge as one of the pivotal figures in the creation of the field of Holocaust studies in America. He was one of the first historians, if not the first, to design a comprehensive program for its study. A Polish-born Jew with a doctorate in history, he survived the war in hiding. After the end of hostilities, Friedman visited death camps, interviewed survivors, collected evidence about major Nazi perpetrators, authored one of the first books on Auschwitz, and assisted the prosecutors at Nuremberg.[41] In 1946, worried about both the increasingly prevalent expressions of Polish antisemitism and growing communist influence, he left Poland and headed west, eventually ending up in New York, where his former teacher Salo Baron arranged for him to be a research fellow and lecturer at Columbia University. During the next decade his advice and counsel were sought by most of the groups doing work in this area, including Israel's newly founded memorial museum of the Holocaust, Yad Vashem, which sent him the minutes of its meetings and consulted with him on an array of issues. Friedman thought about the Final Solution in a singularly holistic fashion. Most striking was his articulation of some of the crucial historical issues, a number of which would become—and remain—flash points in the conversation about and study of the Holocaust.[42] Two stand out in particular. Friedman was among the first to take issue with the already prevalent assumption that Jews had gone "like sheep to the slaughter." He called for a comparative study of Jews' and non-Jews' responses to German persecution and posited that such a study would demonstrate that the two groups responded in a strikingly similar fashion. Moreover, Friedman argued that a redefinition of "resistance" was necessary. Relying on its narrowest meaning— armed uprising—produced a distorted view of Jews' responses. Shortly after his arrival in the United States he was commissioned to write a book marking the tenth anniversary of the Warsaw ghetto uprising of 1943. Of the fifteen chapters in the book, only three dealt with the revolt itself. The remaining chapters addressed actions that, as Friedman argued and as Ringelblum had before him, also constituted resistance. They included the courage shown by children who smuggled food into the ghetto, the women who fiercely protected their families, and the educators who organized an array of classes even though these were strictly forbidden. Friedman believed that Orthodox Jews' study of Jewish religious texts, something that was also forbidden, constituted a form of resistance. He also considered the actions of the internationally renowned educator Janusz Korczak a form of resistance. Korczak, despite repeatedly being offered refuge outside the ghetto, refused to abandon the children in his orphanage and accompanied them to what he knew was a certain death.

After the war some critics castigated Korczak for his "passive" response. Responding to these critics, Friedman argued that it was "unjust" to ignore the "heroism" implicit in such a response. Even smugglers, he argued, engaged in a form of resistance. They "create[d] confusion in the German production and supply apparatus, and thus caused trouble for the Nazis. Every currency smuggler, every contraband carrier, every peasant who delivered his goods not to the Germans but to the black market, produced chaos in the German economy and forced the Nazis to deploy police and military personnel against this sabotage." But, even while calling for a broader definition of resistance, he was cognizant of the danger of too broad a definition. Friedman recognized that if everything became a form of resistance, then in essence nothing was resistance.[43]

But resistance was not the only subject about which he proved prescient. He addressed a topic that became and remains a matter of heated argument. The *Judenräte*, the Jewish Councils, had been created by the Germans to administer the ghettos. They had to parcel out limited living space, food, and jobs. They also had to draw up the deportation lists, essentially deciding who would live and who would die. Friedman observed that there were hundreds of such councils throughout Eastern Europe. Some were composed of people who had been communal leaders prior to the war. Others were made up of people with no leadership credentials but with whom the Nazis felt they could "work." According to Friedman this complex and multifaceted phenomenon could not be condemned with a broad brush. Some members had assisted the Jewish underground while others "degenerate[d] into a fatal oligarchy . . . of mentality unfit to assume any social responsibility."[44] Some were megalomaniacs who demanded praise and adulation from the ghetto inhabitants. Others were forced to take the job and hated every moment of it. Some continued to justify what they had done long after the war ended without showing any sympathy for the victims.[45]

There was yet one additional area where Friedman's musings anticipated debates that would prevail even into the twenty-first century. Though many Jews would insist that the murder of the Jews constituted a link in the chain of antisemitism, Friedman contended it was far more than "just" that. Adopting a scholarly stance that has only become widely accepted by historians in recent years, Friedman argued that Jews may have been the primary victims, but, had the Nazis won, Jews would have merely been the "first obstacle to be removed": other peoples would have been destroyed as well. The Final Solution, he contended, was a crime visited on the body of the Jewish people but also against humanity in general. He was among the few scholars who addressed the persecution and destruction of the Roma (Gypsies) by the Germans.[46]

Ultimately, what may well be most significant about Friedman's plans for future research was how he focused not just on the event itself, but also on the challenges and problems associated with its study. Acknowledging that studying the Holocaust could become a monument to those who had died, he cautioned against allowing sentimentality to cloud a scholarly perspective.[47] But Friedman did more than just call for a sophisticated methodology. He also took aim in rather unforgiving fashion at some of his fellow survivors. He acknowledged that, while the urge of many survivors to write about what they had endured was "a rather elemental passion . . . [with] deep psychological and sociological roots," much of what had been written was "garrulous, naive, and pseudo-pathetic." It was "inferior" material that was not "objective," and it threatened to overwhelm the "serious research" being conducted.[48] It was not just the fault of the survivors. Interviewers who were already conducting oral histories were "not sufficiently trained for this difficult task," and many survivors were presenting, possibly unconsciously, "personal judgments or wishes as facts." (Forty years later, precisely the same critique would be made about other interview efforts.) Even while berating survivors for sometimes veering from the facts, he took exception with those historians who believed documents—and not victims—constituted the only reliable evidence. He cautioned against writing a history of what Jews had endured based only on documents because, he declared, mincing no words, "The German sources are biased." Histories had to be "balanced and complemented by Jewish records and statements—interviews with Jewish survivors, reports by Jewish groups and individuals. . . . The inner Jewish history, the sufferings and the spiritual life, are rarely or falsely reflected in the German sources."[49] Friedman's warning about relying solely on German documents may have been prompted by what happened at the Nuremberg tribunals, which had constituted the earliest comprehensive historical "retelling" of the atrocities of World War II. Prosecutors were particularly suspicious of those witnesses who had a "strong bias against the Hitler regime"—they meant Jews—whom they believed were more biased than other groups of victims. They would, the prosecutors were convinced, "magnify their persecutions" and turn the Nuremberg proceedings into a "vengeance trial."[50]

Creating a Field of Study: Raul Hilberg

Friedman's warnings about not writing history based only on German documents may also have been prompted by yet another factor. He had encountered a doctoral student who would eventually become the preeminent scholar of Holocaust studies and whose imprint on the field would last for decades. For his part, Friedman would become simultaneously one of this scholar's most passionate advocates and intense critics. Raul Hilberg was a thirty-five-year-old Viennese émigré who, after his U.S. Army service and undergraduate studies at Brooklyn College, went to Columbia for a Ph.D. His dissertation would eventually be transformed into *The Destruction of the European Jews*, a nearly 800-page double-column book. The work eclipsed virtually all other surveys of the Final Solution and provided the context for our understanding of how Nazi Germany's bureaucracy carried out genocide. Among scholars there is a rare, if not unique, consensus that Hilberg's research has "shape[d] the academic study of the Holocaust." Forty years after it was published Yehuda Bauer, one of the outstanding historians of the field, believed it was still an "unsurpassed analysis of the Nazi bureaucracy."[51] It also rendered the United States as a new locus for Holocaust studies.[52]

Despite the fact that Hilberg's *Destruction of the European Jews* has served scholars in the field of Holocaust studies and beyond as the starting point for the vast majority of academic discussions about the Third Reich and the Jews, Hilberg's initial steps in the field were hardly smooth. They tell us something about the way in which study of the Holocaust—there was nothing akin to a "field of study" at the time—was perceived in the United States in the 1950s and into the 1960s. Ph.D. advisers generally urge students to find a topic that has not been addressed by other scholars for their dissertations. Hilberg's experience was different. When he proposed making the Final Solution the topic of his doctoral dissertation he was warned away from it by his Columbia adviser, Franz Neumann. Neumann, a noted scholar who had written *Behemoth: The Structure and Practice of National Socialism 1933–1944*, one of the first scholarly studies of its subject, advised Hilberg that he if he studied the murder of the Jews he would be "separating" himself from the "mainstream of academic research" and entering waters that had been studiously avoided by both the academy and the public. When Neumann saw how determined Hilberg was to proceed, he cautioned him, using a rather macabre choice of words given the topic at hand: "It's your funeral."[53]

Hilberg had already encountered similar academic myopia regarding the Final Solution while a student at Brooklyn College. In a class entitled "The Rise of the National State," his professor, Hans Rosenberg, addressed the development of bureaucracy in England, France, and Germany between the years 1660 and 1930. Hilberg recalled how in his student days, courses on European history always seemed to close with 1930 when the topic was Germany: "There was no history after that." One day Rosenberg made what Hilberg described as an "aside," describing the atrocities committed in the Napoleonic period as "the worst in modern history." When Hilberg challenged him by asking, "What do you call . . . six million dead Jews?" Rosenberg's only response was "That is a very complicated question." It was this incident more than any other, Hilberg insisted, that led him to his life's work.[54]

Mainstream historians and other social scientists had shown a decided lack of interest in the topic. In the 1950s and through much of the 1960s, the major history journals, including the *American Historical Review, Journal of Modern History,* and *Journal of the History of Ideas,* published virtually no articles on the Final Solution. American textbooks did only a bit better. Most of the general histories of both Nazism and World War II appearing in the two to three decades after the war devoted, at best, a paragraph or two to the Holocaust. Rarely, if ever, did the authors integrate the annihilation of the Jews into the larger scope of history of the Third Reich. In these texts the fate of the Jews, if addressed at all, was treated as something separate and apart from the greater history of Nazism, the Third Reich, and World War II. It belonged in the more parochial field of Jewish history.

Some textbooks did address the topic but in puzzling fashion. In the 1962 edition of their classic work *The Growth of the American Republic,* Samuel Eliot Morison and Henry Steele Commager described what the Allies found as they pushed across Europe in 1944: "The Allied armies . . . came upon one torture camp after another—Buchenwald, Dachau, Belsen, Auschwitz, Linz, Lublin. . . . These atrocity camps had been established in 1937 for Jews, gypsies, and anti-Nazi Germans and Austrians; with the coming of the war the Nazis used them for prisoners of all nationalities, civilians, and soldiers, men, women, and children and for Jews rounded up in Italy, France, Holland, and Hungary. All were killed in the hope of exterminating the entire race."

Morison and Commager seemed to suggest that the Final Solution was a series of acts of terror and murder directed against a broad swath of peoples, Jews among them. One might argue that the preceding paragraph was simply a matter of imprecise writing. However, their subsequent comments suggest otherwise. The authors noted that "the pathetic story of . . . the diary of the little *German* girl Anne Frank had probably done more to convince the world of the hatred inherent in the Nazi doctrine than the solemn postwar trials" (emphasis added).[55] The obliteration of Anne Frank's Jewish identity at the expense of her German nationality is startling. Anne did come from a relatively acculturated family where Jewish tradition played a limited role. However, the only reason she was in hiding was because she was a Jew. Even the Broadway and Hollywood adaptations of her diary, which deemphasized her Jewish identity, left no doubt that this was the story of a Jewish girl who was persecuted solely because she was Jewish. Yet Morison and Commager stripped her of that aspect of her identity. Students who read this edition of their textbook might have wondered why a German girl had to be hidden in an attic.[56]

This failure by historians to address the murder of the Jews might be coupled with another trend, which, while somewhat on the scholarly fringe, had emerged in the years immediately after the war. Most closely associated with historians Charles Beard, Harry Elmer Barnes, and William Henry Chamberlin, this movement was commonly known as "revisionism." It postulated that America's decision to enter into World War II was a mistake that both allowed Stalin to commit horrendous crimes and ultimately strengthened the Soviet Union's postwar rule over Eastern Europe.[57] Barnes's attempt to "normalize" Germany and its allies, that is, to turn them into a run-of-the-mill enemy, was made more difficult by the murder of European Jewry. Hence, Barnes and some of those who joined him in this cause found it more convenient to deny the existence of the Nazi genocide. They became the earliest purveyors of Holocaust denial in the United States.

Into this atmosphere of scholarly neglect and diminution of Nazi war crimes, particularly those against the Jews, came Hilberg's book. The book would so upend the status quo in historical accounts of World War II and the Holocaust that, with regard to Holocaust studies, one can legitimately speak of "before Hilberg" and "after." One of the first comprehensive surveys of the destruction of the Jews to be produced in an academic setting, Hilberg's work analyzed the Final Solution as an incremental process whose steps included defining who was a Jew, economically isolating and pauperizing Jews, physically concentrating them, and, ultimately, annihilating them. Using an array of documents gathered by the Allies, he demonstrated how the murder program, rather than being the work of a handful of depraved SS officers, was the product of a bureaucracy that, after receiving general orders, acted almost autonomously to destroy Jews. Hitler indicated what he wanted and the vast German administrative structure ingeniously fleshed out his wishes.[58] Once this bureaucracy started down the path of destruction each subsequent step seemed to almost automatically lead to the next: from identification, to isolation, to pauperization, to concentration and segregation, to annihilation.[59] The book precipitated a fundamental shift in Holocaust historiography. If today Himmler's black-uniformed SS are no longer considered the most prominent and crucial players in the killing process, it is, in great measure, thanks to Hilberg's work. If today we understand that behind the Final Solution was a variegated mosaic of dedicated Nazis, outright criminals, "ordinary" Germans, bureaucrats, desk murderers, and cynical killers, it is thanks to Hilberg's work.⁶⁰ If today we know beyond a shadow of a doubt that the documentary record left by the Germans provides extensive and precise details regarding the process of the annihilation of one-third of world Jewry, it is largely because of Hilberg.

Friedman, who sat on Hilberg's doctoral examining committee, thought the manuscript an exceptionally important contribution to the field. (It is questionable whether there really was a "field of Holocaust studies" when Hilberg's book appeared. In many respects both Friedman and Hilberg created it.) Yet Friedman, it is safe to assume, may well have been bothered by one of the hallmarks of the book. Hilberg relied almost exclusively on German documents and made a principled point of eschewing survivors' testimonies because he did not trust their accuracy. But Hilberg offered a more pivotal explanation for his reliance on Nazi documents and his exclusion of survivors as sources of evidence. In the introduction, he asserted that the book did not concern the victims. "Lest one be misled by the word 'Jews' in the title, let it be pointed out that this is not a book about the Jews. It is a book about the people who destroyed the Jews."⁶¹ Hence, there was no reason to examine what the victims had to say. He was only interested in what the perpetrators did.

But, in fact, Hilberg's assertion that his book was only about the perpetrators was inaccurate. He said as much in the introduction. There he declared that when writing about a destruction process, it is insufficient to focus only on the perpetrators. One must also consider the "interaction of perpetrators and victims." Then he proceeded to offer a devastating assessment of the victims' behavior. According to Hilberg, the Jews did more than just fail to resist. They also completely misjudged their enemy. They thought that they could appeal to the Germans on an "intellectual and moral plane" and reason with them. It was, he insisted, a totally useless, if not ludicrous, thing to do. When these appeals produced no results, Jews attempted another futile tactic, which Hilberg branded "anticipatory compliance." When the Germans decreed that there were to be no pregnancies among Jews in the ghettoes, the *Judenräte* forced pregnant women to have abortions. The Germans did not have to demand it, Hilberg observed; the Jewish leadership took care of it for them in a vain effort to appease the Germans. Hilberg described the Jews as having engaged in behavior he termed "automatic compliance." Masses of Jews—in ghettoes, towns, villages, and camps—"reacted to every German order by complying with it automatically" and by "plung[ing] themselves physically and psychologically into catastrophe."

Hilberg offered a painfully simple answer to the question of how it came to be that the Germans perpetrated "one of the most gigantic hoaxes in world history . . . on [a] people noted for their intellect." The Germans did not have to deceive these people; they "deceiv[ed] themselves." Though Hilberg did not explicitly say so, at the heart of his charges was the assertion that Jews were akin to collaborators in their own fate and were responsible, at least in part, for their own destruction. Hilberg found the explanation for these putative compliant responses in years of a diaspora existence. Over millennia Jews were "a minority . . . [that] had always been in danger . . . [but] learned that they could avert danger and survive destruction by placating and appeasing their enemies." He proclaimed that a "two thousand year old lesson could not be unlearned; the Jews could not make the switch."[62] Though occupying only a few pages, an infinitesimally small percentage of the entire book, these assertions were strategically placed in the introduction and conclusion where they were bound to draw readers' and reviewers' attention. It was a heavy indictment. It would ensnare his important work in controversy for over a decade.

We do not know if Friedman was aware of Hilberg's position on Jewish passivity and culpability; Hilberg did not include this argument in his dissertation, adding it only in the book manuscript.[63] Had he known, Friedman might not have recommended the book for publication. As it was, Hilberg faced significant difficulty in finding a publisher, not only because of the manuscript's subject but also because of its length. With these hurdles in mind, Friedman tried to convince Yad Vashem to co-publish the work with Columbia University Press, thereby fulfilling Yad Vashem's mandate to explicate the history of the Holocaust. Yad Vashem agreed in principle to this proposal. But after reviewing the manuscript, its editorial board withdrew its offer. It primary objections were Hilberg's almost total reliance on German sources, his claims about Jews' millennia of compliant behavior, and his appraisal of Jewish resistance.[64] The board might have overlooked the first objection, but not the latter two. In fact, Yad Vashem historians believed that their concerns with the book were linked: had Hilberg not limited himself to German documents, he might have garnered a broader perspective. Instead he swallowed "their story whole" and was therefore "liable to be deceived and to deceive."[65]

Yad Vashem's response surprised Hilberg. He had anticipated that his view of the impact of a diaspora existence on European Jews was completely in sync with Zionist ideology. For the rest of his life, he was sure that his work was rejected because he did not subscribe to the Yad Vashem view of "Holocaust and Heroism." He failed, in other words, to create a balance between tragedy and Jewish resistance and did not sufficiently value—or value at all—Jewish heroism. Unwilling to back down or modify his words, Hilberg told Yad Vashem that the Jewish response during the Holocaust "was not martyrdom. It was not heroism. It was a pure disaster."[66] Many years later, long after his reputation had been well established as a—if not the—preeminent scholar of the destruction process, he still smarted over this rejection, describing it as "parochial self-preservation."[67] But Hilberg was probably wrong in this regard. It was not his failure to celebrate Jewish resistance that got him into trouble with Yad Vashem. It was his claim that the Jews had collaborated in their own murder. His stance, which could easily have been construed to mean that the Jewish people murdered themselves, was repugnant to the Yad Vashem leadership.

Eventually Hilberg found a publisher and the book appeared in 1961 just as the trial of SS Lieutenant Colonel Adolf Eichmann, one of the organizers of the Final Solution, was beginning in Jerusalem. Despite being the work of a relatively unknown recent recipient of a Ph.D., the book gained the attention of a number of influential journals. Precisely as the Yad Vashem historians feared, his discussion of Jewish passivity, which constituted only a small portion of the book, was what many reviewers highlighted. In his review in *Commentary*, Hugh Trevor-Roper, arguably one of the best-read Anglophone historians, fully and enthusiastically accepted Hilberg's thesis that "the Jews of Europe, obedient to their leaders and to their own habits of mind, collaborated in their own destruction."[68] Andreas Dorpalen devoted a significant portion of his review in the *Journal of Modern History,* a publication that had not paid much attention to the Final Solution, to Hilberg's analysis of the victims' reactions, describing it as "one of the finest sections of the book."[69]

Criticism of Hilberg's thesis was inevitable, however. Writing in the *Jewish Quarterly*, A. A. Roback attacked Hilberg's argument that diaspora Jews are "weaklings" and that the *Judenräte* willingly became a "tool for the destruction of [their fellow] Jews."[70] A few months after Trevor-Roper's review, *Commentary*'s pages were replete with letters strongly complaining about both Hilberg and Trevor-Roper, charging that the two historians had ignored a myriad of examples of Jewish resistance. They had also failed to note that no other group persecuted by the Nazis had reacted differently.[71] The letter writers argued that, had Hilberg been more familiar with Jewish history, he would have known that for centuries Jews have demonstrated a wide variety of responses when their physical safety and collective security were threatened. Sometimes they revolted and sometimes they compromised. Sometimes they were submissive and sometimes they were not. Any assertion of a uniform age-old Jewish response was thus invalid. Other letter writers complained that Hilberg failed to consider the extent of Jewish resistance during the

Holocaust itself. In fact, Hilberg considered instances of Jewish resistance, such as the Warsaw ghetto uprising, but dismissed them as irrelevant. Despite being the first armed revolt against the Germans anywhere in Europe, Hilberg contended, the uprising had had no real impact on the Germans.

A number of World War II historians shared Hilberg's dismissive attitude toward the Warsaw ghetto uprising. Gordon Wright's *The Ordeal of Total War 1939–1945* (1968) lauds the Polish people for their August 1944 revolt against the Germans, describing it as one of the "most heroic chapters in the history of the European resistance." But the author makes no mention of the ghetto revolt that had taken place in the same city sixteen months earlier, led by Jews completely untrained in the ways of combat and with little ammunition and few weapons, but who managed all the same to hold out against the Germans for close to three weeks. In contrast to the Polish resisters, the ghetto fighters fought not in the late summer of 1944, when it was already clear that the Germans were on the verge of defeat, but in April 1943, when the final outcome of the war was far less certain. Nonetheless, their efforts warranted no mention by Wright.[72] Contra Hilberg's argument that the Germans were not significantly affected by the uprising, subsequent deportations from other ghettoes employed many more men and resources to ensure there would be no repetition of Warsaw.

Another serious shortcoming in Hilberg's thesis about the Jews' reactions was his failure to take into consideration the fact that millions of other prisoners, including Soviet POWs and forced laborers, responded with the same "passivity and submissiveness" he attributed to Jews. This is particularly true of the Soviet POWs who were trained as fighters. In his refutation of Hilberg's thesis, Saul Esh, a Yad Vashem historian, observed that the idea for the Haganah, the Jewish fighting force that eventually became the Israel Defense Forces, was born among Russian Jews while they were still in the diaspora. After the Holocaust those same "ghetto Jews," the ones Hilberg decried for having absorbed millennia of passivity, arrived in Palestine and immediately joined the Haganah and helped defeat Arab armies. But these protestations notwithstanding, the idea of Jews being responsible, at least in part, for their destruction had by the early 1960s been strongly implanted in the minds of many, both in the scholarly community and outside of it.

Hilberg was certainly not the first person make this claim about Jewish responses to persecution and annihilation. The prominent psychologist Bruno Bettelheim proffered an even more acerbic critique of Jewish responses. In a *Harper's Magazine* essay, which the editors described as "remarkable," he asked: "Why and how did millions of people go passively to their death?" (Notably, the editors treated this assertion as fact.) The author, the editors insisted, had "strong credentials" to address this topic because he had been in Buchenwald and Dachau in 1938.[73] In this essay, drawn from his then unpublished book *The Informed Heart*, Bettelheim treated the Jewish response more harshly than did Hilberg. Writing at the time that *The Diary of Anne Frank* had already achieved great success as both a book and a Broadway play, he criticized the Franks for not having armed themselves with a "gun or two," something, he rather blithely declared, they could have done had "they wished." Then they could have shot the police who came to take them away, he argued. He berated Otto Frank for teaching the children "academic high-school subjects . . . rather than how to make a getaway." Instead of preparing themselves to fight, they "walk[ed] to their death." Like Hilberg, he found the roots of this behavior in the Jewish diaspora mentality. Instead of "march[ing] as free men against the SS," millions of European Jews "grovel[ed], wait[ed] to be rounded up for their own extermination, and finally walk[ed] themselves to the gas chambers."[74]

There were many shortcomings in Hilberg and Bettelheim's arguments, some of which we have already mentioned, for example, their glib and somewhat inaccurate rendition of millennia of Jewish responses to persecution. In addition to portraying Jews as having "behaved homogeneously," they asserted that Jews should have divined what was in store for them. This suggests that German policies developed in a linear fashion. In fact, these policies evolved in fits and starts. Hilberg and Bettelheim's problematic assertions could be traced to their having failed to ask the two questions necessary for properly assessing Jewish reactions: "What did they know?" and "When did they know it?"[75] Holocaust survivors, among those most distressed by arguments similar to those of Hilberg and Bettelheim, expressed a sense of feeling under assault, a sentiment they had experienced repeatedly since their arrival in America.

Survivors in America: An Uncomfortable Encounter

In October 1943 Heinrich Himmler, second in command to Adolf Hitler, declared to SS leaders assembled in Posen that the "annihilation of the Jewish people" was a glorious page in the history of the Third Reich and the SS, but one that would "never be written." Had the Nazis succeeded in their task of wiping out the Jews, Himmler's prediction might have come true. Indeed, the ultimate irony for Himmler's forecast is that much of what has been written on the Final Solution has come from the very people—literally—whom he and his cohorts hoped to exterminate.[76]

The survivors may have escaped annihilation but their postwar road to recovery, including in America, was neither easy nor smooth. The American experience of Holocaust survivors tells us a great deal about them and even more about the society in which they were now trying to find their way. In recent decades, once the Holocaust became firmly rooted in the American narrative, survivors began to be treated with great deference, if not reverence. Invited to various venues to share their wartime experiences, survivors have been videotaped, interviewed, and feted. Their stories have been dubbed "testimonies," giving them an added quasi-forensic gravitas as researchers eventually recognized their value. But such was not always the case.

In an earlier generation, such testimony was treated as dubious, and so were survivors themselves. In 1945, when the war ended and the Jewish survivors were in desperate need of aid, American Jews rose to the occasion in impressive fashion. Jewish organizations of every outlook and stripe raised funds and offered various forms of assistance in order to enable the survivors to rebuild their lives.[77] When the U.S. Congress passed an immigration bill that made it almost impossible for survivors to enter this country, Jewish organizations vigorously fought it. (Ironically, the bill favored Baltic agricultural workers, including those who had allied themselves with the Germans, and even some who had taken part in killing operations.) They did so despite the fact that there was a strong public sentiment in America against admitting Jewish survivors.[78] After intense lobbying, the bill was amended in the early 1950s such that substantial numbers of survivors were able to immigrate. An array of Jewish organizations ensured that these "New Americans," as they were often known, received material aid. When it came to helping and supporting the survivors, American Jews saw themselves "as responsible for 'our European brothers.'"[79] Yet this is only part of the story. To cast this as a purely benevolent relationship, an "unfailingly upbeat . . . postwar narrative of triumph," is to mask its serious complexities. It is, as Beth Cohen observes in her study of how America treated the survivors, "comforting" but not true.[80]

American Jewish attitudes toward survivors could be read in the various labels applied to them, which the survivors did not choose and in fact often resented. Thus these monikers tell us more about those who used them than about the survivors themselves. Initially, survivors in America were often labeled "victims," that is, objects of pity. They were also called *griners*, the Yiddish equivalent of "greenhorn," a newcomer who, unaware of the cultural and sociological mores of the society, is easily duped. One finds a more euphemistic term in some of the literature, especially with regard to what they endured: "the ones who were there."

Even after survivors had settled in America, they were often called DPs or refugees, people who had no place to which to return. This rankled many survivors, as Hannah Arendt noted three years after her arrival in America:

> In the first place, we don't like to be called "refugees." We ourselves call each other "newcomers" or "immigrants." Our newspapers are papers for "Americans of German languages." . . . A refugee used to be a person driven to seek refuge because of some act committed or some political opinion held. Well, it is true we have had to seek refuge; but we committed no acts and most of us never dreamt of having any radical political opinion. . . . Now "refugees" are those of us who have been so unfortunate as to arrive in a new country without means and have to be helped by refugee communities.[81]

Many survivors intuited that, irrespective of what American Jews called them, behind the names lurked feelings of "pity, fear, revulsion, and guilt."[82] While much was offered, certain things were not. Elie Wiesel recounted many survivors' experience: "People welcomed them with tears and sobs, and then turned away. I don't mean parents or close friends; I speak of officialdom, of the man in the street. I speak of all kinds of men and women who treated them as one would sick and needy relatives. Or else as specimens to be observed and to be kept apart from the rest of society by invisible barbed wire. They were disturbing misfits who deserved charity, but nothing else."[83]

They were survivors of genocide, something that fundamentally distinguished them from most other immigrants to these shores. They needed a particular kind of help and in most cases did not get it. One reason for this arm's-length behavior may have been status. At a time when American Jews were celebrating their increased assimilation into the fabric of American society, these new arrivals were foreign, reminiscent of the fact that, but a short generation earlier, Jews had been far from the American mainstream. There was, however, another reason why American Jews might have kept survivors at a distance. Their stories beggared belief. One survivor recalled how in 1951 her American-born Jewish neighbor told her, after hearing her story about selections and gas chambers, that she ought to become a novelist because she had a "terrific imagination." The neighbor even counseled other people in the apartment building to go hear the stories: "She has some imagination." Other people believed the survivors but harbored the suspicion that the newcomers had done something untoward—if not unethical—in order to avoid being murdered. Americans knew of the terrible fight for survival that took place in the camps. Many concluded that "the only people who could have survived were those who would perform the amoral acts necessary to preserve life in the circumstances the Nazis created."[84] There were psychiatrists, some of whom conducted the earliest studies of survivors and of their children, who promulgated the same notion. One doctor who treated survivors declared: "There is reason to believe that a person who fully adhered to all the ethical and moral standards of conduct of civilian life on entering the camp in the morning, would have been dead by nightfall."[85] In other words, to be survivors, victims had to become perpetrators. This perception took a very long time to disappear. In the late 1980s Lawrence Langer, immersed in interviews with Holocaust survivors, was "stunned" when a friend categorically "condemned all Jews who worked in any capacity for the Germans in the camps as 'collaborators.'"[86] The unarticulated corollary of this doubt qua accusation was that the genuine heroes, those who were truly unblemished, were the victims who had not survived.[87]

Yet another common American perception of the "victims" was that, pliant and incapable of taking action, they had let this happen to them. This view, buttressed by the writings of Bettelheim and Hilberg, cast the Jewish victim as weak, passive, and even pitiable. As one survivor recalled, "We were ashamed. We were made to feel ashamed."[88] In addition to the "shame, there was fear—and the reality—of stigma." Many survivors decided that instead of talking, they would keep silent and try to "pass . . . for normal."[89] In the eyes of many of their fellow Americans—including their relatives—survivors now had only one identity. "People would meet me and say, 'OHHHHH! Did you know that he was in a concentration camp?!' That's all it was left to! Nobody asked about it. Nobody asked, 'How was it there?' Just, 'He was in a concentration camp.' It was a pity; that was that. 'This is my nephew,' my uncle would introduce me, 'you know he was in a concentration camp.'"[90]

Upon their arrival in this country survivors were cautioned—often adamantly—by fellow Jews to be discreet about speaking of their experiences. They were explicitly told that if they wanted to acclimate to American society they had best set the past behind them. "Hush up your bad dreams," their American cousins told them. One survivor, having just arrived, was warned by his aunt: "If you want to have friends here in America, don't keep talking about your experiences. Nobody's interested and if you tell them, they're going to hear it once and then the next time they'll be afraid to come see you."[91] Some survivors may not have wanted to talk. But others who did refrained from doing so out of fear that people did not want to listen. "I personally would have felt much better if I could have talked about it. . . . Nobody cared. I mean, people, everyone was talking that they didn't want to hear about it. They didn't want to listen. No, they said 'We heard about it.' Or, 'We don't want to hear about it because we saw the newsreels.'"[92]

There were those among the survivors who refused to be silenced. Ruth Kluger, in her powerful memoir, *Still Alive,* recalls how an aunt cautioned her "to make a new beginning . . . to forget what they did to you. Wipe it off like chalk from a blackboard." The teenage Kluger refused to do so and told her aunt that. "You can't throw away your life like old clothing. . . . Would she want to wipe away her own childhood? I have the one I have."[93] Henry Greenspan, who has interviewed many survivors, describes that silencing as "blunt and undisguised." On occasion it may well have been motivated by good intentions, that healing would be quicker if a survivor were to forget her terrible past. But it also may have been motivated by a typical American sentiment. This country prizes those who seize the opportunities offered them. It celebrates those who take advantage of its gifts and "pull themselves up by their bootstraps" in order to achieve a better life than what they had before. America loves winners, not whiners. Indeed, the one group of survivors who fared better after the war were the resisters. They epitomized not the frightened but the *fighting* Jew. They had reacted and taken their fate into their own hands.[94]

Some survivors recognized the American impatience with dwelling on the past.

> So, so, what are we going to do? Ask the people for sympathy?! Come on! I am a survivor of the Holocaust! . . . NO! We had to adapt ourselves to the mainstream of the country. To make a new life. To fend for ourselves. . . . In the most beautiful country in the world. . . . You come to a big country like this; you're a drop in the bucket. You have to make your own way of life. Here, it's different. It's individual. Everybody is for themselves! And you have to survive.[95]

Thus in the 1950s and early 1960s the survivor story in all its detail was rarely heard outside the circles of fellow survivors and a limited number of American Jews. Survivors spoke about their experiences but primarily "within the family," meaning with other survivors and their offspring. One survivor recalled how in the initial years after arrival in the United States, survivors would gather, not with American friends, but with "five, six couples, survivors coming to our house on the Sabbath, having a little lunch, . . . comparing each other's suffering, telling how it was, talking about how by miracle we survived this selection. . . . I think this was really beneficial to us. . . . We didn't keep it inside."[96]

Then there were those survivors who did not speak out because of a particular fear: "Nobody will *want* to believe us."[97] Primo Levi recalled how inmates all had a dream that, though it may have varied in detail, was "uniform in substance." They would return home and upon telling a loved one what they experienced, they "were not believed, indeed were not even listened to."[98] Levi and his fellow inmates were not wrong. Survivors found that a curtain of silence separated them from the Americans who hosted them upon their arrival in in this country. Even relatives often failed to ask about the fate of close family members. "No one asked," one survivor recalled.

As had Jewish immigrants before them, they formed or joined *Landsmanschaftn,* Jewish benevolent aid societies, composed of people from the same towns and regions. First founded during the mass Jewish immigration of the late nineteenth century, these organizations were generally organized by groups of immigrants in order to provide ties "of sociality and mutual aid." But, in contrast to the typical immigrants, Holocaust survivors were not just waxing nostalgic for a life left behind. They were mourning a community and a family that had been ripped out from under them. That is why for so many survivors the most appropriate term for the Holocaust was *khurbn.* Their world had been completely devastated. It was no more. The safest venue for telling one's story was among those who had shared your experiences and your losses.[99] Even those who in the late 1950s and early 1960s tried to somehow join the survivors in their pain came to recognize that there were barriers that could not be traversed. Rabbi Irving "Yitz" Greenberg recalls going to Yom HaShoah commemorations and services. He quickly discovered that they were organized by survivors for survivors. He was clearly an outsider. "It felt," he recalled, "like we were crashing a funeral."[100]

With few people to talk with about their experiences, survivors often turned to another form of communication: writing. In the late 1950s Philip Friedman told Raul Hilberg that survivors' writings were "too numerous to catalog." He estimated that there already were 18,000 memoirs.[101] Around the same time, when Elie Wiesel tried to find a publisher for his now iconic book *Night,* many rejected the manuscript because, they said, too much had already been written on the topic. In his introduction to the French edition of *Night,* François Mauriac acknowledged that Wiesel's was one among a myriad of Holocaust memoirs when he wrote of "this personal record *coming as it does after so many others*" (emphasis added).[102] As with Wiesel's manuscript, most publishers both in Italy and America rejected Primo Levi's memoir on Auschwitz, which eventually became one of the most cited accounts of camp life, because there already were so many books on the topic.

There is thus no room to assert that there was a blackout in America about the Holocaust during the 1950s. Rather, as Hasia Diner has shown, survivors were conducting an active though unstructured conversation about the Holocaust during this period.[103] Active as it may have been, it does not, of course, compare with what exists today. That, in part, may explain why many people believe there was no interest in the Holocaust at that time. Compared to what exists today it was paltry. Seen in its own context it was hardly that.

"Holocaust" in American Popular Culture, 1947–1962

Holocaust survivors were not alone in grappling with the Holocaust. Popular authors and filmmakers in the United States—Jews and non-Jews, most with no connection to the tragedy—were doing so as well. Understandably, they would take a decidedly different approach from that of the historians discussed above. They would place far greater emphasis on the personal experience of the victims. In so doing they often strayed from history in order to personalize the Holocaust in ways that historians did not. Finally, they were writing as Americans who had experienced the war. All this, of course, would give their books great sway with the public at large. In a certain respect many of the works cited in the following pages were more about America and the American experience than they were about the mass murder of the Jews. Beginning in the first years after the war and continuing until contemporary times, authors of fiction have often relied on the Holocaust as a tool for interpreting America and American culture.

In 1948 five books about World War II were on the *New York Times* best-seller list. As literary critic Leah Garrett observes, all five had Jewish soldiers as their central character, and, of those set in Europe, all made the mass murder of Jews a dominant theme. The five were Norman Mailer's *The Naked and the Dead,* Irwin Shaw's *The Young Lions,* Ira Wolfert's *An Act of Love,* Merle Miller's *That Winter,* and Stefan Heym's *The Crusaders.* There was also a sixth book with a similar theme that sold well but did not make the best-seller list, Martha Gellhorn's *The Wine of Astonishment.*[104] In each of these books a Jewish soldier must contend with the antisemitism of fellow soldiers.[105] These books were not directed strictly to a Jewish audience and, given their sales, were clearly of interest to a broad American readership. What is striking is that, of the four books that are set in Europe, all culminate with the liberation of Dachau.

The fate of European Jews was described in explicit terms. For example, in *The Young Lions* Shaw writes: "The men in the trucks fell quiet as they drove up to the open gates. The smell, by itself, would have been enough to make them silent, but there was also the sight of the dead bodies sprawled at the gate and behind the wire, and the slowly moving mass of scarecrows in tattered striped suits who engulfed the trucks and

Captain Green's Jeep in a monstrous tide."[106] Gellhorn, considered one of the greatest war correspondents of the twentieth century, vividly described the liberation of Dachau in *The Wine of Astonishment*, no doubt recalling having been present when Dachau, Ravensbrück, and Buchenwald were liberated. "On the right was the pile of prisoners, naked, putrefying, yellow skeletons. There was just enough flesh to melt and make this smell, in the sun. The pile was as high as a small house." In Miller's *That Winter* the protagonist, who has been subjected to antisemitic taunts in his army unit, is at Dachau when one of the newly liberated inmates discovers the soldier is Jewish. When the inmate kisses his liberator's hand, the soldier recognizes that he has closer ties to this Polish Jew than to his fellow American GIs who have made his life so miserable.[107] In all these books the European tragedy is not treated as something separate from the war. It is integral to it. As time progressed and interest in the Holocaust grew, however, these two topics would be rent asunder, both in most popular culture and in virtually all scholarly work. Only in the twenty-first century would the two be once again brought together.

In 1950, John Hersey, a Pulitzer Prize–winning writer for the *New Yorker*, author of a groundbreaking report on Hiroshima to which the magazine had devoted an entire issue, made the Holocaust the subject of his next book, *The Wall*. This *roman á clef* told the story of the Warsaw ghetto uprising. Many readers were convinced that this novel, which was over 600 pages, was completely factual and asked Hersey about the ultimate fate of some of the characters. A Book of the Month Club selection and a *New York Times* best seller, Hersey's book was reprinted by publisher Knopf-Borzoi three times alone in its first month of publication and was also serialized in *Harper's Bazaar*. Overall it was the fourth bestselling book of 1950.[108] In order to write the book, Hersey immersed himself in a wide array of historical material on the Holocaust. Critics credited him with having opened for the English reading public "the doors to Holocaust hell."[109] While Hersey had been shaken by the total destruction he encountered in Europe after the war, he also had been uplifted by finding among Jews a "certain optimism . . . for in each case there were survivors . . . [proving] that mankind is indestructible." He was particularly buoyed to learn that in the Warsaw ghetto Jews had created, as he recounted, "a semblance of civilization (theaters, concerts, readings of poetry), and the rituals of everyday human intercourse." In that rich cultural life, Hersey found what he described as "the only hope man has of rising above his unmentionably horrible existence, his foul nest of murder, war, greed, madness, and cruelty."[110] The Jews who created this cultural treasure trove in the face of intense suffering were for Hersey models of hope and optimism.

Hersey injected a universalistic tone into the story of a failed uprising and the tragedies of ghetto life. That may explain why American audiences read it with such enthusiasm. Hersey's Jewish heroes became ideal men and women. After the failed uprising Rachel, one of the central characters who had been forced to take refuge in a sewer, declares that as far as "our religion is concerned, I think there is only one thing: not to hurt anybody. For me, the whole of the Torah is in one sentence in Leviticus: 'Thou shalt love thy neighbor as thyself.'" That verse so formed her life that she posits she would adhere to it even if her neighbor were a Nazi. "How else [can one] cure him of being a Nazi?" Her interlocutor proposes that there might be no cure for someone who is a Nazi: "Maybe you have to kill him." Rachel responds: "I have tried that and where did it get me? Where am I now? In a sewer."¹¹¹ It is this turn-the-cheek universalism that may well have appealed to many Americans in the 1950s. Hersey painted this struggle not as a battle against antisemites who would destroy the Jewish people, but as one against enemies of humanity. At the end of the novel the narrator, a survivor of the ghetto, declares that he wants to survive in order "to contribute my share, no matter how trifling, to the defeat of Anti-Humanity." For Hersey these Jews were the epitome of Western humanism. Interestingly, he did not advocate Jewish assimilation to the point of disappearance. He called for Jews to emerge from the ghetto "*as Jews.*" Having done so, Hersey continued, "*they would then engage—if not lead—in a worldwide 'cultural cross-fertilization.'*" According to Hersey this cross-fertilization offered the only promise "*for human development. Humanity must be the synthesis, the sum, the quintessence of all national cultural forms and philosophies*" (emphasis in original).¹¹²

Hersey's portrait of a people with a *Weltanschauung* rooted in humanistic, as opposed to parochial, beliefs must have spoken to a broad American audience in the 1950s. The book was praised in both the general and Anglo Jewish press. The Yiddish press took a somewhat different view. It credited Hersey, a non-Jew, for taking on this topic and handling it so sensitively, but faulted him for writing a novel "of a universalist, triumphant human spirit" which failed to capture the particular campaign the Germans had waged against the Jews.¹¹³ Most importantly, Hersey had elided the antisemitism that the Yiddish press believed was a critical element of the Final Solution, if not *the* critical element. None of those criticisms, however, affected the way Americans embraced the book.

Laura Hobson's novel *Gentleman's Agreement,* published in 1947, was yet another book with antisemitism as a central theme. It won critical praise and popular acclaim, remaining at the top of the best-seller lists for months. Translated into thirteen languages, it sold more than 1.6 million copies.[114] The film adaptation of the same year, produced by Twentieth Century–Fox and starring Gregory Peck, won numerous awards, among them the Academy Award for Best Picture. The story depicts Phil Green, a reporter for a prestigious New York–based magazine, on assignment to explore the issue of antisemitism. He chooses to do so by posing as a Jew in order to see the problem from the inside. He immediately encounters the vicious but polite antisemitism of upper-crust, wealthy, and privileged Americans. He is turned away from swanky hotels, subjected to taunts by fellow diners in fancy restaurants, and confronted by thinly disguised hostility from the WASP residents of an exclusive Connecticut town. His son is also taunted on the playground. Green's fiancée, a wealthy, privileged woman, becomes exhausted by the turmoil his charade has brought into her life. Agitated by the prejudice he has uncovered among her family and friends, she declares to Green that she is pleased to be "good looking instead of ugly, rich instead of poor, young instead of old, healthy instead of sick."[115] In her eyes being Jewish is naught but an illness, one that cannot be cured. Eventually, as a result of her encounter with Green's Jewish army buddy, she comes to see the error of her ways.

While the Holocaust was not specifically mentioned in the narrative, the entire premise of the plot—the way in which prejudice hurts the victim and distorts the values of this country—only makes sense viewed against the backdrop of the murder of European Jewry. In fact, Hobson had already been writing about the topic. Her first book dealt with the plight of Jewish refugees trying to escape from Europe. More importantly, *Gentleman's Agreement* takes a particularly American slant. It posits that prejudice and hatred, which the men in the story had just spent four years fighting, was alive and well in the United States. Polite, shrouded in innuendo, and nonviolent, it hurt people and negated this country's fundamental principles. Both Hobson and filmmaker Elia Kazan placed the problem of antisemitism within the larger story of prejudice in general. When he is turned away at an exclusive resort Green explodes, describing the hotel management to be "persistent little traitors to everything this country stands for and stands on." He then issues a straightforward challenge to Americans: "You have to fight them. Not just for the 'poor, poor Jews' . . . but for everything this country stands for." (African Americans were decidedly absent from this formulation, however.)

Gentleman's Agreement was not the only movie made in 1947 that had antisemitism as its theme. *Crossfire,* starring Robert Young and Robert Mitchum, is the story of the murder of a Jew by American soldiers who have just returned from Europe. The detective must tease out the fact that antisemitism was the reason for the murder. The movie, which was nominated for five Oscars, conveys the message that, while we may have defeated an enemy overseas, some of the same hatred that motivated this enemy is to be found in our own ranks. The Holocaust and the antisemitism that was its cornerstone became a metaphor here for American prejudice and discrimination.

While neither film addresses the Holocaust head on, together with the aforementioned novels they may rank among the earliest expressions of what has become known as the "Americanization" of the Holocaust. This Jewish tragedy becomes a flashing red light signifying a danger to the fabric of American life. While these works threw down the gauntlet regarding the eradication of prejudice in America, most formulated Jewish identity in a fashion entirely fitting for the 1940s. They transmitted a message that there is nothing distinctive about Jews except for their exposure to antisemitism. This was especially clear in *Gentleman's Agreement,* in which Jews were cast as members of a religious faith not terribly different from Christianity. While passing as a Jew, Phil Green never changes his lifestyle, attends a synagogue, or observes any Jewish practice or custom. When his young son asks him what a Jew is, Green struggles for an answer, eventually telling him that while some of his friends go to church, Jews go to synagogue. In reality, he does not "live as a Jew"; nothing about his life changes except for the fact that everyone around him is told his name is Philip Green and he is a Jew. As Sara Horowitz observes, the only thing that distinguishes him is the antisemitism he faces. His "Jewishness becomes emptied of meaning. [It is] a cipher."[116]

In 1952 *The Diary of Anne Frank* surpassed the great success of both *Gentleman's Agreement* and *The Wall* in the United States. Originally published in the Netherlands in 1947, the diary appeared in German and French editions in 1950 before being published in America with an introduction by Eleanor Roosevelt. It quickly became a best seller.[117] The Broadway adaptation (1955) won a Pulitzer Prize, Tony Award, and New York Critics Circle Award. After over one thousand performances, the play was produced in cities throughout the United States. The Hollywood feature film (1959) led to renewed interest in the book.[118] For many Americans it became and remains an entry point to the Nazi persecution of the Jews and one of its most "enduring popular symbols."[119] Many reviewers and readers seemed to believe that the diary "could really manifest the actuality of the mass murder of European Jewry."[120]

There are various explanations for the way American audiences embraced Anne Frank's diary. It is an endearing story of a young teenager's struggles as she matures into adolescence. She shares her fears, emotions, enthusiastic likes, and intense dislikes in an unaffected style and deals with situations common to teenagers, including sex, "love affairs," parents, and the meaning of life. In that respect, it is not that different from thousands of other books with teenage protagonists. Yet, given that the threat of capture and annihilation was always looming, it bears no resemblance to such books, while still remaining an accessible gateway into the woeful story of the Holocaust. There is limited horror here. No one physically suffers. No one is incarcerated in a camp. No one starves. And no one dies of exposure, starvation, illness, or gassing. Great danger hovers over the eight people hiding in the secret annex, but it never enters until the terrible moment at the end. The fate of those in the annex is now clear, but viewers are left to imagine it.[121] Some critics have been contemptuous of the fact that, given this relatively mild representation of genocide, it has become the iconographic diary of the Holocaust. Political theorist and Holocaust escapee Hannah Arendt, echoing these sentiments, described it in her rather acerbic style as "cheap sentimentality at the expense of great catastrophe."[122]

However, events outside the hiding place do enter Anne's diary in the form of a number of heart-rending entries. She may be an adolescent struggling to figure out the world around her, but she is not unaware of the fate of those Jews who do not have the good fortune to have such a hiding place. On October 9, 1942, she bemoaned the fact that "our many Jewish friends are being taken away by the dozen. . . . Without a shred of decency, being loaded into cattle trucks and sent to Westerbork. . . . If it is as bad as this in Holland whatever will it be like in the distant and barbarous regions [the Jews] are sent to? We assume that most of them are murdered. The English radio speaks of their being gassed." The following month, on November 19, she described what was taking place in Amsterdam. "The Germans ring at every front door to inquire if there are any Jews living in the house. If there are, then the whole family has to go at once. . . . It seems like the slave hunts of olden times." That same month Anne described seeing a group of Jews being marched through the street. They are "good innocent people accompanied by crying children, walking on and on . . . bullied and knocked about until they almost drop. No one is spared—old people, babies, expectant mothers, the sick . . . all join in the march of death." Toward the end of their time in hiding, on April 11, 1944, in a fashion that belied her youth, she wrote about what was happening:

> We have been pointedly reminded that we are in hiding, that we are Jewish in chains. . . . We Jews mustn't show our feeling, must be brave and strong. . . . Who has inflicted this upon us? Who made us Jews

different from all other people? Who has allowed us to suffer so terribly up till now? It is God that has made us as we are, but it will be God, too, who will raise us up again. If we bear all this suffering and if there are still Jews left, when it is over, then Jews instead of being doomed, will be held up as an example. . . . We can never become just Netherlanders, or just English, or representatives of any country for that matter, we will always remain Jews, but we want to, too. (April 11, 1944)

These kinds of observations, while not frequent, call into question the accusation of cheap sentimentality, making it clear that Anne understood the fate that awaited them if they were discovered.

For the purposes of our inquiry, of even greater importance than Anne's poignant comments is what happens to those comments as the book made its way to stage and then to film. Most of them disappeared and were replaced by the playwrights' far more universalized musings: "We're not the only people that have had to suffer. There've always been people that have had to . . . sometimes on race . . . sometimes on another."[123] This was not the only change the playwrights made. In addition to universalizing Anne's sentiments, they gave their rendition of the *Diary* a gauzy optimism. Absent from the production are Anne's declarations that "there's in people simply an urge to destroy, an urge to kill, to murder and rage" and that as a result of the war "everything that has been built up, cultivated, and grown will be destroyed" (May 3, 1944). Instead the play ends with an affirming epigraph. Anne's disembodied voice can be heard proclaiming for a second time: "In spite of everything, I still believe that people are really good at heart." Gone is the line that follows. In it Anne speaks of an "ever approaching thunder" that was already causing the "suffering of millions" (July 15, 1944). A bitter Otto Frank, having just returned from the camps to discover that none of his family survived, shakes his head and sadly notes, "She puts me to shame." It was an uplifting end to a tragic tale. This paean to the power of human goodness, brimming as it is with naïve optimism, has become the iconographic statement of an already iconographic book. It is so famous that, as Lawrence Graver discovered, many people, including the editors of the *Oxford Companion to American Theatre* (1992) and the *Cambridge Guide to American Theater* (1993), believe it is the last line of Anne's diary. It is not.[124]

This universalization and optimism were not present by chance. Despite the fact that, with the exception of Otto Frank, all the residents of the annex had been murdered, the director, producers, and writers wanted the play to be one of affirmation. Expressing a typical American note of optimism, director Garson Kanin told the *New York Times* shortly before the play opened that "Anne Frank was certainly killed but she was never defeated." In a statement that today sounds ludicrous, Kanin insisted that he did not consider the play "a sad play" and had no "wish to inflict depression on an audience."[125] Kanin, along with playwrights Frances Goodrich and Albert Hackett, was not alone in wanting a redemptive play full of hope with room for forgiveness. Otto Frank wanted one as well. While Goodrich and Hackett were working on the script, Frank reminded them that young people from different countries throughout the world "identify themselves . . . with Anne in their struggle during puberty and the problems of the relations [between] mother-daughter." He wanted the production to "reach the masses and influence them," so that they would fulfill "Anne's wish to work for mankind."[126] In other words, in addition to wishing that the play not be sad, he did not want it to be particularly parochial, that is, Jewish.

Otto Frank and the others involved in the production got what they wanted. Walter Kerr of the *New York Herald Tribune* described Anne as "a bird that simply cannot be caged." Echoing Kanin, Kerr triumphantly declared, "Anne is not going to her death; she is going to leave a dent on life, and let death take what's left." The *New York Post* shared Kerr's reaction, proclaiming that the play reincarnated Anne "as though she'd never been dead." The paper seemed delighted that "there isn't a Nazi in it."[127] The *New York World-Telegram and Sun* declared that the genius of "this play is that there is nothing grim or sensational about it." The *Daily News* reported, not without a note of satisfaction, that "the *Diary of Anne Frank* is not in any important sense a Jewish play. . . . It is a story of the gallant human spirit."[128] Brooks Atkinson, the famed theater critic of the *New York Times*, did more than describe it as a "lovely, tender drama." He also praised the playwrights for having presented the story exactly as it is. "They have not contrived anything. They left the tool-kit outside the door of their workroom. They have absorbed the story out of the diary and related it simply."[129] In other words, according to Atkinson, they told the story exactly as it was: optimistic and universal. Except that it wasn't. It did, however, validate postwar American optimism in the notion that "in spite of everything" we can still believe that people are good at heart.[130]

There are legitimate grounds to criticize the decision to gird *The Diary* with an aura of optimism and to privilege the play's famous final line, as opposed to Anne's lament about watching "the world slowly transformed into a wilderness, I hear the approaching thunder that, one day, will destroy us too, I feel the suffering of millions."[131] As Cynthia Ozick, Alvin Rosenfeld, and other critics who have faulted the adaptation aptly observe, Anne wrote her famous line about people being "good at heart" before she had experienced unbearable experiences, including life in a concentration camp, the slow and painful death of her mother and sister, terrible hunger and biting cold, and the conviction that, since her father was almost certainly dead (he was not), she was alone in the world. They rightfully doubt whether she would have expressed such starry-eyed optimism after having endured all this.[132] In fact, in the camps all traces of her optimism disappeared. Her close friend and neighbor, Hannah Elisabeth Pick-Goslar, found her in Bergen-Belsen. She recalled that the Anne she met there "wasn't the same Anne. She was a broken girl . . . it was so terrible. She immediately began to cry and told me, 'I don't have any parents anymore.'" (Her sister, Margot, had not yet died.) Another Dutch girl, Lin Jaldati, described Anne and Margot in the camp as looking like "little frozen birds." She recalled how an ill, feverish, and somewhat delirious Anne cared for an even sicker Margot. When Anne's friend tried to convince her to leave the quarantine bunk because people deteriorated so quickly there, Anne refused, whispering, "Here we can both lie on the plank bed, we'll be together and at peace." When it was clear that Margot was on the threshold of death her friends tried again to get her to leave. Anne replied, "Margot's going to sleep well, and when she sleeps, I won't have to stay up." A few days later they both were dead. The camp was liberated shortly thereafter.[133]

What about the writers' and producers' decision to eliminate the diary's already limited Jewish particularism? In this regard, the critics' complaints notwithstanding, the play's creators may have been quite close to Anne's reality. Anne certainly occasionally expressed pride in her Jewish identity. She knew that her family was in such dire straits because of it. Margot, enamored of Zionism, dreamed of living in Palestine. But Anne was not a knowledgeable or observant Jew.[134] For her to be depicted as a highly identifying Jew would have been as much a distortion as the upbeat ending the creative team gave the diary. It is true, as Robert Alter has observed, that they were "universalizing" a diary that was already pretty universal. Nonetheless, an element of fear pervades her adolescent musings that was deliberately eliminated from the production.[135] Ultimately much depends on how readers choose to read the diary and how they remember Anne Frank from it. They can focus on the numerous adolescent musings and ignore the relatively few, though quite powerful, notes of fear and foreboding. Conversely, they can read the uncharacteristically eloquent declarations about the meaning of life without ever losing sight of what Anne's ultimate fate would be.[136]

While some may criticize Otto Frank, Kanin, and the others involved in the production for playing down and almost eliminating the horror, ultimately they may have had their finger on America's pulse. Would this production have had as great an impact on the American public of the

1950s and beyond if its message had not been universalized to the extent that it was? The legitimacy of the contemporary critics' observations notwithstanding, there is good reason to doubt that American audiences of the 1950s would have as enthusiastically accepted a more assertively Jewish character. Even Jewish leaders, many of whom were admittedly quite assimilated, praised the production. John Stone, chair of the Jewish Film Advisory Committee, liked the movie even more than the play because it gave the story a "more 'universal' meaning and appeal." Without that universalization and Americanization, the story might have become, Stone wrote, "an outdated Jewish tragedy" or, even worse, "a Jewish 'Wailing Wall.'" (Given that it was barely a decade since the end of the war, Stone's use of the word "outdated" may well tell us more about him than the play.)[137] American Jews were certainly pleased by the adulation showered on Anne and her stage and screen depiction. Lawrence Baron argues that the upbeat and universalistic outlook of the play and the movie "enabled people to conceive of the collective Jewish tragedy in individual terms. . . . [Its] appeal transcend[ed] racial, national, and religious differences."[138] As Jeffrey Alexander has argued, instead of the tragedy being relegated to one particular group, the "victims of the trauma became everyman and everywoman, every child and every parent."[139] Now it was a story that was accessible to all Americans.

The problem, of course, was that the historical reality of what happened to Anne Frank and other Jews in hiding was quite different from what American audiences saw on the stage or screen. As historian Tim Cole has observed, none of those Jews in hiding would have been "sought out, arrested, and deported from a hiding place in Amsterdam in spring 1944 if they had been Christians, trade union members, Socialists, handicapped, or members of 'this or that minority.'" They faced their fate solely because they were Jews.[140]

The play's optimistic tone not only reflected the American *zeitgeist* of the 1950s but also contained a political message specific to the moment. Senator Joseph McCarthy and others in Congress were compelling Americans to inform on their friends and colleagues regarding any possible infatuation or connection with communism. This was also the high time of hearings before the House Un-American Activities Committee and the era of the Rosenberg trial and execution. It was also the time of the first stirrings of the struggle against racial discrimination. *The Diary of Anne Frank*, as presented on the American stage and screen, promulgated a liberal and universal message about the persecution of defenseless groups, whether Jews or blacks. It spoke to the dangers of informants, for it was an informant who sealed the Frank family's fate but a few months before the war ended in Amsterdam. This American adaptation also provided uplift—people are good—precisely at a time when the country was emerging from World War II and the Korean War. Americans were having babies, buying cars, and acquiring homes in newly built suburbs. Thanks to the tremendous post–World War II economic expansion, they were attending university, becoming professionals, and entering the middle class at a rate no one—including those individuals who were doing all these things—ever imagined possible. Uplift and optimism were in the American air. This production of the diary provided more of it.

This note of uplift was not unique to *The Diary of Anne Frank*. In the 1950s one of the most popular American television shows was *This Is Your Life*. Every week the host, Ralph Edwards, would invite an unsuspecting audience member to the stage and proceed to tell his or her life story by calling on friends and family. On May 27, 1953, the show featured Hannah Kohner, a Czech survivor who had been incarcerated in four camps, among them Auschwitz-Birkenau and Mauthausen. In the course of the episode Hannah was reunited with childhood friends, a woman who had been in the camps with her, and her brother from Israel, whom she had not seen since their deportation prior to their incarceration in the camps. Hannah's Jewish identity was never explicitly mentioned. (The show did end with Edwards telling the audience that those who wished to help people who had faced the travails Hannah had experienced could contribute to the United Jewish Appeal.) Most significantly, midway through the telecast, Edwards shifted gears and turned to her American experience. He noted how "America had held out a friendly hand" so that "out of darkness . . . terror and despair" she could experience "a new life . . . born in a new world" and "rejoice in the bounties America has given you."[141] Setting the horrors in the past, the show ended on a decidedly positive note. America had given Hannah the opportunity to triumph over adversity.[142]

If *Gentleman's Agreement*, *The Diary of Anne Frank*, and, to a lesser extent, *The Wall* universalized the tragedy of the Holocaust, and if television shows such as *This Is Your Life* celebrated the opportunity America offered survivors, a few years later Leon Uris's *Exodus* (1958) took a somewhat different tack. Otto Preminger, who produced the movie that was based on the book, described it as the most popular American novel since *Gone with the Wind*. Within a month it reached the best-seller list and remained there for a year, spending nineteen weeks at number one.[143] It has been described as a book that "used history to make history."[144] Loosely based on a true incident, it represented the beginning of a distinct change in how Nazi Germany's crimes were presented to Americans. As a result of the British 1939 White Paper, Jewish immigration to Palestine had been severely limited. Even after the Holocaust, when tens of thousands of European refugees expressed a desire to rebuild their lives there, the British would not relent. Jewish groups bought ships, most of which were barely seaworthy, in order to evade the blockade. Uris did not shy away from depicting the Holocaust as a horrific assault on Jews individually and collectively. He introduced the voyage of the *Exodus,* a leaky ship packed with survivors, with an extended and detailed description of what those passengers had endured. The ship manages to evade the British blockade and discharge its passengers, some of whom join in the war for Israeli independence.

The movie, which starred Paul Newman as Ari Ben Canaan, a handsome, chiseled, native-born Israeli Jew (or Sabra), contrasted this modern archetype with the ghettoized European Jew. The most powerful Holocaust "moment" comes when a young Auschwitz-Birkenau survivor, played by Sal Mineo, tries to align himself with a group of Palestinian Jewish extremists. In order to establish bonds of trust and determine whether he can be part of their group, the leader—loosely modeled on Menachem Begin—forces him to articulate what happened to him in the camps. He painfully and reluctantly reveals that, in order to save his life, he had to take one of most reviled jobs in the camp, *Sonderkommando.* In that capacity he had "to shave the heads of other Jews . . . remove dead bodies from the gas chambers . . . collect gold fillings from their teeth." The leader of the resistance group senses that there is something more and pushes him to go on. After great emotional turmoil, he acknowledges that the Germans "used me . . . like you use . . . a woman."[145] While the veracity of such sexual abuse is open to question, this was probably one of the more graphic descriptions of the horrors of the camps to reach Hollywood screens. It is certainly a reflection of the mores of the time that such sexual exploitation is presented as something shameful and awful beyond what else has been done to the Jews. In what Sara Horowitz rightly describes as one of the "best-remembered" scenes of the film, Ari, who has disguised himself as a British officer, listens to a real British officer proclaim that he never fails to detect a Jew because of the particular look Jews have in their eyes. Ari later asks the officer for assistance in removing a bit of dirt that has gotten into his eye. As the officers checks Ari's blue eye from every angle, the film leaves no doubt about the ludicrousness of this antisemitic notion and the officer who promulgated it.[146]

Exodus helped cement in the minds of the American public the notion of a mythic connection between the Holocaust as the tragedy of Jewish life and a people's rebirth in the creation of the State of Israel.[147] It reinforced the notion of the emergence of the Jew from passivity (Holocaust) to self-reliance (Israel). But in many ways this was a quintessentially

American story. The *Los Angeles Times* found the explanation for the book's "universal appeal" for Americans: "our own Revolutionary War . . . transposed to Palestine."[148] Frank Cantor, writing in *Jewish Currents,* a left-wing periodical, observed that "while dealing ostensibly with Israel, *Exodus* is actually an *American* book, which portrays Israel *through American eyes.*" Cantor believed it appealed to American Jews because "it told a *new kind of story* about a *new kind of Jew.*"[149] Philip Roth, who would portray a very different kind of Jew in *Goodbye, Columbus* the following year, believed that Gentiles were so enamored of this book because it lifted from "the nation's consciousness . . . the memory of the holocaust [*sic*] itself."[150] It posed the Jew-as-victim against the Jew-as-fighter and assured audiences that the Holocaust was now never-to-be-repeated history because the new Jews could take care of themselves.[151]

The same year that crowds were filling American movie theaters to see *Exodus,* a new book on the Third Reich shot to the top of the best-seller list. William Shirer's *The Rise and Fall of the Third Reich* sold over one million copies in its first year and another nine million since. A Book of the Month Club selection, it was also serialized in *Reader's Digest,* which boasted a circulation of over twelve million. To the great surprise of the author, his agent, and the publisher, the book eventually sold more copies than any work on European history since the end of World War II. It may rank as "the best-selling historical work ever written in modern times."[152] Yet Shirer, who had covered Nazi Germany for CBS radio and who had published two successful works about his experiences, did not have an easy time getting the book published. He had twice proposed the idea of such a book to Little, Brown, his longtime publisher. Despite their success with his previous books, they rejected the proposal. Shirer then turned to Simon & Schuster, which reluctantly agreed to publish it despite the conviction that there would be limited interest in a book on European history, much less one that was 1,200 pages long, had extensive endnotes, and cost ten dollars, then an exorbitant amount for a book. The publisher demonstrated its lack of faith by initially publishing only 12,500 copies.

The book painted Nazi Germany as a horrific regime, one that governed by fear, persecution, and intimidation. Though Shirer stressed the diabolical nature of the Nazi regime, he almost completely avoided the story of the Jews, reflecting the way in which the Final Solution was still seen as simply part of an array of other wrongs committed by the Third Reich. Shirer argued that within the context of Germany history, Nazism was not an aberration but the natural outgrowth of German tradition. According to Shirer, who as a reporter had watched National Socialism evolve, the Third Reich was a "logical continuation of German history."

This notion was not new to Americans, particularly those who had been adults during the war.[153] In the immediate prewar period and during the war itself, the notion of an intolerant, militaristic, and prone-to-dictatorship Germany was broadly accepted. But within a year or so after the war this perception of Germany had become decidedly out of fashion. This rapid change in attitude had its roots in strategic considerations.

The Soviet Union, America's former ally, had quickly been transformed into its existential enemy. Germany, once an enemy, was now a strategically important friend. It stood alone between the communist bloc and a free democratic Western Europe. The most powerful public manifestation of this reversal of fortunes was the Berlin airlift (1948–49) when the Soviets blocked the Western Allies' land access to Berlin in an effort to gain control over West Berlin. American pilots, who four years earlier had to avoid being hit by German flak, now broke the Soviet blockade of the city and became a lifeline for their former enemies. They supplied the very same people who but a few years earlier had been shooting at them with everything from cooking fuel to candy for children. Germans now constituted "brave souls" standing alone against a communist assault. Throughout the 1950s, when American children practiced "duck and cover," the exercise that was supposed to somehow protect from incoming nuclear bombs, Soviet—not German—weapons were the imagined threat. When supporters of the Genocide Convention discussed the need for a nuclear nonproliferation treaty, more often than not they focused on the potential threat posed by the Soviets.[154]

Around the same time as the publication of Shirer's and Uris' books, there was an outbreak of antisemitic vandalism in various German cities. Though the incidents passed fairly quickly, some observers wondered whether a Nazi resurgence was in the offing. At almost the same time, East Germany began to pass information to the Western press about the high number of former high-ranking Nazis in West German chancellor Konrad Adenauer's government. Some American commentators wondered whether West Germany, America's ally, was beset by "moral amnesia," and had failed to truly sever its Nazi ties.[155] In his review of Shirer's book in *The Nation*, the British historian Geoffrey Barraclough reflected on the political and intellectual embargo—he called it a "smoke screen"—extant in the West regarding German crimes. Mention of Nazi Germany's nefarious deeds was decidedly unwelcome. Those such as Shirer and Barraclough who wished to speak of Nazi wrongs were treated as "the club bores, no one wants to listen to us and people whisper that we are obsessed, hysterical, and neurotically anti-German."[156] This critique came from those on the political left who felt that both the USSR's contribution to the victory over Nazi Germany and Germany's crimes had been conveniently forgotten. Political conservatives took a different stance, depicting this critique as an attempt by the left to obfuscate the threat the USSR posed to the West.[57]

The "club bores," who were buoyed by Shirer's approach, must have found equal solace in Abby Mann's *Judgment at Nuremberg*. First broadcast in 1959 as a television play on the highly respected *Playhouse 90* and then as a Hollywood movie (1961), it was based on the 1947 Nuremberg trial of Nazi-era judges. Though it addressed issues such as "race defilement"—sexual relations between Aryans and Jews—and the murder of the handicapped, its essential message was that America, beset by strategic Cold War fears of the Soviets, had committed a miscarriage of justice by prematurely abandoning any serious efforts to punish Nazi war criminals.

These plays, novels, and movies that captivated Americans during the 1950s and into the early 1960s played down the Jewish character of the victims and universalized the message of the Final Solution, treating it as a sidebar. Nonetheless, they helped lay the foundation for a far more serious examination of what would soon become known as "the Holocaust."

2 State of the Question

The Eichmann Trial and the Arendt Debate

In May 1960 Israel kidnapped former SS Lieutenant Colonel Adolf Eichmann in Argentina and took him to Israel. Right after the war he had escaped from an Allied prisoner of war camp and had been "hiding"—many people knew he was there—in Argentina since 1950. The kidnapping, the trial, and a debate about it all served to alter dramatically how Americans would understand the Holocaust for decades thereafter.

Eichmann had been a pivotal player in the realization of the Final Solution. He had overseen the deportation of Jews from places as diverse as the Reich, Western Europe, Greece, Hungary, and Italy. He had coordinated the roundup, evacuation, transportation, and myriad other details involved in moving people out of their homes and countries. He had traveled to the death camps to ensure that they were ready to "absorb" these new arrivals. Singularly committed to his job, Eichmann was so intent on killing every Jew possible that toward the end of the war he contravened an order from SS Führer Heinrich Himmler to halt the deportations. He wanted to dispatch one more trainload of Jews to be gassed at Birkenau before ending the deportation process. He also sought out individual Jews with the same vigor that he dispatched entire communities to their deaths. At one point the German Foreign Office inquired about the status of a Jewish woman then interned in the Netherlands. She was married to an Italian Catholic, and the Italians wanted her returned to Italy. As soon as Eichmann received the requests he took action. "I have therefore instructed my office in The Hague to transfer the Simons woman immediately to the East," that is, to the death camps. Eichmann had simply been asked about her status. Yet he responded by having her deported.[1]

The dramatic nature of his capture by Israel, which had not yet marked its bar mitzvah year, hit the front page of newspapers throughout the world. Interest in the event was enhanced by the Jewish state's ability to find, capture, and spirit Eichmann out of Argentina without being stopped. When his trial began in April 1961 more reporters were present in Jerusalem than had attended the Nuremberg tribunals. But there were other far more important contrasts between these two legal proceedings. At Nuremberg the story of the Jews was a sidebar. The crime that the

Allies prosecuted there was the killing of European civilians, and some of those civilians happened to be Jews. In his report to President Harry Truman prior to the trial, Justice Robert H. Jackson, America's chief prosecutor, never mentioned Jews as victims.[2] A German Jew killed on German soil was not counted as a victim. The "controlling criterion" for who was a victim was the individual's nationality or the site of their murder and not their religious or ethnic identity.[3] In contrast, at the Eichmann trial the story of the murder of European Jewry was front and center from the outset. The first counts of the indictment against him were for crimes against the Jewish people. The latter counts cited his crimes against other peoples. But this was not the only contrast with Nuremberg. There, virtually no survivors testified. In Jerusalem, one hundred did. If Nuremberg represented the "triumph of the written over the oral," the Eichmann trial represented the triumph of the victims' evidence.[4] The prosecution ensured that these witnesses told the story of Jewish persecution from its beginnings in 1933 through its end in 1945. By having each witness "reproduce" a small "fragment of what he had seen and experienced," Gideon Hausner, the chief prosecutor, aimed "to superimpose on a phantom" a dimension of reality.

For the first time the comprehensive story of the Final Solution, or Holocaust, as the translators often referred to it, was presented on a public platform. (Much of that testimony had little to do with Eichmann specifically.) It was the first trial to be recorded for television. Segments were shown each night in America during primetime. As a result, the trial, in the words of critic Susan Sontag, "made the comprehensible incomprehensible. . . . Masses of facts about the extermination of Jews were piled into the record; a great outcry of historical agony was set down."[5] Dorothy Rabinowitz of the *Wall Street Journal* described it as a "galvanizing" event that brought people "face to face with emotions theretofore repressed, with events whose full scope and reverberations had been kept, rumbling beneath the surface of consciousness."[6] Yale scholar and Holocaust survivor Geoffrey Hartman, who would go on to found the prototypical collection of Holocaust victim testimonies, remembered hearing on the radio the testimony of a survivor. "It was then," he recalled forty years later, that he "understood for the first time the power of witnessing, of testimony."[7]

The sheer number of survivors who testified and the power of the stories they told almost made Eichmann shrink in importance. Sitting in a glass booth for his protection, he "was eclipsed by the victims."[8] Haim Gouri, a poet and journalist who covered the trial, observed that "the events being described were larger than he [Eichmann] was." Survivors occupied the center of the trial. "They served as faithful proxies of the

Holocaust. They were the facts."[9] Ironically, the judges at the trial had a very different perception of the survivor testimony. Basing their verdict on the written record, they dismissed survivor testimony as a by-product of the trial. In the opening pages of their decision they noted that while the survivors "poured out their hearts as they stood in the witness box," what they had to say was of interest to the historians but not to them. The trial accelerated the process whereby survivors became, rather than victims, "bearers of history."[10] The number of survivor testimonies and memoirs submitted for publication increased exponentially. During the trial spectators would be told, "You came on a good day," that is, when survivors were speaking or, conversely, on a "bad day," that is, when only documents were under consideration.

While the degree of interest in the Holocaust in general and survivors in particular increased markedly after the trial, this spike was not solely the result of the trial itself. One of the most intense intellectual conflicts the contemporary scholarly world has ever witnessed erupted in the trial's aftermath. It created an intellectual maelstrom from which the field of Holocaust studies has not yet quite emerged. In 1963 the *New Yorker* published a series of articles about the trial by Hannah Arendt, which subsequently appeared as *Eichmann in Jerusalem: A Report on the Banality of Evil*. The book became the prism through which many people's view of the Holocaust was refracted. Arendt provoked what has rightly been described as an "unparalleled public airing of historical issues relating to the Holocaust."[11] Scholars, journalists, historians, theologians, intellectuals, religious leaders, and an array of others weighed in on what they thought she meant. More than just an intellectual debate, it was also personal and vituperative.[12] Her critics condemned her and her writings as "wicked," "pervaded by vanity," "unfeeling," "distorted." Hugh Trevor-Roper, who had so affirmed Hilberg, considered her "arrogant" and her book as filled with "half-truths . . . [and] double standards of evidence."[13] At the other end of the spectrum her fans waxed rhapsodic, describing her work as "brilliant," a "masterpiece," and "splendid and extraordinary." They condemned the attacks as a "pogrom." Incorrectly suggesting that only the Jews were upset by her comments, they dismissed the hostile reviews as "Jewish patriotism." She was painted by her supporters as having been persecuted by an "army of inferior male detractors."[14]

Arendt, a highly assimilated German Jew with a Ph.D. from the University of Heidelberg, left Germany in 1933 when the Nazis were poised to arrest her for her work with a Zionist organization. She spent the next years in Paris helping Jewish refugee children. In 1941, after a brief internment in a French detention camp as an "enemy alien," she escaped to the United States. There she wrote for the German Jewish newspaper *Aufbau* and was an editor at Schocken Publishing. In the postwar era, together with Professors Salo Baron and Gershom Scholem, she worked as the director of the Jewish Cultural Reconstruction, which sought to retrieve and then distribute heirless Jewish religious and cultural artifacts in the American zone. Her *Origins of Totalitarianism* (1952) established her scholarly reputation. In it she argued that totalitarian regimes such as Nazism and Stalinist communism could successfully compel ordinary people to do extraordinarily horrible things by making these actions the norm. Less interested in the ideological underpinnings of the totalitarian system than in its *modus operandi,* she focused on the means, as opposed to the ends, of these state terrors. As a result, radical racial antisemitism, one of the distinctive features of Nazism, fell to the side. For Arendt, death camps were a product of the totalitarian regime's desire for "absolute domination," and not, as many other scholars argued, a place for elimination of all European Jews and others the Germans considered inimical to their regime.[15]

Teaching positions at Berkeley, Princeton, and the University of Chicago followed. Her book became a sort of manual for graduate students in the social sciences. The historian Michael Marrus notes that the copy he used when he was a graduate student in the early 1960s was "about as heavily underlined and annotated as any in my library." He recalled that he "read every word, so important did my colleagues and I believe her work to be. I went back to it often." Amusingly, and in a rare expression of academic candor, he confessed that when he returned to the book thirty years later, "I found the work practically impenetrable, her prose dense and cumbersome, replete with long-winded, unsubstantiated and highly abstract formulations." Why then did virtually every social science student read the book with the seriousness and reverence Marrus describes? It may have been that she was willing to address subjects which students thought critically important and which no one else was addressing at the time.[16]

In truth, much of what she actually said about the Eichmann trial has been distorted or ignored by both her critics and supporters. Today it is quite common to hear her painted as an opponent of the trial from the outset. That is not correct. Immediately after Eichmann's capture, a debate erupted about whether Israel had the right to try him. The opponents contended that, since Israel did not exist when the crime took place and it was not committed against Israeli citizens, the trial could not legitimately be held there. Arendt thought otherwise. Jerusalem was the correct venue. She dismissed these objections as "formalistic [and] out of tune with reality and with all demands that justice must be done." Israel was the "country in which the injured parties and those who happened to survive are." According to Arendt, to argue that it did not have the right to try a perpetrator was "legalistic in the extreme." When a German friend suggested to Arendt that the trial be held outside of Israel, she used the first-person plural to respond: "*We* kidnapped a man who was indicted in the first trial in Nuremberg. . . . *We* abducted him from Argentina because Argentina has the worst possible record for the extradition of war criminals. . . . *We* did not take the man to Germany but to our own country" (emphasis added).[17] She insisted that Israel "had as much right to sit in judgment on the crimes committed against their people, as the Poles had to judge crimes committed in Poland." She was particularly rankled by the oft-voiced contention that Jewish judges would be biased. Why had that question not been raised when Polish or Czech judges presided over war crimes trials immediately after the war? Were the critics masking their conviction that Jews were inherently unable to be fair?

But there was much about the trial that she fervently disliked. She fundamentally disagreed with the prosecution's argument that Eichmann's crime had been simply a link in the centuries-long chain of antisemitism. While rooted in antisemitism, the Holocaust was, she argued, something far "larger" than just that. Anticipating what would become a much-accepted approach to the Holocaust, she argued that the attempt to annihilate an entire people was unprecedented. It lacked the utilitarian criteria generally associated with aggressive wars. It did not aim to conquer or enslave a hostile population. It did not further Nazi world rule. In fact, Arendt had long contended that the Nazis' actions were not just non-utilitarian, but anti-utilitarian. They hampered the conventional war, diverted men and materiel from the fighting to the killing process, and murdered useful and accomplished workers who were aiding the war effort.[18]

Fitting Eichmann into the context of her argument in *The Origins of Totalitarianism,* she declared that he was not an avowed antisemite but a typical bureaucrat who would follow any order that was given to him by a totalitarian regime. In contrast to prosecutor Hausner, who thought Eichmann was a talented desk killer, she believed him to be a killer but one without the talent or intellect to take initiatives. "Everybody could see that this man was not a 'monster,' but it was difficult indeed not to suspect that he was a clown."[19] It was in this regard that she introduced a concept that would become known as the "banality of evil." By that she did not intend to suggest that what he did was banal, but that a banal person, one with no particular talents and without an "insane hatred of Jews," could be motivated to do evil. Many of her critics took issue with her on this point. But they were not alone. Decades later historians such as Christopher Browning, who based much of his theories regarding perpetrators on her work, would argue that regarding Eichmann she was wrong. Eichmann's demeanor at the trial fooled her. She dismissed him as a "clown." He was, in fact, a committed antisemite.[20]

Recent research has all but given the death knell to Arendt's theory that Eichmann was a man who was simply following orders "in all his bizarre vacuousness" and did not understand what he was doing. Utterly committed to his task of killing Jews, over a decade after the war he was still boasting of it and only regretted that he had not finished the job. In Argentina he told a group of Nazi fugitives, "To be frank with you, had we killed all of them, the thirteen million, I would be happy and say: 'all right, we have destroyed an enemy.'"[21] Arendt also took issue with Hausner's decision to build much of his case on survivors telling their stories. By doing this, she argued, Hausner highlighted the victims' suffering rather than the perpetrators' crime. Taking a formulaic view of trials, she argued that a trial must be about what the defendant did and not what happened to the victims. Today her failure to give any weight to victims' rights would sound quite dated. But it was not just victims' rights to which she failed to give weight. She refused to acknowledge that there was any value in the prosecutor's decision to make history rather than simply to do justice. In fact, she was convinced that bringing history into the courtroom is what rendered this a "show trial," a term which, in the wake of the Stalinist era, was pregnant with accusation. History and forensics are often not the most compatible of bedfellows when the setting is the courtroom. Nonetheless, to think that a man who was accused of genocide could be tried without bringing history into the courtroom seemed strangely short-sighted for such an astute thinker.

While these particular criticisms rankled her critics, they were not the ones responsible for precipitating the barrage of withering attacks on her. It was what she said about the *Judenräte,* the Jewish councils. Appalled by the fact that they prepared the lists of those who were to be deported, she contended that they facilitated the Nazis' murderous objectives. She held Jewish leaders responsible for the death of millions. One of her book's most oft-quoted proclamations was that "if the Jewish people had been really unorganized and leaderless, there would have been chaos and misery but the total number of victims would hardly have been between four and a half and six million people." She declared their "pathetic and sordid" behavior to be the "darkest chapter" of the Holocaust. This assertion left many of her critics dumbfounded. Was she saying that the actions by Jewish leaders were darker than mass killings by the Germans? Was she holding Jews or their leaders responsible for the death of their coreligionists? In fact, she was. She was essentially painting them as collaborators.

She was wrong on a number of salient facts. The *Judenräte* were not free to act but were under Nazi control. Moreover, she used a sword to skewer the councils when a scalpel would have been more appropriate. She painted a multitude of different leadership entities with one broad brush. Philip Friedman had already pointed out, as we have noted, that the various *Judenräte* did not all act in the same fashion. Some cooperated. Some resisted (and were punished accordingly). She also ignored the fact that in the summer of 1941 over a million Jews were shot on the eastern front, where in most cases there was nothing akin to a *Judenrät* at all. In her defense, however, many of her critics failed to note that she was not holding the masses of Jews responsible. It was the leadership that was in her crosshairs, not the masses of victims. The Germans' ability to compel members of a group to act against their own was vivid proof for her of what a totalitarian regime could accomplish. It could turn victim against victim.

In what may have been an attempt to add historical heft to her condemnation of the councils, she noted that the story of the *Judenräte's* activities had now been "exposed for the first time in all its pathetic and sordid detail by Raul Hilberg, [in his] standard work *The Destruction of European Jews.*"[22] That sentence inexorably linked her view of the Final Solution to Hilberg's. Within a short time after the publication of her critique of the trial, two different articles in *Yad Vashem Bulletin* treated her views as identical to Hilberg's and Bettelheim's. They were jointly accused of "castigat[ing] the victims," "sympathize[ing] with the misunderstood murderers," and "help[ing to] implement the murder of their fellow Jews."[23] Alexander Donat, writing in *Judaism,* equated her with Bettelheim and accused her of "mercilessly" continuing the "vicious assault on the memory of the six million Jewish victims . . . [which had been] initiated by Bruno Bettelheim." Donat acknowledged that Arendt had "leaned" on Hilberg's research to reach her conclusions. Donat found Hilberg's conclusions "mainly wrong." However, he excused him because this "conscientious scholar" had mistakenly relied on German materials to the exclusion of Yiddish, Hebrew, Polish, and other primary sources. He offered no such excuse for Arendt.[24]

There are a number of ironies here. First of all, Arendt was hardly alone in her criticism of the *Judenräte.* Her view of them was precisely the one held by many ghetto inhabitants. Emanuel Ringelblum, the historian who was interned in the Warsaw ghetto and created the famed *Oyneg Shabes* archives, refused to work with the *Judenräte.* Resistance fighters in both Warsaw and Vilna accused the *Judenräte* of having betrayed their cause. When Hausner asked ghetto fighters Yitzhak Zuckerman and Zvia Lubetkin-Zuckerman to testify at the Eichmann trial, they demanded to know whether he would include in his prosecution the story of Jewish complicity and the *Judenräte*. In a paper given at Yad Vashem in 1957, Philip Friedman noted that more than just facing "widespread distrust," the *Judenräte* were "hated, despised, and reviled" by Jews in many places.[25] In essence, Arendt's view of these Jewish leaders did not differ from that held by many victims and survivors. Yet in the uproar over her work that fact seemed to be forgotten or plowed under.

Most importantly, from a historiographical perspective, Arendt's assertions about Jewish responses were not identical to either Hilberg's or Bettelheim's. In fact, other than on the matter of the *Judenräte*, they were quite at odds with one another. While she agreed with them that Jews had acted with "submissive meekness," she dismissed as "foolish," if not "pretty stupid and crazy," Bettelheim's and Hilberg's notions about the roots of this compliance being found in diaspora behavior patterns. Arendt privately described Hilberg as "babbl[ing] about a 'death wish' of the Jews." As she explicitly and repeatedly noted, while Jews may have failed to resist, so too did every group the Germans persecuted. "The sad truth of the matter is that . . . no non-Jewish group or people behaved differently." Every group, whether possessing a diaspora background or not, had acted in the same fashion. Arendt rejected Bettelheim's suggestion that Jews went "like sheep to the slaughter" because the evidence demonstrated that under "these conditions all groups, social and ethnic, behaved alike." She accused Bettelheim of suffering from "inverted chauvinism," that is, believing that Jews should have been prescient and acted differently than every other group persecuted by the Germans. That is why she grew so angry with Hausner for repeatedly asking witnesses: "Why did you not resist?" Arendt felt it illegitimate to expect of Jews behavior that was entirely different from all other victims. Whereas Hilberg dismissed the Warsaw ghetto uprising as irrelevant, Arendt saw "glory" and "heroism" in their actions.[26] These were serious differences between Arendt on one hand and Hilberg and Bettelheim on the other. Nonetheless, critics melded their positions on the putative Jewish response to persecution into a unified theory.[27]

The fact that Arendt was so frequently coupled with Bettelheim infuriated her. Arendt was particularly peeved because Bettelheim cited her own experience in a French detention camp as proof of his theory about Jews' "ghetto thinking." He told the story of what he claimed happened to Arendt in the French concentration camp Gurs in 1940, when seven thousand Jewish women interned in the camp failed to take advantage of the chance to escape before the camp was "handed over to the Germans."

According to Bettelheim, the French underground arrived at the camp in the short interval between the French withdrawal and the German arrival. Despite being offered a "chance to get away to all who wished," most of the women refused to go. What was particularly damning to Bettelheim was that they refused, despite the fact that what "lay in store for them had been vividly described." Bettelheim condemned the women for not believing what they were told and for "show[ing] no interest in the chance to save their lives." He reserved his praise for the 200 women who did leave, Arendt among them.

The problem was that Bettelheim's version of her story was, in Arendt's words, "altogether wrong." In 1940 there was not yet any French underground to arrive at the camp and warn the women about what "lay in store" for them. Bettelheim was clearly suggesting that they had been explicitly told that they were headed to their deaths and nonetheless refused to leave Gurs. The problem with this claim is that at the time of this incident, no German killing program yet existed.[28] No one could have warned them what lay ahead. Arendt also noted that those who left had to do so with "nothing but a toothbrush since there existed no means of transportation." This would have made leaving beyond the reach of many of the women. Most of the women who remained behind were indeed killed, but not for another two years.[29]

Why did her critics fail to notice that Arendt's views were so at odds with Hilberg's and Bettelheim's? Why did they wrongly tar them with the same brush? Some critics' views may have been shaped by her tone that was often sneering and judgmental, if not contemptuous. Even her staunch defenders acknowledged that she "caused pain and anger" and sounded "imperious."[30] It was this tone that was at the heart of the criticism of her from the noted Jewish scholar and her long-time friend Gershom Scholem. He found what she wrote to be "heartless," "malicious," "lighthearted," and "flippant."[31]

The anger against her was further compounded by not just what she said, but where she said it. The *New Yorker* was one of the more respected magazines of the time. It epitomized a "goyish" or WASP mentality despite the fact that its editor was a Jew. Arendt claimed that she purposely chose a non-Jewish publication in order to maintain her objectivity. (There is a question as to whether this is entirely correct. It seems that she had initially asked *Commentary*, which was published by the American Jewish Committee, to send her to Jerusalem for the trial but it could not afford to do so.)[32] Her tone and the immense megaphone at her disposal left many Jews—survivors in particular—convinced that she, who had never faced the worst of the Holocaust, was pontificating to them from a lofty perch outside the community.

Her critics were so incensed that most of them ignored one paragraph in which she pointedly articulated the historical significance of this trial. It is likely that most of them would have fully agreed with her:

> For the first time (since the year 70, when Jerusalem was destroyed by the Romans), Jews were able to sit in judgment on crimes committed against their own people, that for the first time they did not need to appeal to others for protection and justice, or fall back upon the compromised phraseology of the rights of man—rights which, as no one knew better than they, were claimed only by people who were too weak to defend their [rights] . . . and enforce their own laws.[33]

Also ignored by most of her critics were her piercing criticisms of West Germany's record on war criminals. At a time when it was not politically popular for a Western commentator to be critical of America's ally the Federal Republic of Germany, Arendt did not hesitate to do so. She roundly faulted Germany's record regarding its Nazi past. While Israel had to "ferret out criminals and murderers from their hiding places," in Germany the murderers were "flourishing in the public realm." Those war criminals that were tried generally received "fantastically lenient" sentences.[34]

David Engel suggests that the hostility toward her was so intense because she was the first major voice to dissent from the almost universally accepted opinion that Eichmann was a monster who joyfully and purposefully murdered Jews.[35] Furthermore, at long last, the Eichmann trial had appeared to offer a corrective to the Nuremberg rendition of Germany's crimes against humanity. The German attempt to destroy the Jewish people was put front and center. The horrors of antisemitism were finally being given their due in the public sphere. Then came Arendt, a respected, well-known voice and a German Jew, to say this was not the result of age-old Jew hatred; this was a function of the development of the modern nation-state.[36] Rather than being motivated by deep ideological, antisemitic commitments, the killing of the Jews was the result of totalitarianism, modernity, and bureaucracy.[37]

Many Jews felt blindsided, if not betrayed, by her critique. Incensed at her putative failure to see the reality of antisemitism and to recognize Eichmann as an antisemite, they ferociously lashed out at what she wrote as well as at what they *claimed* she wrote. The anger toward her could only have been exacerbated by the fact that Arendt was both an assimilated German Jew and a woman. Though World War II had certainly upended her life, she had, for the most part, escaped the harsh fate of those who had been in concentration camps or ghettoes. Survivors were incensed that, despite this, she felt entitled to judge those who had endured these hardships. Thanks to her scholarly achievements, she had access to the pages of the *New Yorker*, a publication capable of reaching influential non-Jews and convincing them that Jews got it all wrong when they blamed antisemitism for their travails and were, at least partially, responsible for their own deaths. This was precisely what happened when people such as R. H. Glauber, writing in the *Christian Century*, reflected on the "part Jews played in their own destruction" and wondered: "If Eichmann was guilty . . . are not those Jews also guilty?"[38]

Yet in addition to the Arendt debate and the public's growing awareness of the vast homicidal nature of the Final Solution, the Eichmann trial had other, equally far-reaching consequences. The word "Holocaust," meaning the German attempt to liquidate European Jewry, entered the American, if not the Western, lexicon. During the Eichmann trial Paul Jacobs, writing from Jerusalem, used it in his reports, explaining to his readers that this was what "the Nazi annihilation of European Jewry is called in Israel."[39] The *New York Times* also noted at the time that the trial had recessed for "Day of the Holocaust," as Israel had begun to call Yom HaShoah. If there was any doubt about the meaning of the word, it would be laid to rest by subsequent developments on the Broadway stage.

The Arendt debate was still underway in America when *The Deputy*, a play by German playwright Rolf Hochhuth, opened on Broadway in 1964. The play, which had already premiered in Berlin, presented a searing indictment of Pope Pius XII for failing to protest the fate of the Jews despite knowing precisely what was being done to them. It portrayed Pius as someone who put the Vatican's narrow interests ahead of moral and ethical considerations. The pope's defenders argued that he had aided many Jews but had done so quietly and secretly. Thousands of articles addressed the issues raised by the play.[40] Arendt, one of the participants in the debate, unequivocally condemned the Vatican's hypocrisy and noted that the Vatican repeatedly claimed that it had no control over the actions of local Church hierarchies, such as when Dutch Church leaders turned over to German authorities those Jews who had converted to Catholicism. Yet it happily took credit when other local hierarchies, such as those in southern France, helped Jews escape by distributing forged documents. Arendt observed that the Vatican failed to stop local hierarchies from accepting Nazi doctrine of separating Jews out from the rest of society and failed to use the resources at its hand to save Jews. While many Allied and neutral leaders failed to speak out, Arendt wryly observed that the Vatican was in a different category. "The man on St. Peter's chair is no ordinary ruler but 'the Vicar of Christ.'"[41]

A radical theological shift had begun for Christians—both Catholics and Protestants—with the Second Vatican Council, also known as

Vatican II (1962–1965). It repudiated the charge that all Jews were responsible for the death of Jesus. It further asserted that, in contrast to the way Catholic liturgy had depicted Jews for millennia, "the Jews should not be presented as rejected or accursed by God," and it condemned all expressions of antisemitism. *The Deputy,* coming as it did in the wake of this historic Vatican gathering, pushed the question beyond the general role of the Church in generating and perpetuating antisemitism and forced the focus upon the pope himself. Historian Tom Lawson credits the play with generating the "Pius Wars," in which the pope's role was hotly debated.[42] Fifty years later these wars continue. At the heart of the matter are two pivotal questions that became central to America's encounter with the Holocaust. What was the rest of the world doing while this annihilation was underway? What could those who were not directly involved in the fight have done to stop it, had they cared to do so? While the first query was entirely within the bounds of traditional historical inquiry, the second was not. The question, which remains a matter of increasingly virulent debate, brought America and its history into the heart of the conversation about the Holocaust. Now there were three players on the historical stage: victim, perpetrator, and bystander. The term bystanders, introduced into the conversation about the Holocaust in a *New York Times* editorial about *The Deputy,* was used to describe those who, while not poised against one another on the battlefield, might have made a difference.[43] The debate about bystanders in general would shape the way many Americans—Jews in particular—examined not just the Holocaust, but also the way their country responded to contemporary moral tragedies.

"Holocaust": Shedding Light on America's Shortcomings

While *The Deputy* sought to elucidate the tragedy, other works did the opposite. They used the Holocaust to shed light on an array of American issues, including discrimination against women, nuclear war, racism, poverty, slavery, suicide, and even failed marriages. Some of these— including book-length studies, films, plays, novels, and poems—achieved a near legendary status in American culture. Among them were works by both Jews and non-Jews, including Betty Friedan's *The Feminine Mystique,* Stanley Kubrick's *Dr. Strangelove,* Arthur Miller's *After the Fall,* Sidney Lumet's *The Pawnbroker,* Stanley Elkins's study of slavery, Sylvia Plath's "Holocaust poems," Kurt Vonnegut's *Mother Night,* and Stanley Milgram's obedience studies. All these authors and directors relied on the Holocaust as a means of enabling their readers to better understand "the brutality of ordinary American life."[44] As we trace the history of the construction of the Holocaust narrative in America, these works constitute important markers, not for what they tell us about the Holocaust, but for the degree to which their creators assumed audiences were aware of this event and used it as a vehicle for shedding light on America's failures and challenges.

In his study of slavery, Stanley Elkins compared the behavior of Nazi concentration camp inmates and slaves in the American South. He posited that the concentration camp and plantation system rendered both slaves and camp inmates docile and compliant. They were reduced "to complete and childish dependence on their masters" and exhibited inherently and unnaturally submissive behavior.[45] In 1962 Sylvia Plath wrote three poems that compared the suffering she had experienced as a woman with that of European Jews during the Holocaust. Plath imagined herself suffering as a Jew, "A Jew to Dachau, Auschwitz, Belsen." Her pain was so great that "I think I may well be a Jew."[46] In *Mother Night* Kurt Vonnegut drew a direct parallel between Nazi crimes and those committed by America in subsequent years. For him these crimes had become "indistinguishable from one another."[47] Betty Friedan, widely considered one of the "mothers" of American feminism, cited Bettelheim's description of concentration camp inmates' behavior. She compared the "millions who walked to their own death in the concentration camps" to the compliant American housewives who lived in suburban homes that were but "comfortable concentration camps." Just as Jews were imprisoned in camps, American women were imprisoned in suburbia.[48]

At the same time, Yale researcher Stanley Milgram was beginning his now well-known obedience experiments. Anxious to ascertain how far people would go in fulfilling amoral, if not immoral, orders, he asked volunteers to take the role of "teacher," posing questions to another person who was cast as a "learner." Each pair was situated in different rooms such that one could not see the other. If the learner answered the question incorrectly, the teacher was to administer an electric shock for the express purpose of effecting greater learning. After each wrong answer the "teacher" was to increase the level of the shock, although the "teachers" were told that the "learners" would suffer no permanent harm. Unbeknownst to the "teachers," however, the "learners" were paid actors and the machine a phony. The actor was instructed to scream as if in increasingly excruciating pain. Milgram, who had been influenced by Arendt's contention that ordinary people could be made to do extraordinarily awful things, believed he was creating a setting akin to the Nazi death camps. He wanted to see if Americans, participating in an experiment in a Yale lab, would replicate the behavior of concentration camp guards. Milgram believed his experiments showed that adults have an extreme willingness to "go to almost any length on the command of an authority."[49]

While Milgram's work ostensibly concerned the Holocaust, his real focus was American society. He acknowledged wanting to know whether in "all of the United States a vicious government could find enough moral imbeciles to meet the personnel requirements of a national system of death camps." He contended that his experiments proved that Americans were capable of committing the same evil deeds as the Nazis. Critics pointed out that the laboratory conditions did not in any way approximate the situation in the death camps and that the experiment elided any historical context for the Holocaust, particularly European antisemitism. In addition, Milgram ignored or failed to give sufficient weight to the fact that 40 percent of the "teachers" refused to continue, while others vehemently protested when encouraged to administer higher levels of shocks.[50] But these critiques have today all but sunken into oblivion. Milgram's work has become a popular benchmark to explain immoral behavior by those in power. That it ignores the historical context of Nazism has proven irrelevant to many social scientists and pundits. The fact that his study appeared just as the Vietnam War was escalating led many commentators to cite it as proof that any group— Americans included—was capable of atrocities. They pointed to the 1968 My Lai massacre, "the most shocking episode of the Vietnam War" in which American soldiers murdered approximately 500 civilians.[51] Milgram's work buttressed one of the ways in which Arendt's work was understood: that there's a little bit of Eichmann in all of us. Yet Arendt herself found such a glib interpretation of her work to be ludicrous. She believed it ignored both the cultural context within which Eichmann operated and his exceptional self-deception and thoughtlessness.[52]

Stanley Kubrick's classic film *Dr. Strangelove or: How I Learned to Stop Worrying and Love the Bomb* (1964) is a comic elegy about the world's enhanced ability to destroy itself. Co-written, directed, and produced by Kubrick, it focused on the scientists and military personnel necessary to make this happen. The title character, played by Peter Sellers, was modeled on the many German scientists whom the U.S. government had brought to this country under Operation Paperclip in order to keep the Soviets from repatriating the selfsame talent.[53] In the film a rogue army general sends a squadron of planes to bomb the Soviet Union. Three of the planes are intercepted; one is not. Were it to drop its bombs, the earth's surface would be contaminated and rendered uninhabitable for many generations. The U.S. president turns to Strangelove, his scientific advisor, for advice. Strangelove, who speaks with a thick German accent, suggests that several hundred thousand people—more women than men—be sent down deep mineshafts where they would participate in a controlled breeding program. Once the radiation had dissipated, the off-spring, products of the breeding program, could return to earth's surface. (The original settlers would long since have died.) For Kubrick, Strangelove's notion of a breeding program and his lackadaisical attitude toward the death of tens of millions of people were meant to remind viewers of Nazi behavior. Lest there be any doubt about whom Strangelove represented, he addresses the president as "Mein Fuhrer" while involuntarily giving the Nazi salute. (The salute was an improvisation added by Sellers.)

In *The Pawnbroker* (1964), directed by Sidney Lumet based on the 1961 novel by Edward Lewis Wallant, the Holocaust is far more than a distant reference. Although flashbacks include graphic descriptions of the destruction and torture of a Jewish family, the film's real focus is on the tortured postwar existence of the family's sole survivor. Operating a pawnshop in Harlem, then a quintessential American urban slum, Sol Nazerman interacts with blacks, Hispanics, and poor whites. Both the shop and the streets around it are raw, gritty, unforgiving, and, like a concentration camp, promise no hope, no future even to those who survive them. Despite the fact that the film contains some of the rawest descriptions of the Holocaust produced thus far, at its heart it is a lament about America's urban ghettoes and the poverty, dehumanization, and cruelty of life endured by their inhabitants.[54]

Arthur Miller, author of *Death of a Salesman*, also used the Holocaust as a metaphor for suffering in *After the Fall* (1964), widely considered to be based on his failed marriage to Marilyn Monroe and her subsequent suicide. The central character, a New York intellectual, bereft after a failed marriage and the suicide of a former wife, is struggling over whether to begin life anew with another woman. It is a difficult and painful play. Miller's stage directions call for a "blasted stone tower of a German concentration camp" to be onstage for the entire play. The lights on the tower come ablaze during the play's bleaker moments. *New York Times* theatre critic Howard Taubman described it as the story of "any and all courageous enough to hunt for order in the painful and joyous chaos of living."[55] Years later Miller called it a play that "is looking into a void where there is nothing and trying to invent something to stop the world from killing itself." He also recalled how he learned about the Holocaust: "It entered my work through my bones. . . . It leaves the human being utterly alone with his pain."[56] As for American antisemitism, Miller had already directly confronted the subject in his 1945 novel *Focus*. During World War II he worked at the Brooklyn Navy Yard where he encountered raw antisemitism, made all the more painful by the very "existence of Nazism." The experience was exacerbated by the fact that his antagonists with whom he worked had almost no "comprehension of what Nazism meant." Years later he recalled "the sense of emergency" he felt when he wrote the novel.[57]

By 1965 Friedan, Kubrick, Lumet, Milgram, Plath, Vonnegut, and Miller—all iconic or soon-to-be iconic figures on the American intellectual and creative landscape—were convinced that the Holocaust and its imagery needed no explication. They believed it was well enough understood that it could be utilized to explicate other issues.[58] This again gives the lie to the notion that the Holocaust was simply absent from the American cultural landscape prior to the 1970s. Those consuming these works could do so against a background of the Eichmann trial, the Arendt debate, *The Deputy,* as well as works discussed in the previous chapter, *The Wall, The Diary of Anne Frank* (book, play, and movie), *The Rise and Fall of the Third Reich, Judgment at Nuremberg,* and *Exodus* (book and movie). All these brought the Third Reich and its attendant horrors into sharper relief on the American intellectual, scholarly, and cultural—both high and low—scene. They would constitute the fertile soil from which would emerge an explosion of interest in the Holocaust in the late 1960s.

A Post-Holocaust Protest Generation Creates Its Memories

As the cultural historian James Young has observed, "Memory is never shaped in a vacuum."[59] Regarding the construction of the Holocaust narrative in America, this observation was never truer than during the 1960s and 1970s. Interest in the Holocaust spiked both within the Jewish community and outside of it. That spike was not engineered or decided upon by anyone. It came about as a result of a confluence of generational, social, and political circumstances, some of which were internal to the Jewish community while others were totally removed from it. Yet as this confluence of circumstances came together to precipitate a cultural revolution in America, no social, political, ethnic, or sexual group was immune. The way in which many Americans—young Jews prominently among them—thought about themselves and their relationship to the larger society changed dramatically. Part of that change involved embracing one's particular national, religious, historical, or group identity in an unapologetic and uncompromising fashion. Therefore, while the next few pages may seem like a digression, they are of critical importance to our understanding of how the Holocaust came to occupy such an important place in American popular and intellectual realms. (I am fully aware of the problematic nature of the much used [if not overused] term "identity." It can encompass both far too much and far too little. It brings under its rubric people who don't belong there and often leaves out those who do. At the same time, despite its shortcomings, it serves as a useful tool for understanding much of what follows in this chapter.)[60]

For close to two centuries immigrants to America had an implicit agreement with the majority culture. America was a melting pot and newcomers, particularly if they were considered white, were invited, if not expected, to jump in. They were to acculturate, if not assimilate. That began to change in the 1960s as the children and grandchildren of these immigrants became increasingly intent on highlighting their distinctiveness. They did not necessarily reject American culture, but they sought to find a *modus vivendi* that would allow them to embrace both their majority and minority identities. This trend was rooted in great measure in the civil rights movement that, in the period since the Supreme Court's 1954 decision rendering school segregation illegal (*Brown v. Board of Education of Topeka, Kansas*), had grown in prominence and strength. For African Americans, what began as a legal struggle had morphed, by the mid-1960s, into a broad-based movement. In great measure it is in the civil rights movement where we find the origins of what would become known as "identity politics" as well as, in great measure, the catalyst for growing American interest in the Holocaust.

Increasingly, the once-loathed hyphenated American identity would become more than just acceptable. It would become a desideratum. This was evident among individuals who occupied the most elevated stations in America. In 1963 President John F. Kennedy, a Catholic with strong Irish roots, visited Ireland. While there he declared, "This is not the land of my birth, but it is the land for which I hold the greatest affection." To grasp the full import of Kennedy's statement one need only compare it with his father's reaction a few decades earlier when a reporter referred to him as an "Irishman." He erupted: "I was born here. My children were born here. What the hell do I have to do to be called an American?" If Kennedy Sr. was astonished to hear his son's comment, he was probably not alone. Only a few years earlier sociologist Will Herberg had definitively proclaimed that "the ethnic group . . . had no future" in American life and that "ethnic pluralists were backward-looking romantics . . . [who] were out of touch with the unfolding American reality."[61] Herberg's proclamation of the death of ethnicity was not just premature, however. It was wrong.

Symptomatic of the early stirrings of this change was the ad campaign run by a New York–based bakery, Levy's Real Jewish Rye, which was anxious to broaden its customer base beyond the Jewish community. It placed posters in New York City subways, each one featuring a decidedly ethnic figure—black, Asian, Native American, and Irish among others—happily eating a deli sandwich made with Levy's. Emblazoned on the poster was the line: "You Don't Have to Be Jewish to Love Levy's Real Jewish Rye." This was a celebration of ethnicity unlike anything seen before, even in ethnically diverse New York. (The ads were so popular that when the bakery was sold to a larger corporation, long after this advertising campaign had ended, the *New York Times* reported the sale with the following lament: "You don't have to be Jewish to mourn a bit over the passing of Levy's Real Jewish Rye Bread from Brooklyn, after 91 years, to Connecticut.")[62]

But identity politics was not just about celebrating diversity. It was also about demanding redress of past wrongs.[63] Taking their cues from the civil rights movement and its offshoot, the Black Power movement, minority groups that had long felt themselves marginalized or stigmatized began to become more vocal. Gays, women, Hispanics, and other groups challenged the notion that they occupied a lesser stratum in American society than their WASP heterosexual male contemporaries. This social upheaval—some would call it a revolution—was to change the face of American society. The country was awash with protest movements, many of which highlighted the abiding inequalities in American life. At the same time, the anti–Vietnam War movement was transmitting the message that authority—irrespective of whether it came in the form of draft boards, police departments, elected officials, or university presidents—could be challenged.[64] The civil rights movement became stronger and far more broadly based than ever before. The women's movement demanded that proper attention be paid to domestic violence, unequal pay, and sexual harassment. It also celebrated women's creativity and often unheralded contributions to society. The homosexual community began to emerge from living in painful and sometimes dangerous shadows. On a September night in 1969 New York City police raided Stonewall Bar, which attracted a homosexual clientele. These raids were not uncommon. Generally patrons cooperated with the police in the hope of keeping their names and images out of the paper. That night was different. The patrons decided not to submit to being arrested on the flimsiest of charges and publicly humiliated. They determined that they would fight back. This is generally considered the birth of the gay rights movement. Over the course of the following evenings, as word of this unprecedented resistance spread, crowds gathered in support of homosexuals' civil rights. Riots ensued when the police tried to disperse the crowd. Many gay participants in these gatherings spoke of the exhilaration they felt at no longer being the passive victim.[65]

Italian Americans were also part of this evolution, though in a less dramatic fashion. It was not until 1966 that an Italian American became the CEO of a major bank in New York State. Mario Cuomo, who would eventually become governor of New York, was counseled in the late 1950s by well-intentioned law school officials to change his vowel-laden surname if he wanted to land a good job. Legendary auto executive Lee Iacocca attributes the fact that he was fired as president of Ford Motor Company to Henry Ford II's conviction that Iacocca had mob connections. (Ford reportedly spent $2 million investigating the charge and found no evidence of any such links.)[66]

While many Jewish baby boomers joined the civil rights, anti–Vietnam War, women's liberation, and gay rights movements, a significant cadre of them also turned their energies to the revitalization of Jewish communal life. American-born and well educated, they were equally at home in their American and Jewish skins. Empowered by the world of identity politics, they felt free to be "boldly Jewish in very angular ways." They challenged their parents' generation about almost everything, energized by the same tactics that were propelling many of the protest movements in America.[67] Regarding forms of worship and religious observance, they accused their parents of having stripped Jewish tradition of many of its distinctive elements in a misguided effort to fit into non-Jewish America. They also pushed for women's rights, created new and more participatory modes of worship, and embraced rituals long rejected by their parents because they were "too Jewish," and lobbied for Jewish studies programs at America's finest universities.

Faith in the Wake of Auschwitz: Shifting Theologies

This new generation of American Jews was also reading and listening to intellectuals, rabbis, and leaders such as Abraham Joshua Heschel, Emil Fackenheim, Elie Wiesel, Richard Rubenstein, and Irving "Yitz" Greenberg, all of whom by the mid-1960s were struggling with how to integrate the Holocaust into the arc of Jewish tradition, theology, culture, and community. What, they wondered, were its implications for contemporary Jewish life? They knew it had to be a part of the Jewish story. However, just as Salo Baron had cautioned many decades earlier, these theologians did not believe tragedy should dominate or become the sum total of that story. By 1966 Rubenstein's *After Auschwitz: Radical Theology and the Future of Judaism* was causing a stir among theologians—Jewish and non-Jewish—who were grappling with the nature of an omnipotent God. He spoke of the "death of God" in the wake of the Holocaust and rejected the notion of a transcendent God.

At the other end of the theological and ontological spectrum was Heschel, who had lost much of his immediate family in the Holocaust. Through his writings and his teaching he would shape the *Weltanschauung* of much of the leadership of the next generation of American Jewish spiritual leaders and, through them, their followers. Writing in the euphoria that followed the Six Day War in 1967, Heschel offered a resolution that was quite different from Rubenstein's:

> What should have been our answer to Auschwitz? Should this people, called to be a witness to the God of mercy and compassion, persist in its witness and cling to Job's words: "Even if He slay me yet will I trust in Him" (Job 13:15), or should this people follow the advice of Job's wife, "Curse God and die!" (Job 2:9), immerse itself into the anonymity of a hundred nations all over the world, and disappear once and for all? . . . We did not blaspheme, we built. Our people did not sally forth in flight from God. On the contrary, at that moment in history we saw the beginning of a new awakening, the emergence of a new concern for a Living God theology. Escape from Judaism giving place increasingly to a new attachment, to a rediscovery of our legacy.[68]

But Heschel did not reflect only on humanity's relationship with God in the wake of this tragedy. He also addressed the question of memory and its impact on the collective identity of a people. This was not a new idea for Heschel. Already in the very aftermath of the Holocaust he had written, "Just as an individual's memory determines the nature of his personality, so the collective memory determines the identity of nations. . . . The power of collective memory is one of the characteristics of Israel. . . . It is incumbent upon us to remember those events that occurred to our ancestors."[69] "Israel," the nation and the people, had to remember and integrate those memories into their identity. During the 1960s it was not just Heschel's theology that spoke to these students. He was an activist, marching with the Reverend Martin Luther King Jr. in the Selma-to-Montgomery civil rights march and co-chairing the antiwar group Clergy and Laity Concerned with Vietnam. As American Jewry's representative to Vatican II, he was one of those greatly responsible for persuading the Catholic Church to change those portions of its liturgy that vilified Jews and anticipated the conversion of the righteous and insightful among them to Christianity. This period and Heschel's influence on a small number of young, activist Jewish students marked the beginning of what anthropologist Riv-Ellen Prell describes as a "shift in the discourse of American Jewish life." An essential part of that shift involved a critique of American Jewish culture and a conviction that religion could be, in the words of one of Heschel's students in the late 1960s, "a positive force for social change."[70]

This shift in Jewish theologians' thinking was paralleled by the simultaneous efforts of a group of Christian theologians to confront their faith's role in paving the road to the Holocaust. A few of them had been struggling with this issue since the 1940s and 1950s. Franklin Littell, a pioneer in this field, had seen the devastation wrought upon the Jews when he worked in Europe in the period immediately following the war. By 1949, after sustained encounters with survivors, he began to focus upon the Christian failure to resist the "tragedy of the physical assault on the Jewish people." Roy Eckardt, writing from Europe in 1946, declaimed against the "religion of Nazism" and its attempts to annihilate the Jewish people. His Ph.D. dissertation at Columbia began by depicting how the Nazis had murdered the population of the Lodz ghetto.[71] Hubert Locke was a graduate student in theology in the 1950s in Chicago. He quickly recognized that all the leading contemporary theologians were Germans. It was early in the civil rights movement and Locke, a black man, wondered: What did "these great minds say and do about their own society when it was coming apart at the seams?" He soon discovered that, rather than castigate what they saw around them, many of them had been ardent supporters of the Third Reich. Shocked by this realization, he began to more closely examine the record of German Christians during the Holocaust. This brought him in touch with Littell and, together in the 1970s, they founded the International Scholars Conference on the German Church Struggle and the Holocaust. At Wayne State University in Detroit, Locke would also teach one of the first university courses on the topic.[72] Eva Fleischner, who was born in 1925 in Vienna to a Jewish father and Christian mother, was sent to England at age thirteen on a *Kindertransport* when the Nazis entered Vienna. She spent the war years in England and, after graduating from Harvard and spending time in Paris as a Fulbright scholar, she joined the Grail, a Catholic ecumenical organization, which independent of the Church hierarchy aimed at reaching women who could "transform the world." She not only joined this conversation but within a short time after beginning her Ph.D. work at Marquette was publicly challenging a Christian theologian who, while decrying the Holocaust, questioned whether it was in fact a "deed of Christian society." Writing in the *Journal of Ecumenical Studies* Elwin Smith argued that those who committed this heinous act had stopped being Christians and therefore Germany had not been a Christian state. Fleischner considered this "a preposterous maneuver to shift the focus of blame from ourselves, the henchmen, to the victims."[73] Littell, Fleischner, Eckardt, and their compatriots shared the conviction that the "Shoah is no more than / no less than the logical, moral (immoral) climax of some nineteen hundred years of Christian anti-Semitism."[74] Such direct challenges by Christians to their own faith and its history were unique at the time.

Soon a "second generation" of Christian thinkers began to struggle with the implications of the Shoah for their own tradition. John Roth, whose courses on the Holocaust would lead to his being named National Professor of the Year by the Carnegie Foundation for the Advancement of Teaching, acknowledges that the more he learned about the Holocaust the clearer it became to him that his "own Christian tradition was implicated."[75] James Cargas, a professor of English who eventually came to describe himself as a post-Auschwitz Catholic, devoted much of his scholarly career to writing about the Holocaust. He was brought to the topic by a chance reading of an excerpt from Elie Wiesel's *Night* that was published in a Catholic periodical. The son of a "passively racist and passively anti-Semitic" father who made it clear to his son that "Negroes were not welcome" in their home and taught him what it meant to "jew someone down," Cargas points to the "momentous Saturday afternoon" when he bought the magazine because the father of a young boy on a team he coached was the editor. He happened upon Wiesel's work. At that moment, he recalled over thirty years later, "the direction of my life began to change." After reading *Night* in its entirety, he turned to other books on the topic and very quickly came to the "crashing realization that probably every Jew killed in the Holocaust was murdered by a baptized Christian."[76] For Eugene Fisher, who would eventually serve as executive secretary of the Secretariat for Catholic-Jewish Relations of the National Conference of Catholic Bishops, U.S.A., it was also *Night* that "riveted his attention" on the Holocaust.[77]

For these theologians the Holocaust posed a great theological challenge to their faith.[78] Echoing Littell, Fleischner, Locke, Roy Eckardt and others, Alice Eckardt declared the Shoah to be far more of a Christian problem than a Jewish problem. But this was not just a theological issue and something to be mourned. It demanded action on their part. Rosemary Radford Ruether, a committed Christian and a veteran of the civil rights movement, was not alone when she asserted that the Holocaust compelled Christians to undertake a "profound reassessment of this whole heritage [of Christian teachings regarding Jews]. . . . The church . . . must take responsibility for the perpetuation of the demonic myth of the Jews that allowed the Nazis to make them the scapegoat of their project of racial purity."[79] These scholars and activists, for whom Christianity shaped both their professional and personal lives, became Jewish theologians' conversation partners. By 1974 Robert McAfee Brown, a member of the faculty of Union Theological Seminary in New York, was teaching a course on Elie Wiesel. His students, among them Mary Boys, a member of the religious congregation Sisters of the Holy Names of Jesus and Mary, attended Wiesel's lectures at the 92nd

Street Y.[80] Jewish scholars welcomed and sometimes marveled at these Christians' willingness to confront their own tradition in such a forceful manner. (Some cynics wondered if these theologians were being closely listened to by Jews and virtually ignored by their fellow Christians.)[81]

Carol Rittner, who entered the convent just as Vatican II was under-way and who eventually became the founding director of the Elie Wiesel Foundation for Humanity, "confronted" for the first time the horror that was Auschwitz when she read Viktor Frankl's memoir, *Man's Search for Meaning*. Because none of her professors in graduate school, which she began in 1971, seemed interested in her questions about the Holocaust, she proceeded to read on her own. She eventually read Jules Isaac's *Jesus and Israel*, an exploration of the centuries of the Christian "teaching of contempt" for Jews and an explication of the way the Gospels presented a distorted picture of Jesus' attitude toward Israel. (When she first read the book Rittner did not know that Isaac's pivotal audience with Pope John XXIII had served as a major impetus for the convening of Vatican II.)[82] This Catholic nun began to struggle with such questions as "Where were the churches? Where were the Christians? Why didn't they help the Jews?" In the mid-1970s, after extensive reading, attending lectures by Wiesel, taking McAfee Brown's course, and studying at Yad Vashem, she offered one of the earliest courses on the Holocaust to be taught at a Catholic college. To this day she sees the Holocaust in terms of the "contradiction" between her commitment as a nun to giving her "whole life to being of service to people" and her horror at how the "underside of Christian theology with its anti-Judaism and anti-Semitism" was a cornerstone of genocide.[83]

These Christians were confounded to learn that over the course of centuries some of the Church's most pious adherents had engaged in overt expressions of hostility—if not calls for physical violence—toward Jews. Decades later, Peggy Obrecht, a Presbyterian who would become the founding director of the United States Holocaust Memorial Museum's (USHMM) Committee on Church Relations and the Holocaust, and who laid the foundation for many of the museum's interfaith programs and seminars, still recalled her teenage shock when she learned how centuries of venerated Church leaders had engaged in virulent expression of anti-semitism: "I had never heard such things." But it was not just the historical record of the Church that upset her and numerous others. Alice Eckardt recalled how in 1938, right after *Kristallnacht*, a Christian neighbor in her hometown of Bethlehem, Pennsylvania, expressed satisfaction that Hitler "was putting the Jews in their place."[84] And Obrecht was appalled to encounter antisemitism in high school in the 1950s. Warned away from a particular school because "it's where the Jews go" (it had precisely two Jewish students), she was taken aback by these overt expressions of contempt for Jews. In the 1970s, while conducting a Christian-Jewish dialogue, she experienced a "perfectly horrible moment" when a participant asked: "Where were you when I was being called 'Christ killer' on the schoolyard? Where were you when I encountered anti-Semitism in the workplace? Where were you when my life as a Jew was repeatedly being marked by encounters with hate from Christians?"[85] For these people questions such as "Where were the Christians?" may seem admittedly naïve today. But as Rittner has observed, in the 1960s when she and others like her began their explorations, they had not yet come to the realization that Hitler and his henchmen built their "deadly ideology on the twin foundations of racist anti-Semitism and anti-Judaism in Christian theology."[86]

Father John Pawlikowski, who describes himself as a "child of Vatican II," was an early participant in the Christian–Jewish dialogues that began in the immediate aftermath of the gathering. Reflecting on those early exchanges that took place in the 1960s, Pawlikowski recalls that, rather than the Holocaust, the topic of antisemitism was more likely to be on the agenda. But by the end of the 1960s, in the wake of the Six Day War, that changed as the Holocaust became a more frequent topic. Social ethics, the focus of his graduate work, became his entry point to the field. While he recognized the Catholic Church's failures during the war, he concerned himself not with excoriating Pius but with exploring the pope's failed vision of leadership at a time of social crisis: "Pius' record can't be changed but the contemporary response of the church to crisis could be." According to Pawlikowski, the World War II Vatican was too much dominated by juridical ideas, institutional concerns, and tools of diplomacy and too little dominated by ideas of mercy, service, and social justice. By 1968 he was integrating the Holocaust into his courses on social ethics. For a number of years he was one of the few instructors in Catholic institutions or, for that matter, any other institution, to do so.[87]

Victoria Barnett is part of the second generation of Christian theologians who entered and, to some degree, helped build the field that studies the German Church during the Holocaust. The director of the USHMM's Programs on Ethics, Religion, and the Holocaust, she first encountered the Holocaust when she was a graduate student in 1978 at Union Theological Seminary and took McAfee Brown's course on Wiesel. By the following year she was in Germany doing research on Protestant churches and the Holocaust.

Ultimately these scholars, theologians, and activists came to the topic of the Holocaust from different directions. Some, such as Obrecht and Alice Eckardt, began with the context of Christian–Jewish relations.

Mary Boys entered through a theological door. Others, such as Reuther, Locke, and Roth, who describes himself as a "philosopher who was tripped up by history," were propelled by a desire to uncover the historical record of their faith and its contribution to this crisis. Irrespective of how they entered the field, virtually all of them expressed a sense of "shock" and "surprise" at discovering their tradition's deep-seated moral failure, its anti-Jewish polemics, and dismal record of antisemitic actions.[88] Years later, as they looked back on their discovery of this "dark side" of the Church's history, many of them seemed uniformly bemused by their shock. The evidence had been there all along but they had never seen it. Eva Fleischner, who had attended Catholic schools and whose life had been animated by her faith, was completely taken aback—"What," she wondered, "was going on here?"—when, upon beginning her doctoral work in the late 1960s, she encountered the "persistent animosity on the part of Christians—many of them canonized saints in my church—to the people to whom they owed the origins of their faith."[89]

They took varied paths to the topic and expressed their interest in a multiplicity of ways. What cannot, however, be emphasized enough is the role they played in the evolution of the American encounter with Christianity's role in the Holocaust. Long before many students of Jewish history and theology were confronting this issue, they were.[90] While for Jews it might have evoked feelings of sadness and loss, for them it evoked, in addition, a sense of shame and disappointment in the theological system that so undergirded and shaped their lives. As Fleischner noted in her comments at the important 1974 conference held at New York's famed cathedral Saint John the Divine, in the post-Holocaust era it was easier on some level to be the heirs to the victims than the heirs to the perpetrators.[91]

At the same time a radical shift in theological thinking regarding the Holocaust was occurring among Jewish thinkers. In March 1966 the editors of *Judaism,* then one of the premier journals of Jewish thought and contemporary affairs, convened a symposium. Participants included the literary critic George Steiner, the philosopher Emil Fackenheim, and Elie Wiesel. It was here that Fackenheim, who had thus far dedicated most of his scholarly work to Hegel, first articulated an idea that would shape many Jewish attitudes toward the Holocaust. Fackenheim argued that after the Holocaust there was a new commandment for Jews. Whereas Jewish tradition posits that Hebrew Scripture contains 613 commandments, a 614th had been added in the wake of the Holocaust: "Thou shalt not hand Hitler a posthumous victory. Thou shalt live as a Jew." In the decades to follow, Fackenheim's teaching would become the rationale for a broad array of activities including observing the Sabbath, giving *tzedakah* (charity), and marrying a Jew. His actual teaching was, in fact, far more nuanced:

> We are, first, commanded to survive as Jews, lest the Jewish people perish. We are commanded, secondly, to remember in our very guts and bones the martyrs of the Holocaust, lest their memory perish. We are forbidden, thirdly, to deny or despair of God, however much we may have to contend with him or with belief in him, lest Judaism perish. We are forbidden, finally, to despair of the world as the place which is to become the kingdom of God, lest we help make it a meaningless place in which God is dead or irrelevant and everything is permitted. To abandon any of these imperatives, in response to Hitler's victory at Auschwitz would be to hand him yet other, posthumous victories.[92]

But the subtlety of Fackenheim's statement would be lost, as the Holocaust became a ubiquitous part of Jewish life.

Yitz Greenberg, an Orthodox rabbi who taught at Yeshiva University, also had a profound impact on bringing the topic of the Holocaust into the discourse of American Jews. Initially his audience was, in the main, Orthodox Jews, particularly the baby boom generation. (By the 1980s he would have an even greater following outside the Orthodox community than within it.) Greenberg argued that the Holocaust was of tremendous religious significance, far more than previous Jewish tragedies, and called for both a communal and religious response. He challenged American Jews to engage in a "communal and theological effort . . . to confront the challenges of the Holocaust." It had to be "integrated" into and shape contemporary Jewish life.[93] It was, in fact, Greenberg's argument about the integration of the Holocaust into contemporary life that prompted Pawlikowski to rethink his theological stance and begin to see the Holocaust as both a challenge to all covenantal religions and as an exemplar of the failure of religious institutions at a time of social crisis. Most contemporary social ethicists were then concerned primarily with the meaning of evil. Pawlikowski credits his expansion of the parameters of the question to his interactions with Greenberg and his encounters with Holocaust survivors, which began at a 1972 conference at Saint John the Divine in New York. He began to struggle not just with evil, but also with the degree of human responsibility in face of evil.[94]

The Baby Boom Protesters

The rabbis and theologians may have engaged in "revolutionary" discourse. But, as was the case in much of the Western world during this period, it was the students who were the foot soldiers who transformed this discourse into facts on the ground and who spearheaded a countercultural revolt against established American Jewish religious and communal life. From the Jewish Theological Seminary, its neighbor Columbia University—which was in the throes of its own revolution—and beyond came activist students who wanted to change the nature of the American Jewish world. Instigating a period of tremendous creativity, they called for courses in Jewish studies (following the lead of African American students), challenged the entrenched communal leadership, and created all sorts of homegrown nontraditional worship groups that were decidedly not aligned with the organized Jewish community. Soon Jewish women, who played a formative role in the general women's movement, were also calling for changes in the Jewish community. They wanted to participate more fully in religious activities and did not want to be shunted aside from top leadership positions in Jewish communal organizations. When young Jewish women demanded that the Conservative movement count them in a minyan (prayer quorum), the *New York Times* covered the story. Admittedly, it placed it on the "Food, Fashion, Family, and Furnishings" page. But a little over a year later, in September 1973, when the Conservative movement announced it would indeed begin to count women in a minyan, the story made the front page.[95] Reform Jews responded as well. Pushed by its younger members, including students, campers, and emerging leaders within Reform, the movement's governing body slowly began to embrace Jewish rituals and practice that generations of Reform Jews had proudly abandoned. Kippot (skullcaps) and talitot (prayer shawls) became a common sight in Reform synagogues. Hebrew Union College, the Reform rabbinical seminary, began to offer a vegetarian food option for students who did not want to eat non-kosher meat. New rituals built on traditional sources, such as a simchat bat, the celebration of the birth of a girl, became commonplace. Sales of books on Jewish topics—particularly on living a Jewish life—skyrocketed.

This baby boom generation also critiqued the community's exterior life, that is, how Jews related to those around them, especially those in power. With a certainty that bordered on self-righteousness, they condemned their elders for being afraid to "speak truth to power," particularly when it came to the welfare of other Jews. Using the Holocaust as means of differentiating between their behavior and those of their parents, they pointing at the perceived failings of American Jewish leaders during the war years and asked, why had they not done more?

Their use of the Holocaust to differentiate between their response to Jewish persecution and that of previous generations was fueled by such books as Arthur Morse's *While Six Million Died: A Chronicle of American Apathy*, which, in a rather sensationalized approach, accused America and American Jews of having failed to rescue European Jewry.[96] Forgotten in

Morse's account, which British historian Tony Kushner has described, not inaccurately, as "semi-journalistic and angry in tone," were the protests and boycotts that were conducted by American Jews.[97] Nonetheless his book became the template for many American Jews' perception of what happened in America during the Holocaust. Within a few years other studies of the topic—scholarly, journalistic, and polemical—appeared. David Wyman's *Paper Walls* built on Morse's argument. He traced the State Department's use of bureaucratic and administrative minutiae, the "paper walls" of his title, to keep Jews out of this country during the prewar period. But, as Wyman demonstrated, behind those walls flourished numerous instances of overt antisemitism by many of the officials who oversaw the immigration process. Henry Feingold's *The Politics of Rescue* made a similar argument.[98] Both Feingold and Wyman contextualized their criticism within the political realities of the 1930s and 1940s, reminding their readers that much of the explanation for America's failure to act lay in the social and political realities of the day, including unemployment, xenophobia, rampant antisemitism, and growing isolationism. These books were followed by yet others, many with an increasingly shriller tone. In many cases one had to read no further than the title to grasp the author's argument, as in *The Jews Were Expendable, No Haven for the Oppressed,* and *The Failure to Rescue.*[99] The authors painted a dismal picture of America and its refugee/rescue policy. Rather than a heroic America that ousted evil tyrants, defeated nefarious regimes, and freed oppressed peoples, these critics depicted an America that had callously stood by while Jews were oppressed and killed. Some of the books accused the White House, State Department, and Congress not just of standing by but of erecting roadblocks to rescue. President Franklin Delano Roosevelt was cast as the primary culprit. Given the reverence for him held by so many American Jews, this vigorous critique was striking.

But Morse and these other critics did not have only Washington officials in their rifle sights. They also took the American Jewish establishment to task for adhering to a policy of quiet diplomacy when far more strident behavior was called for. The critics accused "uptown," acculturated, wealthy, and religiously liberal Jews of caring more about what non-Jews would say than about the fate of their fellow Jews; they did not protest or demand action when government officials failed to act. These critics—of whom I was one—helped forge many of the "central features of the historiographical landscape" concerning America's response to the Holocaust.[100]

Their accusations were, of course, not entirely new. They had been made during the war itself by a small, active, and energetic group of Jews who eschewed the established Jewish community's quiet behind-the-scenes diplomacy.[101] But after the war these accusations lost their potency.

Roosevelt was dead. The camps were opened and survivors had to be assisted. A new Jewish state desperately needed support. The Cold War was brewing. Most importantly, Americans had embraced an image of their country as having fought "the good war." The wartime debate that had so roiled American Jews about the failure to rescue did not just end. It disappeared and was virtually forgotten until the late 1960s with the confluence of the emerging protest movements and this literature of critique. It would become and remain a historical marker that demonstrated why contemporary American Jews must never be like their World War II–era predecessors.

But it was not only young Jews for whom study of the Holocaust became a means of sorting out some of the upheavals that marked American society beginning in the late 1960s. Among those who would go on to play a major, if not critical, role in shaping Holocaust studies in the United States were a group of non-Jewish baby boomers. For them it was not Eichmann, the Six Day War, Vatican II, or any other assertion of their religious identity that brought them to this field. It was what they were witnessing around them. Historian Peter Hayes, who would become one of the world's experts on the role of German corporations during the Holocaust, felt sympathy for African Americans, shame at segregation, and anger at the Vietnam War. Hayes saw Vietnam as "a racist effort by the United States to inflict pain and [bring about the] destruction of people depicted as 'gooks.'" Watching police officials such as Birmingham's infamous Bull Connor direct the use of police dogs and fire hoses against civil rights activists reminded the young Hayes of what he had read about the SS. Learning of the My Lai massacre left him fearing that the Final Solution "could happen here."[102] A similar story surrounds John Roth. While a theological struggle about the role of Christianity in the Holocaust may have ultimately brought him to this field of study, his self-described "seedbed" experience came years earlier—although, he acknowledges, he "did not know it then." He was in high school when his father, a Presbyterian minister in southern Indiana, was forced out of his pulpit because he wanted to open the church to people of all races. His parishioners thought otherwise. After his father lost his job, the family had to relocate. Looking back decades later, Roth described this experience as "one of those things that aroused [in him] a passion about racism." It was the "ignition" of his commitment to the study of "racism's genocidal logic" and made him "a ripe candidate" for a "professional and personal turning" toward the topic of the Holocaust. That turning came when, as a Yale graduate student, he encountered the work of Rubenstein and Wiesel. Reading Wiesel changed his life "personally and professionally."[103]

Civil rights also formed the context for Karl Schleunes, whose *Twisted Road to Auschwitz* was the first American book to argue that the Holocaust was not the result of a single order from Hitler but the work of a multitude of bureaucrats. As a graduate student in the early 1960s he explored the evolution of the Final Solution and the role antisemitism played in it. At the same time the civil rights movement's battle against racial prejudice served as a "moral inspiration." When he marched with the Reverend Martin Luther King in Chicago he felt that on some level he was engaged in a contemporary manifestation of the fight that should have been waged against antisemitism. "It felt," he told me as he looked back on those years, "as if it were the same thing."[104]

Christopher Browning, one of America's premier historians of the Final Solution, credits the Vietnam War with providing a crucial context for his interest in studying the Final Solution. Reading Arendt while the war was raging, he found her notion of the banality of evil particularly "applicable to the American misadventure in Vietnam into which the 'best and the brightest' of the Kennedy and Johnson administrations had led the country." He subsequently turned to Hilberg's book, which he found "electrifying and exhilarating" and one that "changed his life." When he began his Ph.D. studies in 1970 he told his advisor that he wanted to study the Nazi bureaucracy, particularly the "Jewish experts" of the German Foreign Office who were the official liaison to Eichmann and the SS. He was cautioned by his dissertation adviser, as Hilberg had been in the 1950s, that while the topic was good, it had "no professional future" because there were no universities offering courses on the topic, few academic journals seeking papers on the subject, and few colleagues working in that field. Browning persisted and found that by the late 1970s things had changed dramatically.[105]

Robert Ericksen, who has done path-breaking work on the Protestant church and German theologians, had similar experiences. As an undergraduate he witnessed the American civil rights struggle and developed "a sensitivity" to America's failures. He credits his interest in the behavior of German intellectuals and theologians during the Holocaust to his "amazement at how smart people in the LBJ cabinet could support the Vietnam War. . . . How could they have gotten it so wrong?" While Ericksen, the son of a Lutheran minister, credits his religious heritage for his specific interest in German church leaders, there was one additional context that shaped both his and Browning's career paths: Watergate. Ericksen recalled being in Gottingen doing research as Congress investigated the unfolding Watergate scandal. The corruption in his own government echoed for him the corruption he was reading about in the Third Reich.[106] For Browning "the parallels between the criminal bureaucrats of the Nazi regime whom I was studying and the criminal political operatives of the Nixon regime were . . . inescapable." He had documented the work of the most important members of the Jewish Desk of the German Foreign Office, all of whom were well educated. Three had law degrees and one a doctorate in anthropology. All joined the Nazi party in 1933, not because they were antisemites, but because they saw career opportunities. They distinguished themselves, as Browning observed, as "self-made, professional anti-Semites," willing to do whatever was necessary to advance their careers and the Nazi cause. Though well aware that there was no "moral or historical equivalency" between the crimes of the Final Solution and the Nixon White House, Browning saw a bureaucratic parallel between those who helped run the Final Solution and those in the Nixon White House who engaged in various "dirty tricks." They all considered themselves above the law. Both sets of bureaucrats needed no explicit instructions from on high to figure out what they had to do. They would do whatever was necessary. Browning recalled how "one of the most ambitious and vicious among them, Charles Colson, later admitted he would have run over his grandmother to get the president re-elected."[107]

By the early 1970s the Holocaust had become a means for a cadre of both Jews and non-Jews, some of whom were self-identifying religious Christians, to make sense of the political and social upheavals in their own country.

From the Mideast to Moscow: Holocaust Redux?

Unexpectedly, in the spring of 1967 developments on the international scene gave the Holocaust a newfound relevance among a broad swath of American Jews. In May of that year Egyptian President Gamal Abdel Nasser mobilized his army and ordered the United Nations troops stationed on the Israeli–Egyptian border to withdraw from Sinai and from Gaza. The troops had been stationed there since the 1956 Sinai War to ensure there were no border violations and that Israeli ships would be able to pass freely through the Straits of Tiran, at the tip of the Sinai Peninsula. The U.N. Secretary General immediately complied. Egypt then massed troops and tanks along the Israeli border and closed the straits to all ships headed to or from Israel. On May 26 Nasser declared that, if there was a war, its main objective would be the destruction of Israel.[108] Other Arab nations, including Jordan, Syria, Saudi Arabia, and Iraq, aligned with Egypt in anticipation of what some of their leaders were calling a "holy war." Responding to a reporter's question about what would happen to the residents of Israel when the Arabs conquer it, Palestine Liberation Organization (PLO) chairman Ahmad Shukeiri matter-of-factly stated: "Those who survive will remain in Palestine. I estimate that none of them will survive."[109]

American Jews, deeply frightened by these developments, began to fear that a tragedy was in the offing. The Holocaust became the metaphor that gave both expression and context to those fears. It seemed to be on every American Jew's mind. Lucy Dawidowicz described the period as a "trauma" that included "a reliving of the Holocaust." American Jews were beset by feelings of "anxiety . . . tension . . . irritability . . . [and] nervousness," and as the days dragged on they felt a "frightening sense of impotence." They feared that a "collective Auschwitz" was in the offing for Israel.[110] Literary scholar Robert Alter recalled how the Jewish community feared that three million Jews "might be annihilated."[111] "Gloom and despair" prevailed.[112] Professor Saul H. Lieberman of the Jewish Theological Seminary, the era's preeminent historian of the Talmud, gave voice to that anguish. "The Jewish people have never in its history passed through an hour of such dangers. Its entire existence is gravely threatened."[113] That those who were deeply connected to the Jewish community should have felt this way was not surprising. More striking was the number of unaffiliated Jews, people who had shown no connection to any form of organized Jewish life, who responded similarly. Rabbis and Jewish communal workers reported that among those who came forward to donate funds were people they had either never known before or who had previously rejected invitations to affiliate with the Jewish community. In less than a month the United Jewish Appeal raised over $100 million, though it is unclear how people thought their money would be used. (American law prohibits charitable donations from being used for foreign military purposes.) Many contributors likely assumed their funds would help bolster the Israeli economy, which was essentially shut down for nearly a month. But the sums raised far exceeded those needs. Dawidowicz wondered if "perhaps for many their contributions were in expiation for their indifference 25 years earlier."[114]

Young people, members of the protest generation who had previously expressed pointed disdain for the established community and its leadership, also volunteered in unprecedented numbers to travel to Israel and fill jobs that had been left open because of the nationwide call-up of reserve soldiers. They picked fruit, washed floors in hospitals, delivered the mail, and, in so doing, deepened their relationship with Israel. According to Milton Himmelfarb, a wry observer of American Jewish life and an editor of the influential publication *Commentary*, these young Jews suddenly realized "that genocide, anti-Semitism, a desire to murder Jews—all those things were not merely what one had been taught about a bad, stupid past, not merely the fault of elders who are almost a different species. Those things were real and present. . . . Suddenly the Jews of Israel were seen to be potentially as wretched as anyone can be."[115] Though not everyone saw the young people's heightened interest and identification in such cynical terms, the spike in their Jewish self-identity was undeniable.

It was not, however, just fear and foreboding that reminded American Jews of the Holocaust. There was also frustration—if not outright anger—at the response of other nations to this potential Jewish tragedy. As the situation grew more severe, the Western democracies, including the United States, France, and Great Britain, seemed to be reacting with great equanimity. France, until then Israel's main supplier of arms, instituted an embargo on all weapons to the area, thereby depriving Israel of weapons. While the Soviet Union provided a steady supply of arms to the Arabs, America seemed reluctant to help.[116] For many Jews this resembled the world's response to the dangers the Jews faced in the 1930s and 1940s. Abraham Joshua Heschel captured this sentiment: "The world that was silent while six million died was silent again, save for individual friends. The anxiety . . . grueling, the isolation . . . dreadful."[117]

Expectations of a Holocaust redux notwithstanding, Israel achieved notable military victories. American Jews who had not been on the battlefield felt like vicarious soldiers. Even more important than the unprecedented amounts of money they had donated was the way they had openly and unashamedly called for American support of Israel. If prior to the war they had used Holocaust analogies to give expression to their fears, now they used them to articulate a newfound sense of security and to highlight how much Jewish life had changed. As never before, American Jews saw Israel's response to the military threat it faced as a historical corrective. While most other nations sat silently by as the threat to Israel mounted, Israelis, who in the eyes of many American Jews were extensions of themselves, had not. Knowing they were about to be attacked, Israel had delivered the first strike. Some Jews openly expressed the wish that Jews had acted this way twenty-five years earlier. A Jew who had previously been completely unconnected with the Jewish community or its traditions told sociologist Marshall Sklare, "No more does the Jew march to the oven." This woman, a successful professional who, much to the consternation of her Jewish and even her non-Jewish colleagues, worked on Yom Kippur, easily slipped into the first-person plural as she described how things had changed. "*We* never fought back before. *We* always picked up our bundles and ran. *Now* we can fight back." Her son, a graduate student, told his mother he could not comprehend why Jews had "walked to the gas chambers." He believed in "fighting back."[118]

Jews' self-image was not the only thing that changed as a result of the war. The world's image of the Jew did as well. Robert Alter described how the image had been transformed from a "grim" vision of "endless lines of wan, gaunt figures trudging off to the factories of death" into "the counter-image of Jews in armored columns rolling across the Sinai to crush the massed army that intended their destruction."[119] Jews heard these sentiments throughout the United States. A Georgia gas station employee declared: "I always thought Jews were 'yaller,' but those Jews, man they're tough."[120] One Jew reported that a Gentile business associate with whom he had done business for many years made a long-distance call (which in 1967 was still considered out of the ordinary) to tell him, "You Hebes really taught those guys a lesson." Sklare described the reaction that Israel's possible obliteration and eventual victory elicited in May and June 1967 not as "a response to Israel in the conventional sense but rather a response to events of Jewish history from the 1930's onward."[121] In the United States a poster that gained popularity during this period perhaps best epitomized this idea. A man in Hasidic garb is shown emerging from a phone booth; as he does so, he tears opens his shirt to reveal a Superman costume underneath. Rather than the letter *S* on the middle of his chest, however, there is a large *J*. From super fears to Super Jew. But within a brief six years, the euphoria over Israel's 1967 victory would be eclipsed by the losses sustained in the 1973 Yom Kippur War. Once again the shadow of the Holocaust loomed large, as both Egypt and Syria mounted surprise attacks on the Day of Atonement, appearing to put Israel on the brink of military collapse before the tide eventually turned. By this time the image of Israel as the symbolic counterpoint to the Holocaust, so evident in 1967, had become firmly fixed among American Jews.[122]

Events in the Middle East were not alone in giving Holocaust imagery contemporary relevance. The increasingly difficult situation of Soviet Jews, then the third-largest Jewish community in the world, did so as well. Communist ideology posited that religious identities were obsolete and a danger to society. Jews faced serious discrimination and overt anti-semitism. In addition to their rights to worship or to learn about their tradition being severely constricted, they encountered professional and personal obstacles just for being Jewish. As reports on their increasingly difficult situation reached America, a relatively small group of Jewish students made it into a cause. With the civil rights movement engaging in massive protests and the concept of identity politics gaining momentum, some American Jews, primarily students who had a strong Jewish communal and religious affiliation, began to protest on behalf of Soviet Jews. In May 1964 the first rally for Soviet Jews was organized in just four days, with 1,000 students gathering outside the Soviet Mission to the United Nations and chanting—with clear reference to the Holocaust—"History Shall Not Repeat."[123] These developments rattled the American Jewish community, whose unwritten policy since the establishment of Israel was to avoid mass protest rallies in favor of quiet diplomacy. Younger Jews, increasingly schooled in protest activities, dismissed these efforts as ineffective and outmoded.[124] (For its part, Israel also eschewed public protests. It assumed it could accomplish more by quiet action.)

Then came the crisis of May and June 1967. The USSR sided with the Arabs and broke relations with Israel. It also began to disseminate virulently antisemitic propaganda. Internally it pressured Jews to eschew all expressions of Jewish identity. A few Jews, rather than be frightened into silence, took a different tack. They held open protests, an unheard of tactic in the USSR. Small groups began to study about their history and tradition. Relying on official Soviet policy, which allowed for the limited reunification of families, they requested permission to immigrate to Israel. They were refused and thus gained the appellation *refuseniks*. Soon they were fired from their jobs and subjected to an array of governmental recriminations. The more they enhanced their Jewish identity, the more likely they were to be subjected to KGB surveillance and persecution.

Efforts on behalf of Soviet Jews received an added boost by the publication in 1967 of Elie Wiesel's *The Jews of Silence,* a report on his visit to Soviet Jews. Wiesel wrote that prior to his trip he was convinced that their situation was "not so unbearable." His encounter with them altered his perception. People sidled up to him at the synagogue and in voices that were "choked and fearful" asked him, "Do you know what is happening to us?" People quietly whispered in his ear but as soon as they sensed someone was watching, ended in mid-sentence and slipped away. When he returned he described the "community of terrorized captives, on the brink of some awful abyss" that he had found there.[125] In the wake of the Six Day War, Soviet pressure on Jews increased and the policy of "quiet talks and quiet diplomacy" was understood by the American Jewish community to be outmoded and irrelevant. Israel, which no longer had relations with the USSR and no means to engage in quiet actions, turned to select American Jews and asked them to travel to the Soviet Union. They were to contact *refuseniks,* bring them educational supplies, and, most importantly, tell their story when they returned home.

Throughout this period—both before and after the community changed its policies—activists drew parallels between the fate of European Jewry during World War II and Soviet Jews. Although Soviet Jewry activists soon replaced the mantra "History shall not repeat" with the catchier slogan "Never again," both directly tied the situation of

Soviet Jews to the Holocaust. Underneath this two-word phrase was the message that American Jews were resolved to never again let another Jewish community be wiped out, physically or even spiritually, as had been the case in the 1940s. But there was a secondary meaning to the slogan. It was directed not at the perpetrators (the Soviets) but at the bystanders. Never again would Jews in other countries, the United States in particular, sit idly by as harm was done to their fellow Jews. Given that the students who first chanted these slogans had not been born during the Holocaust, there was an added import to their message: We won't respond as our parents purportedly did. We will not be cowed into silence. We will march. We will protest. We will not put our safety and security ahead of the suffering of our fellow Jews.[126] As the historian Ismar Schorsch has observed, one cannot fully understand the efforts on behalf of Soviet Jewry without taking into account the "powerful guilt feelings" over American Jews' "timid and inept" behavior during the Holocaust.[127] These sentiments were seething just under the surface for many, regardless of whether they had been in a position at that time to do anything about the situation in Europe, or had even been alive during World War II. The Vietnam protest generation found it easy to castigate their parents' generation.

In his report on Soviet Jewry, Wiesel had excoriated American Jews for responding with a shrug when he told them what he had found. They insisted, according to Wiesel, that his story must be "exaggerated." Echoing what American Jewish leaders had said during World War II, contemporary Jewish leaders told him "we can do nothing about it; or we must not do too much lest we be accused of interfering in the cold war." He told American audiences that he was tormented, not by the silence and fear he found among Soviet Jews, but "the silence of the Jews I live among today."[128] As he told a meeting of 500 Conservative rabbis in 1966, just as Jews had been "abandoned" by American Jewry during the Holocaust, so too Soviet Jews were now being abandoned by them.[129] For the next two decades, until the collapse of the USSR, the link between the Holocaust and the protests on behalf of Soviet Jewry remained explicit. When American Jews chanted "Never again" at Soviet Jewry marches and protest meetings, and when they emblazoned it on T-shirts, placards, and banners, the slogan was about them as much as it was about Soviet Jews. Jewish activists had accused the previous generation of sitting silently by as a community of their fellow Jews faced communal extinction. The same would not be said of them.[130] "Never again" became and remains a fixed part of the American Jewish lexicon.

There was no surer sign that by the end of the 1960s the Holocaust, both the word and the topic, had become established on the American cultural and scholarly agenda than the Library of Congress's decision in September 1968 to create a new classification in its Humanities Section: "Holocaust. Jewish (1939–1945)." Prior to creating a classification, the LOC must be convinced that the topic is neither a fad nor the province of a small group of authors. It has to be important in and of itself and have staying power. With this action, it was clear that, in the eyes of this scholarly and cultural gatekeeper, the word was now firmly linked to the annihilation of European Jewry.[131] Ironically, the LOC has not retained its notes on how precisely the choice to use the dates 1939–1945, as opposed to 1933–1945, was made. In the 1990s, once the field had expanded and developed far more than anyone had anticipated, the LOC would return to the issue. Some scholars pointed out that the euthanasia of those the Third Reich deemed handicapped or disabled as well as numerous antisemitic actions of the 1930s were being separated into a different designation. Though there does not seem to have been much discussion of the LOC's 1968 decision at the time, undoubtedly most scholars welcomed it, its complexities and shortcomings notwithstanding.[132]

Yet public awareness was still, even among scholars, highly attenuated. In the late 1960s the *Encyclopedia Americana* was preparing its 1968 edition. It turned to Raul Hilberg, then already recognized as the leading historian on the destruction of European Jewry, to write about concentration camps. Intent on making his contribution more comprehensive than that in the *Encyclopedia Britannica*, Hilberg labored over the assignment. The editors were pleased and asked for two additional small articles, one on Buchenwald and the other on Dachau. Hilberg waited to be asked to write a similar submission on Auschwitz or Treblinka, two camps that, in the historical context of the genocide, were far more significant. But no such request ever came. And no such articles were included in that edition.[133]

Survivors: From DPs to Witnesses

As noted, survivors had found the Eichmann trial to be a "profoundly liberating event." For the first time the Holocaust narrative was broadly discussed and heeded outside of their immediate circles. In the wake of the trial the perception that survivors' stories were exaggerated or even false began to dissipate. After the trial they were increasingly seen as a coherent group with a story worth telling.[134] However, to root the changes in the survivors' situation solely in the Eichmann trial is to ignore other important factors. By the end of the 1960s, survivors themselves were in a very different position. At the time of their liberation many were in their late teens and early twenties. They focused their energies on rebuilding their lives, finding jobs, acquiring spouses, having children, and making new friends. Some were naturally reluctant to speak of the past because of the trauma they endured. Others kept silent because they doubted, correctly, that Americans wished to listen. Paula was one such survivor, interviewed by Henry Greenspan repeatedly in a longitudinal study over many decades. Age fifteen when she was liberated, she then told a room full of Allied soldiers and former POWs that "the crematorium remains our nightmare. We are telling everybody about it, whether we want to or not." A few years later, after settling in the United States, she told Greenspan something quite different. She now felt a "stigma and silence" imposed upon her. Survivors were not just told to "keep it to yourself"; they silenced themselves. "Because we were trying to find a place in the community. We had to survive again, in a new country."[135] But by the 1970s survivors were settled into their new lives. This certainly made them more comfortable about speaking out.

American attitudes toward survivors of war, illness, and a variety of traumas were shifting as well. Americans were beginning to think about catastrophe survivors in general, from Hiroshima to cancer to sexual abuse, in different terms. The beginnings of these changes were evident in Robert Jay Lifton's *Death in Life,* a study of the survivors of Hiroshima. Winner of the National Book Award for 1967, the book was part of a growing body of literature of critique that reevaluated America's past. Lifton observed that, though Hiroshima may have brought an American victory, it had left many victims. It behooved us, he argued, to understand the impact of this event on them. Lifton found that, rather than pathetic and terribly damaged individuals in need of help, they were people who, after having "come in contact with death in some bodily or psychic fashion" and emerged alive, possessed a certain resilience. Deliberately eschewing the term "victim," he argued that they had much to teach us, the bystanders. Years later he reflected on this transition. "When you use the term victim you wonder what's wrong with the person but when you use the term survivor you wonder what's wrong with the person who did this to them."[136] He compared the Hiroshima survivors with Holocaust survivors and found that both had emerged with resiliency and dignity from their near death experiences.[137]

Lifton broke new ground in his methodology as well. Many scholars had thus far treated survivor testimony with a great deal of skepticism. Hilberg felt it could not be trusted and, therefore, had little to offer the historian. In contrast, Lifton privileged it over documents and official reports. According to Lifton, survivors' recollections constituted "authoritative descriptions" of these tragic events. He argued that, rather than documents, their "encompassing narrative" gave "strong articulation" to what they had endured.[138] Shortly thereafter, Terrence Des Pres began to work on *The Survivor: An Anatomy of Life in the Death Camps.* The book would be one of the first scholarly works that treated Holocaust memoirs as worthy literary products. Since it served as one of the foundation stones for what would become a highly sophisticated field of critical studies of Holocaust memoirs from both a literary and psychological perspective, it is worth nothing that Des Pres was not Jewish. The field was not the concern of only those seeking to publicize the woes of their coreligionists.

The Survivor, a collective biography of survivors which, like Lifton's *Death in Life,* stressed the survivors' dignity and resiliency, was shaped by Des Pres's intention to use "the survivor's own perspective" to reach his conclusions.[139] Des Pres predicted that this would disturb historians, who were trained to "distrust personal evidence." He contended that when a survivor's account of an incident is reiterated by "dozens of other survivors, men and women in different camps, from different nations and cultures, then one comes to trust the validity of such reports."[140] Admittedly, neither Lifton nor Des Pres were conducting their work as historians. Eventually, however, historians would also become persuaded that the survivors could be important sources of information. The first step came with Dawidowicz's *The War Against the Jews: 1933–1945,* an accessibly written narrative. At the same time she compiled and published a documentary source reader on the Holocaust. Both appeared in the mid-1970s just as courses on the Holocaust were beginning to be offered at American universities. Instructors now found themselves with texts they could use to teach a course. Hilberg's book, which had become the standard text in the field, was far denser and more comprehensive than Dawidowicz's. Hilberg also focused exclusively on the perpetrators, with the exception, as we have noted, of some disparaging remarks about the victims. What made Dawidowicz's book so different from Hilberg's was the degree to which she relied on Jewish sources. In addition to telling the story of the destruction, though not in nearly as much detail as Hilberg, she painted a portrait of the Jewish experience. Above all, she treated Jewish diaries and documents as reliable sources. Though historians would eventually question and reject many of her assertions, such as that Hitler had hatched his plan to kill the Jews in the 1920s, she helped place the victim at the center.[141] Her work brought Holocaust studies back to the approach that had been advocated by Philip Friedman two decades earlier. Gradually the documentary evidence, which was once considered entirely sufficient for writing the historical record, began to vie for authoritative resonance with the "testimonies," as interviews were increasingly called.[142]

The testimonies were not evidence in the juridical sense. As with any testimony, particularly that of a traumatic event years after the fact, many were not completely factual. (Even historians who relied on them knew to treat them with the same caution they would treat any oral history.) Nevertheless, testimonies had a unique power. Geoffrey Hartman believed they alone could "recreate the emotional and psychological milieu of survivor experience, what was done and suffered daily."[143] Bettelheim took issue with this approach and with depictions of survivors, particularly in Des Pres's work, as "active agents responsible for their own survival"; Bettelheim claimed that they often survived because of their passivity or simple luck.[144]

For survivors, the introduction of Holocaust courses and the interest in their testimonies must have seemed a long-awaited salve to their unbridled anger toward relatives who told them not to talk about their problems; toward social workers who instructed them that healing came by leaving the tragedy behind; and toward those scholars who, despite never having experienced the worst of Nazi persecution, nonetheless wrote, as one survivor described it, "learned works about the way the Jews became accomplices to their own murder." People such as Hilberg, Arendt, and Bettelheim, survivors complained, claim to know "exactly how Jews should have behaved in order to save themselves."[145]

By the 1970s those who had previously been considered victims were beginning to perceive their suffering not as a badge of shame but as a source of honor. (The same was true for survivors of cancer, rape, incest, and a host of other maladies and tragedies.) In 1979 a *New Yorker* cartoon captured this change. Two men sit on a small desert island stranded and alone. A single scrawny tree provides traces of shade. One says to the other: "You know what we are? Real survivors! People will say, 'Those two guys are real survivors!' I mean when it comes to survivors we really. . . ." As the cartoonist rightly understood, by this point in time in America a "survivor"—irrespective of what the person had survived—had become not an object of pity, but "a kind of fashion possessed of a particular moral stature, if not heroic pride."[146] Rather than feeling silenced, survivors now found themselves "increasingly celebrated as a group" and endowed with "paradigmatic value as embodiment of a moral force." No longer were they "greenhorns" or even "refugees," but "esteemed" or "heroic" people who had important lessons to impart to younger generations of Americans.[147] Some among them would use their newfound status, authoritative voice, and financial means to help shape how America remembered and commemorated the Holocaust in the coming decades.

It was not just survivors who emerged from their DP status during these years. Their children, many of whom took to calling themselves the "Second Generation" or "2G," did as well. Most of them had grown up or were born in America, so it was not the status of DP that they were shedding. During the 1950s and 1960s groups of psychoanalysts based primarily in New York began to write about their patients who were children of survivors. Many people, including some of these analysts, used these cases to generalize about all 2Gs, painting them as inherently damaged children.[148] In the turmoil and introspection of the late 1960s and 1970s, other 2Gs began to rebel against the notion that because their parents were survivors they necessarily were damaged. A few 2Gs, who themselves were training as psychologists and who had also participated in feminist consciousness-raising groups, began to organize support groups for children of survivors. This was happening even as women and other ethnic groups were gravitating to the notion of owning one's history of oppression. There were, of course, thousands of 2Gs who did not seek out these groups but, having become more aware of their specific identity and its "legacy," began to turn to other causes, including the political left, opposition to the war in Vietnam, support of Israel, environmental activism, and other activist causes. While they did not share a common *Weltanschauung,* many among them made a point of linking their activism and commitment to change to their 2G identity.[149] Reacting to the earlier psychological studies that had so shaped the initial impression of 2Gs, they eschewed the notion that as a result of their parents' trauma they were flawed in some way. Most importantly, they insisted that it was a mistake to focus on the psychological problems they might have, problems that were probably common to other children whose parents had been traumatized by war, if not to many adolescents. Rather, the focus should be on the "strengths [they] had observed in their parents," who, despite having faced unspeakable traumas, had survived and gone on to build new lives.[150]

Severed Alliances

In the late 1960s, alliances American Jews had established or thought they had established with other ethnic, religious, and political groups began to fray.[151] Once again many Jews found the Holocaust to constitute a potent symbol, if not tool, for understanding what was happening.

Since the time of Vatican II, whose liberalizing influence was felt across religions and denominations, many rabbis and Jewish communal leaders had become actively engaged in Christian–Jewish dialogue. A significant portion of that dialogue was devoted to exploring the roots of Christian antisemitism and the significance of Israel for Jews. These Jewish leaders were nonplussed that most of their Christian dialogue partners remained conspicuously silent in May and June 1967 when it appeared that Israel's existence was imperiled. These theologians justified their silence by explaining that they did not want to get entangled in what they deemed a political issue. For many of the Jews partaking in this dialogue it was, at the least, a response to the devastation of the Holocaust. As a Reform rabbi observed, "The survival of the Jewish people is not a political issue."[152]

The sense of abandonment was further compounded by the fact that there were Christian leaders who, despite having supported Israel prior to the war, took a very different position in the wake of its victory. In July 1967 the National Council of Churches (NCC) executive committee met in special session to issue a statement which sharply criticized Israel's "territorial expansion by armed force." A former president of Union Theological Seminary was even more aggressive in his criticism. In a letter to the *New York Times* a few weeks after the war, he described Israel's military action as an "assault" and an "onslaught." It was, he declared, the most "violent, ruthless (and successful) aggression since Hitler's blitzkrieg across Western Europe in the summer of 1940 aiming, not at victory, but at annihilation." He predicted that, given Israel's actions, there well might be an "even more murderous and tragic holocaust." His historical analogies (Hitler's blitzkrieg) as well as his choice of language ("annihilation," "murderous," and "holocaust") shocked many Jewish leaders, particularly those who had advocated ecumenical dialogue. There were Christian theologians and scholars who were deeply disturbed by this behavior. Not surprisingly, among the most articulate and outspoken of them were those, such as the Eckardts, who had already begun to struggle with the conundrum of Christianity's role in and response to the Holocaust. Not only did Roy Eckardt condemn this in a letter to the newspaper, but he and Alice wrote a two-part article for *Christian Century* that provocatively asked why the churches were once again silent when Jews faced destruction.[153]

But it was not just religious dialogue partners whom Jews saw as having gone on the assault. Over Labor Day 1967 the National Conference on New Politics (the "New Left") passed a resolution that held Israel responsible for the war, which it described as an "imperialist Zionist war."[154] Many Jews who believed there to be a natural alliance between liberal politics and Jewish beliefs experienced a sense of "overwhelming aloneness." In an article that heralded the beginning of a political shift by some Jews toward the political right, Milton Himmelfarb, who moved decisively rightward himself, wrote, "We learned the old, hard truth that only you can feel your own pain."[155] However, the Jewish community's growing rift with the African American community had a far broader and more significant impact. More than any other white group in America, Jews had long perceived of themselves as maintaining a sustained relationship with blacks on issues of civil rights. Their shared history of discrimination had shaped "the Jewish vision [of themselves] as an ally to the underdog."[156] The relationship had not been tension-free. As Jews entered the middle class in the 1950s and 1960s and left the urban neighborhoods in which they had once lived, Jewish shopkeepers and landlords often stayed behind. Their tenants and customers were mainly African Americans. Yet for many American Jews supporting the civil rights movement was akin to an eleventh commandment. The tension and hostility in that relationship were given prominent voice in a 1967 essay by noted African American author James Baldwin in the *New York Times Magazine*. He lashed out at the Jewish landlords and shopkeepers whom he felt defrauded their African Americans tenants and customers. Even Jews who reached out to help African Americans were depicted as doing so in a paternalistic, if not self-righteous, fashion.[157] His comments provoked an outcry among many Jews. One of the most trenchant responses came from Rabbi Robert Gordis. He pointed out that although Baldwin acknowledged that he did not know if the shopkeepers or landlords who cheated blacks were Jews, he identified them as Jews nonetheless. According to Gordis, Baldwin was guilty of the same kind of prejudicial stereotyping to which blacks had long been and were still subjected in the United States.[158]

Long simmering tensions had emerged around a series of interrelated issues. In urban centers there were pronounced differences in the quality of public schools between white neighborhoods and African Americans neighborhoods. Jews, along with many white families, opposed the busing programs that were instituted as part of integration efforts and affirmative action programs. Furthermore, in predominantly black neighborhoods in New York it was not uncommon for the teachers and principals to be Jewish. (In the 1940s and 1950s many Jews found they could have fulfilling jobs teaching in public schools and thereby avoid the discriminatory barriers that barred them from other fields, such as medicine and law.) In the late 1960s, community leaders in minority areas demanded local control of the schools, a move that many principals and teachers opposed. As a result, teachers were transferred, leading to teacher dissatisfaction and strikes. African Americans associated with the "Black Power" movement issued sharp—some were overtly antisemitic—rebuttals to Jewish groups who had once partnered with them. The head of the teachers' union, Albert Shanker, reprinted some of these pamphlets and circulated them citywide, further exacerbating tensions and anger.[159] Julius Lester, an African American radio talk show host, invited a black teacher to read a student's poem on the air. Dedicated to Shanker, it began, "Hey Jew boy with that yarmulka on your head / You pale faced Jew boy I wish you were dead." Sometime thereafter a black high school student appeared on the show and in a casual manner commented, "Hitler didn't make enough lampshades out of them." (Within a decade Lester would convert to Judaism, a move that in some small way had its roots in this incident.)[160] Poet LeRoi Jones, later known as Amiri Baraka, penned a poem that included the lines "brass knuckles in the mouth of the Jewlady."[161]

By this time the putative African American–Jewish alliance was severely frayed, if not severed.[162] The Student Nonviolent Coordinating Committee (SNCC), a radical group that played an important role in the civil rights struggle, published an article that included a photograph supposedly portraying Zionists shooting Arab victims lined up against a wall. The caption read: "This is the Gaza Strip, Palestine, not Dachau, Germany."[163] Irrespective of how extensively these feelings permeated the African American community, many Jews felt frightened and betrayed. They believed that they had devoted themselves to the cause of civil rights and saw this work as an extension of their Jewish identity. Julius Lester contended, probably accurately, that Jews worried about the collapse of this "alliance" far more than did blacks. Supporting the cause of civil rights was one of the means by which, he argued, they defined themselves, not just as liberals but as Jews. He related how a Jewish woman he met had explained how she knew she was Jewish. "I read the *New York Times* and give to the NAACP."[164] There was a world of difference in how each community perceived their relationship, and a tremendous gap in how the world perceived their respective suffering. As Baldwin perceptively observed:

> The Jew can be proud of his suffering or at least not ashamed of it. His history and his suffering do not begin in America, where black men have been taught to be ashamed of everything, especially their suffering. The Jews' suffering is recognized as part of the moral history of the world and the Jew is recognized as a contributor to the world's history; this is not true of the blacks. Jewish history, whether or not one can say it is honored, is certainly known; the black history has been blasted, maligned and despised.

Baldwin ultimately traced the source of this tense relationship to the Christian world. "The crisis taking place . . . in the hearts and minds of black men everywhere is not produced by the star of David but the old rugged Roman cross where Christendom's most celebrated Jew was murdered. And not by Jews." Yet at the same time he relied on negative stereotypes of Jews, who increasingly felt shut out of the movement.[165]

Engendering a similar sentiment among Jews, a group of black feminists declared that, no matter how passionately one might care about another person's cause, it is not the same as advocating for your own cause: "We believe that the most profound and potentially most radical politics come directly out of our own identity, as opposed to working to end someone else's oppression." Their identity was rooted in the "historical reality" of their experience. Those who had not had these experiences were, at best, onlookers, they stated.[166] While some Jews felt rebuffed, others had a different reaction and turned their energies inward. In the words of historian Clayborne Carson, director of the Martin Luther King Jr. Papers Project, they had entered the civil rights movement "as whites" but "would leave as Jews."[167]

It was not just developments on the domestic scene that left Jews feeling alone and rather adrift, however. That sentiment was exacerbated in 1974 when the United Nations granted observer status to the PLO and gave an enthusiastic welcome to its chairman, Yasser Arafat, who delivered a speech to the UN General Assembly with a holster on his hip. (The holster was empty but for many the symbolism was still potent.) A year later the UN General Assembly passed, with the strong support of the Eastern bloc, a resolution equating Zionism with racism. This resolution was emblematic of a growing chorus of hostility toward Israel from groups and institutions that American Jews had always seen as liberal and consequently more resistant to antisemitism. Matters at the United Nations only became worse when in 1976 a Saudi representative gave a speech denying that the Holocaust had occurred.[168] Despite the fact that, from the perspective of income, education, and class standing, Jews hardly fit the profile of an aggrieved group, they increasingly felt under siege. Cynthia Ozick, writing in *Esquire* after the Yom Kippur War, expressed this sentiment, albeit in fairly extreme if not sensationalist fashion: "Day by day it became more and more plain how alone—the aloneness of those who feel themselves condemned, the aloneness of, after so much America, the stranger." In fact, one did not have to read her article to glean her message. The title alone was enough: "All the World Wants the Jews Dead."[169]

In 1978 the sense of being under siege was disproportionately heightened by the actions of a motley group of American neo-Nazis. They precipitated a lengthy legal battle when they announced their intention to organize a march through the town of Skokie, a Chicago suburb that was home to thousands of Holocaust survivors. Skokie officials tried to prevent the march by instituting a series of municipal regulations, including the need to obtain $350,000 liability and property insurance that would prevent this ragtag bunch of misfits from holding their march. The town also issued an injunction against religious and racial incitement and the wearing of military uniforms.[170] The Nazis claimed that these regulations constituted roadblocks that were designed specifically to prevent their march. Believing that their civil rights had been abrogated, they turned to the American Civil Liberties Union (ACLU) to help them mount a legal challenge. There ensued a long, drawn-out, and convoluted legal battle that eventually reached the Supreme Court. Frequent news reports, often on the front page of prominent newspapers, kept this story in the press for well nigh two years.[171]

The vast majority of Americans had utter disdain for the Nazis. About that there was little debate. It was the decision of the ACLU to defend the Nazis' right to march that became a matter of tremendous dissension. Many Jews found it ironic at best that the Nazis were being represented by an organization whose membership ranks included a disproportionately high number of Jews. The ACLU repeatedly protested that it too abhorred the Nazis, but reminded its critics that this was a straightforward freedom of speech case. There were other ironies. Frank Collins, the leader of the Nazi Party, was, in fact, the son of a Jew who had been imprisoned in Dachau by the Nazis.[172] ACLU director Aryeh Neier, who was skewered in much of the Jewish community for "defending" Nazis, was a German-born Jew whose family had managed to escape only in the late 1930s. Neier protested that while he was "unwilling to put anything, even love of free speech, ahead of detestation of the Nazis," he nonetheless felt morally obligated to defend them. One could not, he cautioned, relegate to the powerful, which in this case constituted Skokie officials, the power to decide who had the freedom to speak and who did not. Someday the tables might be turned and that power could be used against Jews. This, he told his critics, was what he had experienced in Germany.[173] His protestations fell on deaf ears, particularly among survivors. Thousands of Jewish members left the ACLU. Donations plummeted. Critics of the ACLU's decision argued that carrying a swastika through the streets of a community filled with Holocaust survivors constituted "fighting words," an incitement to violence.[174] Many American Jews once again found their liberal leanings tested. The more disenchanted among them believed, as a pundit once observed, that the ACLU's "open mind" had allowed its brains to fall out. For many Jews the ACLU's position concerned more than a debate over legal issues. They could not grasp how the ACLU and Neier, in particular, could expend their energies defending those who venerated the very regime that had inflicted devastation on so many people, Jews in particular. It was one thing not to approve of stopping them, but it was quite another to provide them with a vigorous legal defense.

During the protracted imbroglio, survivors, particularly in Skokie, insisted that while the ACLU might be oblivious to the lessons of the Holocaust, they themselves were not. They contrasted their response to Nazis with that of European Jewry during the 1930s. German Jews had failed to see the handwriting on the wall, they said, and consequently failed to show a strong face to their enemies. Unlike the Jews of the 1930s, the survivors insisted that they would not fall into that trap. (Their perception of what German Jews understood of the threat facing them and what they did in response was rather naïve and unnuanced, however. It was a skewed, if not self-serving, interpretation of history that to some extent remains dominant among American Jews to this day.)[175] One of the leaders of the Skokie battle exhorted a gathering of thousands of Chicago area residents not to behave as Jews supposedly had in the 1930s and 1940s: "Don't go into your homes. Don't lock your doors. Don't pull the drapes. Don't go into the basement. Evil will triumph only when decent human beings are silent."[176]

The Skokie case demonstrated Holocaust survivors' newfound communal clout. Initially the national Jewish organizations, together with Chicago's rabbinic leadership, advocated that the same policy they generally used when dealing with extremist fringe groups be followed: work quietly behind closed doors. Reasoning that these Nazis were few in number and hardly a formidable organization, they wanted to avoid giving them undue publicity. They counseled that waging a confrontational legal and media battle would not be efficacious. Instead, let the Nazis march but be totally ignored. Jewish organizations, both national and local, and Jewish leaders proposed that everyone—Jew and non-Jew—stay off the street at the time of the march and that storeowners shutter their business establishments. An entire city should turn its back on these purveyors of hate. A handful of Nazis marching down abandoned streets would, the leaders reasoned, only serve to highlight the pathetic nature of their cause. The Jewish communal leadership working together with the leadership of the village of Skokie assumed that this policy would be adopted.

They failed, however, to anticipate the reaction of Holocaust survivors. At gatherings organized by communal leaders in order to explain the approach they advocated, survivors rose up in open revolt. They left no doubt that the suggested course of action was not something they could abide. Their unequivocal opposition forced a change in policy, not just within the Jewish community but outside it as well. Struck by the survivors' opposition, the Irish Catholic mayor, who had initially proposed ignoring the Nazis, was one of the first to change his position. He acknowledged being particularly influenced by the personal stories of Holocaust survivors, including the gentleman who related how he had watched his two-year-old daughter killed by a Nazi prison guard. The man asked the mayor to understand how it would feel to him to see Nazis marching down the streets of the town he now called home. The mayor credited that conversation with convincing him to change his stance.[177]

The Nazis eventually won the right to march. However, they decided that they would instead hold what turned out to be a rather lackluster rally in downtown Chicago. The fact that the Nazis decided not to come to Skokie was considered a victory. Some survivors mused that it might have been otherwise. Had they marched, the survivors would have been there: "It is important to show the Nazis that Jews can't be pushed off to the side, hiding in cellars."[178]

Though the legal battle grabbed most of the headlines, something else was happening as well. Many of the participants, including village officials, remarked that, though they had lived alongside these survivors for many years, only now were they hearing their stories. After the battle ended, one town official who had worked with the survivors wondered whether the experience of standing up and fighting had "made it possible for the [survivors] to unburden themselves about many things that had occurred in their past." Once again we see how both the survivors and the America in which they lived had changed. It is likely that, had this controversy taken place in the 1950s or even in the early 1960s, survivors would have been equally upset but would not have felt as emboldened to challenge the Jewish establishment or the political leaders of the village. One of the Skokie town officials, reflecting on these events twenty years later, mused: "The survivors won their battle." In fact, he contended, they did more than win. "Whenever we travelled, we were always treated a little bit like celebrities because we were from Skokie . . . 'Oh, you're from that community that kept out the Nazis.'"[179] Survivors had taken on a weak, though noxious, scrum of American Nazis. Though they lost the legal battle, they won the war. They demonstrated that they would not sit idly by when confronted by antisemites. They left no doubt that they were a force with which to be reckoned.

The Holocaust and the Small Screen

At the same time that the debate about Skokie was filling the news, another Holocaust-related effort was grabbing headlines as well. In April 1978 NBC's broadcast of the television miniseries *Holocaust* garnered an audience of over 120 million people. By this time the word "Holocaust" was so commonly understood to mean the destruction of European Jewry that NBC saw no need to provide a subtitle to explain what the word referred to. The miniseries, though a rather cheesy and melodramatic soap opera, enthralled critics and audiences throughout America. It was a media event of national proportions, generating reviews, news articles, classroom discussions, and communal gatherings.[180] Tom Shales, chief television critic of the *Washington Post*, described it as the "most powerful drama ever seen on TV." Writing in the *Wall Street Journal*,

Dorothy Rabinowitz called it "a television event with the power that may be without peer." In *Time*, Frank Rich predicted that it was likely to "awaken more viewers to the horrors of the Third Reich than any single work since *The Diary of Anne Frank*." Even historian Ismar Schorsch, who questioned the efficacy of the newfound emphasis on the Holocaust, credited the show with penetrating the "double veil of Christian ignorance and indifference." It had, Schorsch believed, a "resounding pedagogic effect."[181]

The chorus of praise was not universal, however. Elie Wiesel, by then one of the most prominent survivors in the world, found the production "untrue, offensive, and cheap" and responsible for trivializing the reality of the horrors. A number of scholars agreed. Lawrence Langer considered the series' upbeat ending out of sync with reality, while Alvin Rosenfeld condemned the rendering of a real-life tragedy into entertainment.[182] While scholarly disdain for the Hollywoodization of the Holocaust was not unexpected, other scholars argued that the show, though certainly flawed, had important redeeming qualities. Film scholar Judith Doneson believed that the miniseries was far more sophisticated than many critics charged. It depicted an array of different responses on the part of Jews and non-Jews to Nazi persecution. In addition to the familiar stereotypes of Jews and Germans, the show included Jews who complied with the Nazis' orders as well as Jews who resisted. There were Germans who participated in the murders despite having no deep-seated ideological commitments. There were Germans who expressed virulent antisemitism and others who assisted Jews.

The broadcast also marked a generational shift in the American public's remembering of the Holocaust. Whereas many of those who had seen *The Diary of Anne Frank* onstage or in its film adaptation had lived through the war years, for a new generation in the late 1970s the Holocaust had moved from "social memory" to "historical memory," from memory of events personally recalled to memory filtered through the media and national commemorations.[183] Regardless of one's opinion about the quality of the miniseries, there was no question regarding its impact. The American Jewish Committee conducted a poll and found that over 60 percent of American viewers believed the film made the Final Solution explicable.[184] Geoffrey Hartman believed that it was the miniseries, of which he was not a fan, that prompted many survivors in his community to come forward to tell their story: "Bad art had a good result."[185] Most importantly, Doneson observed, "people in Idaho, North Dakota, New York—throughout the United States—were now initiated, albeit in a simplified manner, into the world of the Nazi genocide against the Jews."[186] Film scholar Lawrence Baron postulated that seeing the responses of ordinary people to the Final Solution "helped viewers draw connections with the consequences of not opposing similar injustices in the present."[187] This was not evil committed solely by "higher ups" in resplendent uniforms. Plain people—Germans citizens and their compatriots—had a direct hand in the tragedy.

What may have been even more striking than the buzz the miniseries created in the United States was the reaction in Germany the next year. Approximately fifteen million viewers tuned in to the broadcast there, with widespread impact. A subsequent book on the production and its German reception bore the subtitle *Eine Nation ist betroffen* (A nation is stunned). Many scholars and political analysts credited the miniseries with doing more to make the general German public aware of Nazi war crimes than all the academic studies that had preceded it. It stimulated a conversation in German society that had been studiously avoided for over thirty-five years.[188] As Anton Kaes noted in *From Hitler to Heimat:*

> An American television series, made in a trivial style, produced more for commercial than for moral reasons, more for entertainment than for enlightenment, accomplished what hundreds of books, plays, films, and television programs, thousands of documents, and all the concentration camp trials have failed to do in the more than three decades since the end of the war: to inform Germans about crimes against Jews committed in their name so that millions were emotionally touched and moved.[189]

On a concrete level *Holocaust* prompted the Bundestag to repeal the statute of limitations on war-era crimes. Furthermore, the government-sponsored language association, Gesellschaft für deutsche Sprache, declared "Holocaust" to be the "word of the year." (Prior to this point Germans tended to use *Mord an den Juden, Judenmord, Vernichtung der Juden,* or *Judenvernichtung,* often with the adjective *systematisch.*) It is doubtful that any other American middlebrow television production ever had such an impact on another country.

America and the Holocaust: Playing the Blame Game

Increased interest in the Holocaust led to an increased interest in America's response to the Holocaust, which had been a matter of debate since Arthur Morse's work in the mid-1960s. In 1984 David Wyman wrote *The Abandonment of the Jews,* his second contribution to the field, a book that was an unrelenting indictment of both the Roosevelt administration's and the established Jewish communal leadership's response to the persecution of the Jews during the war years. The failure of the world in general and America in particular to respond to this persecution had left

Wyman deeply shaken. He made a point of identifying himself at the very outset of the book as "a Christian, a Protestant of Yankee and Swedish descent," and, in his short biography on the website of the David S. Wyman Institute, as "the grandson of two Protestant ministers."[190] One cannot help but wonder if Wyman believed that identifying himself as not coming from an "interested party" gave his critique added clout.

That same year there was yet another manifestation of the increasing contempt among segments of the American Jewish community for the behavior of World War II–era Washington officialdom and Jewish communal leaders. Jack Eisner, a wealthy Holocaust survivor, funded a commission chaired by former Supreme Court justice Arthur Goldberg. Its mandate was to explore American Jewry's response to the Holocaust. Ostensibly, this was supposed to be a balanced investigation. However, the organizers' biases, their conviction that American Jewry had failed during the war, were revealed in the very questions the group was supposed to investigate: not "Were American Jews passive about the plight of European Jews?" but "Why were so many American Jews passive or relatively unconcerned about the plight of European Jews?"

The composition of the commission also pointed to the fact that this investigation was not designed to conduct nuanced historical research. The members were not scholars but local politicians and leaders of Jewish organizations. The team of researchers who carried out the investigation itself began their work by already ascribing to American Jews some responsibility for the Holocaust: "The question of their responsibility for the catastrophe is a legitimate one for historical inquiry." Eventually the commission collapsed because of internal disagreements. What is remarkable about this enterprise, however, is its investigatory and juridical tone. The organizers, claiming to speak for American Jewry, were essentially putting the leaders of the community during World War II on trial.[191]

By the last decades of the twentieth century the notion that America and American Jewry had abandoned European Jews had become almost axiomatic. Within the Jewish community it was so universally accepted that there was virtually no debate as to its accuracy. At a meeting of the United Jewish Appeal Young Leadership Cabinet in the summer of 1993, an Ohio lawyer intoned in an invocation: "Give us strength to lead our people like Joseph and Esther, and not like Henry Morgenthau and Felix Warburg. . . . They could have influenced Roosevelt but they chose not to." As one journalist who was present observed: "No one raised an eyebrow."[192]

Indeed, there was much that America did not do that it might have done. The White House and the State Department could have instructed its European-based consuls to be more lenient in distributing visas. A total of approximately 190,000 quota slots for immigrants from German and Axis-dominated countries went unused during these years. This was not because of a lack of applicants but because of the "paper walls" American officials erected. American officials placed so many barriers in applicants' paths that for most of the 1930s the limited number of entry visas for Germans were not fully allocated. Of course, changing the entry regulations would have raised the ire of isolationist and anti-immigrant forces. FDR determined, possibly correctly, that it was not realistic to try and that it might be detrimental to his efforts against the Axis powers, such as the Lend-Lease program to help Great Britain. That is not to suggest there was not more—much more—that FDR could have done. And, of course, American Jewish communal leaders could have been far more forceful in their demands.[193]

Yet the critics have often gone too far. They rooted their analysis not in available political and strategic options, but in what the critics would have wanted FDR, political leaders, and American Jews to do. As Henry Feingold has observed, the critics' complaints lacked "historicity." The World War II–era leaders were condemned as having failed because they did not, in the words of Michael Marrus, "live up to our standards."[194] These critics were indulging in what historians call presentism, relying on standards that were applicable to contemporary American political life and not the context of the times. They projected backward from the present into the past and contended that American Jews should have adhered to tactics that, although fitting for the present, were not appropriate or even available during World War II. Ignoring pressing political realities, they seem to be taken by the heroic fantasy that FDR, or any president, could have altered history by virtue of his own will.[195]

The early scholars, among them Morse, downplayed the protests and boycotts that in fact took place during the war years. In retrospect such efforts may seem paltry when held up against both the genocide that was the Holocaust and later political activities by many groups, including Jews. While there was certainly more that American Jews of that era could have done, it is important to note that they lived in a very different America, one that was isolationist, highly antisemitic, and antagonistic to anything that smacked of what today might be called identity politics. Jews feared being held responsible for "pushing America into war" in order to "save" Jews. Over half of them were immigrants who were still struggling to establish themselves in America. Moreover, casting the Allies as the Nazis' passive accomplices in the act of genocide, as much of this literature is wont to do, is historically indefensible. It ignores the existing reality in America during the 1930s—isolationism, xenophobia, and unemployment—and, during the war itself, the fact that a two-front war did not go well for a number of years.[196]

The efforts during the last decade of the twentieth century to cast America's leaders and American Jews as accomplices with Nazi genocide had less to do with history and more to do with contemporary American politics. As noted, excoriating the World War II American Jewish community became a way of highlighting the fact that by the 1980s the contemporary Jewish community had adopted a different modus operandi, one that was not afraid to speak truth to power. It had become the counterpoint for the contemporary Jewish community to celebrate not just its sagacity, but also its refusal to be cowed by fears of what others might say. But highlighting the complacency of the World War II Jewish leadership served another end as well. By the 1980s sectors of the American Jewish community had begun to shift to the political right. Jews had until then almost reflexively believed in and supported the Democratic Party. Yet it could be argued that at the most crucial moment for Jews in American history, that same party had failed them. This trope became a means of rationalizing and justifying the rightward political movement of many American Jews. There is a certain degree of irony inherent in the fact that this shift began to gather strength during the administration of the same Democratic president who would be most responsible for ensuring that the Holocaust became rooted in the overall American narrative.

The White House: Whose Holocaust?

But for a political conundrum faced by the White House during the administration of President Jimmy Carter, the United States Holocaust Memorial Museum (USHMM) might never have come into being. It owes its existence, in great measure, to Carter's troubled interactions with the American Jewish community.

Shortly after his inauguration in 1977, Carter's relations with the organized Jewish community began to fray over the White House's policy toward Israel. The White House announced it was entering into discussions with the PLO, an organization openly and actively engaged in terrorist activity. The situation continued its downward spiral when the Carter administration and the Soviet Union issued a joint statement regarding "the legitimate rights of the Palestinian people" and indicating their intention to work on the Palestinian issue together. American Jews were shocked that Carter considered the Soviet Union an appropriate partner for negotiating a Middle East peace agreement given its overt antisemitism and intense hostility toward Israel. Indeed, the USSR had a long track record of disseminating materials that relied on traditional antisemitic themes and imagery. It was one of the major purveyors of the false assertions that Zionists collaborated with the Nazis in the persecution and destruction of the Jews and that the Jewish people were intent on "achieving world domination."[197]

In 1978 matters reached their nadir when President Carter announced his proposal to sell F-15 warplanes to Israel, Egypt, and Saudi Arabia. Israel considered the acquisition of such attack planes by Egypt and Saudi Arabia a direct threat to its security. Matters grew even tenser when Carter said that, should Congress reject the sale of planes to any one of the countries, he would withdraw the entire package. American Jews, who had never felt particularly close to Carter, were distressed. White House officials recognized the severity of the situation and instructed Mark Siegel, the White House's special liaison to the Jewish community, to sell the package to the community. At a large gathering of young American Jewish leaders, Siegel, repeating what the White House had told him, categorically declared that the planes were solely defensive weapons and thus posed no threat to any country, Israel included. His audience knew otherwise and bluntly informed Siegel that, more than just being wrong, he had been misled by his White House colleagues, apparently deliberately. Siegel contacted the Pentagon to ascertain whether the jets were indeed strictly defensive. Years later he recalled Pentagon officials' reaction: "When they stopped laughing, I realized I had been lied to."[198] He resigned shortly thereafter.

It was against this background that Carter's Middle East policy became a factor in the decision to create an American Holocaust museum. Shortly after Carter's election, Siegel had asked Ellen Goldstein, a White House staffer, whether there were any national memorials to the Holocaust in the United States. Goldstein reported that, while there were local memorials, there was no national memorial. She mused that building one might begin to "heal the rift" that had developed between the president and the Jewish community.[199] Goldstein's memo languished and nothing happened.

Then, a year later, the battle erupted over the proposed neo-Nazi march in Skokie. Goldstein read a column in the *New York Times* by William Safire in which he observed that "America has no vivid reminder of the Final Solution but we have a reminder that not even Israelis can boast: our own homegrown handful of Nazis."[200] She then wrote a second memo on the topic to her boss, the president's domestic advisor, Stuart Eizenstat, who himself had lost family in the Holocaust, noting that an announcement of a plan to build a memorial would be "an appropriate gesture" to mark the upcoming thirtieth anniversary of Israel's independence. She warned that, while the idea "deserves consideration on its merits," some people might dismiss it as a political ploy. The White

House decided it was worth the risk, and suddenly a suggestion that had gone nowhere for a year was now firmly on the presidential agenda. A few weeks later, in May 1978—shortly after 120 million Americans had watched NBC's *Holocaust*—President Carter stood before a gathering of Jewish leaders who had been invited to the Rose Garden and announced his intention to appoint a commission that would be entrusted with responsibility to create a memorial "to the six million who were killed in the Holocaust." It would be chaired by Elie Wiesel who, the White House staff felt, was the "one person" capable of this job. He "has the stature," Eizenstat said, and "had become the worldwide spokesman for Holocaust survivors and indeed for the victims."[201]

During the 1960s Wiesel's prominence had spread in the American Jewish community. His book *Night,* which was published in the United States in 1959, carried an introduction and strong personal endorsement from the Nobel laureate and French literary hero François Mauriac.[202] Though the book initially sold quite modestly, it received positive reviews from various scholars and intellectuals. Then Wiesel took to the road. Wiesel described this as a time when a "very small group of people," himself included, "would go around literally from conference to conference, from convention to convention, from community to community to speak about this. Because nobody else did."[203] By "community" Wiesel was, of course, referring to Jewish communal settings. In fact, others were speaking about it but virtually no one, with the exception of Simon Wiesenthal, was gaining the same attention as Wiesel. By the mid-1960s his place in American Jewish communal life was secure, as evidenced by the packed houses drawn to his yearly lecture series at New York's famed 92nd Street Y.[204] His reputation soon began to expand beyond the confines of the Jewish community. That trajectory was accelerated by his ongoing literary output that was meeting with critical acclaim. Literary critic Robert Alter believed Wiesel's singular achievement to be his ability to "realize the terrible past imaginatively with growing artistic strength in a narrative form that is consecutive, coherent . . . and in a taut prose that is a model of lucidity and precision."[205] While some of Wiesel's critics claim he only became a prominent figure after the Six Day War when he began to trade on his identity as a survivor, in fact on June 4, 1967, just before the war broke out, he received an honorary doctorate from the Jewish Theological Seminary of America and gave the commencement address.[206]

Well before then Wiesel was increasingly treated as someone who needed no introduction. In spring 1966 Steven Schwarzschild, the former editor of *Judaism,* had called Wiesel the "*de facto* high priest of our generation."[207] Robert Jay Lifton repeatedly referred to Wiesel in his book on

Hiroshima but, obviously convinced that his readers would know him, did not bother to identify him precisely.[208] Nor did Isaac Bashevis Singer when he reviewed Wiesel's *Jews of Silence* in the *New York Times.* Both Singer and the editors at the *Times* clearly assumed no identification was necessary.[209] By this point Wiesel's stature had spread to the other side of the Atlantic. In a lengthy assessment of the Paris literary scene written for the *New York Times Book Review,* editor and critic Herbert Lottman singled out three young authors, Wiesel among them, and credited them with doing some of the best work in French literature. (Though Wiesel had by this point in time moved to New York, he still wrote most of his work in French and spent extended periods of time in France.)[210] The *New York Times* interviewed him in February 1970, ostensibly in conjunction with the publication of his ninth novel, *A Beggar in Jerusalem.* Far from concentrating on Holocaust-related matters, the interview was a free-wheeling discussion of contemporary issues, including events in Biafra and Vietnam.[211] It was one of the early signs of how Wiesel would use his increasingly high profile to speak about human rights abuses in general. Eventually, as chair of the Holocaust memorial commission, Wiesel would have the opportunity to play a singular role in shaping the American narrative of the Holocaust.

As noted at the outset of this book, the commission did not represent the first attempt in the United States to build a Holocaust memorial on public land, though all previous proposals had been rejected.[212] And now, only a little more than a decade after New York officials had decidedly denied the appropriateness of a memorial to the Holocaust built on public land, the president of the United States was standing in the White House Rose Garden proclaiming that a memorial to Holocaust victims on public property was fitting and that it should be built under the aegis of the federal government.[213] Carter offered a series of explanations as to why an event that had occurred in Europe should be commemorated in America or, to use James Young's formulation, why this event was of *Americans'* history as well as of *American* history. The president, who had unsuccessfully tried to have Congress ratify the Genocide Treaty, posited that a memorial might remind Americans why that effort was so necessary. Americans, as a "humane people, concerned with the human rights of all people . . . [should feel] compelled to study the systematic destruction of the Jews so that we may seek to learn how to prevent such enormities from occurring in the future." But Carter also offered explanations that were rooted specifically in American history. American soldiers had "liberated many of the death camps" and many of the former inmates had found a haven in this country. (Actually, Americans liberated concentration camps but not death camps.) In addition, he told the Rose

Garden gathering that, after visiting Israel in 1973, he read Morse's *While Six Million Died*, which demonstrated that "six million people, most of European Jewry," had been killed "not only because of Nazi brutality but also because the entire world turned its back on them." He would return to this theme of America's failures on other occasions and argue that America bore some of the "responsibility for not being willing to acknowledge forty years ago that this horrible event was occurring."[214] His references to *While Six Million Died*, the way America "turned its back" on the victims, America's role in the liberation of the camps, and the refuge many of the victims found in this country put the Holocaust in an American context in a way that New York City officials in the previous decade would have considered implausible. There are few, if any, clearer indications of how much America's relationship to remembering the Holocaust had changed than the contrast between the fate of the New York memorial in the 1960s and the words uttered in the Rose Garden in the 1970s.

Ironically, the president's announcement of an official American memorial opened a Pandora's box of issues that would roil the world of Holocaust commemoration and scholarly study for many decades. Fundamental to the various imbroglios was a basic definitional question: What precisely was the Holocaust? Embedded in this relatively straightforward question were an array of political, ideological, and historiographical issues. Was the Holocaust the German attempt to murder European Jewry, or did it constitute the vast array of bestial crimes against humanity committed by the Germans? Were its victims limited to Jews, or did they include all other peoples who were subjected to Germany's brutal hand? Some of these questions had been percolating in scholarly circles well before the Rose Garden announcement. However, now that this was a presidential matter, the stakes rose exponentially. Moreover, there was a far larger media spotlight.

For many Jews, particularly survivors such as Wiesel, there was nothing to debate. Survivors and those in the Jewish community who had concerned themselves with this event considered it a given that, irrespective of its name—*Shoah, Khurbn,* Catastrophe, Final Solution, or Holocaust—this enterprise constituted the German attempt to wipe out European Jewry. The Germans had been quite clear about that when they spoke of "The Final Solution of the Jewish Problem" (*Endlösung der Judenfrage*). Beginning with the Nazi Party platform, they had made noxious antisemitism one of the cornerstones of their ideology. Jews were, they argued, the root cause of Germany's troubles and a real threat to its very existence. Nazis did not speak of other peoples in a similar fashion. Holocaust survivors did not deny or ignore that there had been countless other victims—groups and individuals—of Nazi crimes, many of whom had suffered bestial treatment. Some, such as the Roma and the Sinti, had been gassed or shot. But it seemed apparent to those who had been directly touched by this genocide that, while many had suffered horribly, there was something distinctive about what the Germans tried to do to the Jews. It differed from both the other horrific actions taken by Germans against a myriad of civilians groups, and it also differed from millennia of other antisemitic actions. To Wiesel and those around him, it was self-evident that the Holocaust was the state-sponsored attempt to wipe out European Jewry. The Germans ferreted out every Jew they could find irrespective of where they lived, their age, or their socioeconomic status. The German did not care if a Jew was in her dotage or an infant in arms, rich or poor, or profoundly religious or intensely secular. The only factor that was relevant to the Germans was the answer to this question: Did they have Jewish parents or grandparents? Non-Jews, with the exception of the Roma and Sinti and the handicapped, had to do something—it could be the mildest and most benign of things—in order to be punished or murdered. They had to have some sort of public position, knowledge, or stature that made Germans imagine them to be potential enemies. Jews, on the other hand, were targeted because of what they were: Jews. Portions of the Roma were similarly targeted, though in the 1970s there was far less public recognition of that fact. In an apparent effort to explain how, if the Holocaust was an attempt to destroy European Jewry, other victims were part of these atrocities, Wiesel offered the following dictum: "While not all victims were Jews, all Jews were victims."[215] This attempt to differentiate did not placate those fighting for representation.

Today there is an emerging historical consensus that, had the Nazis won the war, other groups of peoples, particularly those in the "east," would probably have been subjected to a fate similar to that of the Jews. All Roma, including those who were initially left alone, would have been annihilated. Millions of other people would have also been murdered. "Useless eaters," people whom the Nazis determined had nothing to offer to the "thousand-year Reich," would have been eliminated. (We see the beginnings of this in the T-4 program that was responsible for the murder of hundreds of thousands of Germans who had hereditary diseases, were mentally disabled, or in some way did not fit the Nazi vision of an Aryan society. This program and the medical personnel who ran it would lay the foundation for the gas chambers that eventually took many additional lives.) Had a victorious Third Reich had the opportunity to conduct these other murder programs the death toll would have dwarfed that of the Jews. However, only in the case of the Jews did Germans feel compelled to begin their murder campaign immediately. The other murders, with the exception of portions—but not all—of the Roma, could wait until after the war. Those writing about the Holocaust pointed to this all-inclusive, comprehensive, cross-border, and immediate attempt to wipe out an entire people as a singular characteristic of the killings of Jews, rather than the numbers or means.

There is an axiom in American political life that "all politics are local." A corollary of this principle is that if the White House is involved, everything becomes political. That is precisely what happened as Carter and his aides entered this definitional quagmire. Various Eastern European national groups began jockeying for representation on the presidential commission. Polish Americans, Lithuanian Americans, Latvian Americans, and Ukrainian Americans all argued that they too had been victims of the Holocaust. Jews and particularly Holocaust survivors found these demands to be ludicrous, if not cruelly insulting. Many of these Eastern European nationals, motivated in part by antisemitism as well as their hatred of Stalin and communism, had sided with the Germans and actively assisted with the Final Solution. Other Eastern European nationals participated in the killings, not because they hated Stalin or communism, but to prove to the Germans that they were loyal to the new regime.[216] The record of these Eastern European peoples' wartime cooperation with the Germans was not a matter of historical dispute. Latvian and Lithuanian police units were actively involved in murdering Jews in their countries. Ukrainians units had been used by the SS in ghetto "cleaning" operations in Warsaw, Lublin, Galicia, and many other portions of Eastern Europe. In Hungary the situation was similar. In short, the Germans could not have done what they did to the Jews without the extensive help of national and local groups in virtually all of the East European countries in which they operated.[217] What made these requests even more infuriating to survivors and others on the commission was that among the members of these groups were war criminals who had entered the United States under false and illegal premises.[218]

Some of these groups were surprisingly candid as to why they were so anxious for membership on the presidential commission. A representative of the Ukrainian Anti-Defamation League told the director of the United States Holocaust Memorial Council that Ukrainians were intent on being included so that they could "block any historical references to Ukrainian collaboration with the Nazis" in the proposed memorial. Sometimes their intentions were less overt. The president of the Polish American Congress sent the director of the Holocaust Council an article by the vice president of the organization that, he said, would explain why non-Jewish Poles should be included as members. The article defended the Poles' failure to help Jews by asking how could Poland have "help[ed] people who are themselves resigned passively to accept their fate." In other words, what happened to the victims was their own fault. Ultimately this debate over membership and definition morphed into a political battle that pitted Carter and his advisers against Wiesel and many of the other White House appointees to the council. The White House, feeling that it had done enough for the Jews, urged Wiesel to convince the Jews to share the Holocaust with other groups.[219] Survivors were nonplussed by this glib suggestion for rewriting history. What had started out as an attempt to mend fences had become something else entirely.

The Kremlin versus Wiesel: Identifying the Victims

Upon their return from an official investigatory visit to Eastern European Holocaust sites, Wiesel and the other members of the White House commission prepared a report for the president. Accompanied by a cover letter from Wiesel, the report and the letter were characterized by a note of distress, if not defensiveness. In his letter Wiesel defined the six million Jews as "the principal target of Hitler's Final Solution" and insisted that it was a "moral imperative" for any memorial that emerged from the commission's work to place special emphasis on their murder. The report took matters further. More than just singling out the Jews as the central victims of the Holocaust, it stressed the unique character of the Holocaust and declared that to be the primary "philosophical rationale" for the commission's work.[220] This genocide was, it insisted, fundamentally distinct from all others that had preceded it. "Never before in human history had genocide been an all-pervasive government policy unaffected by territorial or economic advantage and unchecked by moral or religious constraints." The goal of killing Jews was pursued even when it hindered the war effort, as when skilled factory workers were killed despite the fact that they were producing products commissioned by the Wehrmacht.[221] The report noted that when it concerned Jews, "genocide was an end in itself independent of the requisites of war." It contrasted that German goal with the fate of Gypsies. While Gypsies had been annihilated, the Nazis' attitude toward them was inconsistent. Some were allowed to serve in the Wehrmacht while others were consigned to the gas chambers.[222]

The emphasis in the report on Jews as the central victims and the uniqueness of what was done to them was prompted not just by the commission's struggles with the White House staff over definitions, but by what happened on the trip to Eastern Europe. Communist government officials in both Poland and the USSR repeatedly insisted to the delegation that the Holocaust was not about Jews. Jews may have been among those killed but their death had little if any correlation to their being Jewish.[223] Wiesel described what happened in a rather elegiac lament in the *New York Times Magazine:*

> High-level meetings, discussions, ceremonies. The scenario is every-where the same. The hosts refer to victims in general, of every nation-ality . . . we speak of Jews. They mention all the victims, of every nationality, of every religion, and they refer to them en masse. We object: Of course they must all be remembered, but why mix them anonymously together? . . . [Jews] alone were fated to total extermina-tion not because of what they had said or done or possessed but because of what they were.[224]

Communist officials insisted that during World War II Jews were simply one among an array of members of the proletariat who had been murdered by the fascists. This perspective emanated naturally from Marxist ideology that eradicated ethnic distinctions. Moreover, Soviet officials were annoyed by the attention lavished on the Jewish death toll during the war. Such attention, they believed, came at the expense of the far larger number of Soviet citizens who had died or been murdered in the course of the war. Commission members discovered that at sites of Jewish massacres there was no mention of the fact that the victims were Jews. Even at sites where Jews were the only ones buried there, for example, mass graves in Jewish cemeteries, there was no reference to their Jewish identity. They were identified as "victims of the fascists." At Babi Yar, the ravine outside of Kiev where over 33,000 Jews were mur-dered in the course of two days, it was the same. The memorial omitted any mention of Jews.[225] The delegation encountered the same resistance in Poland. Government officials had prepared an official itinerary that included visits to Polish national sites but omitted visits to sites of Jewish importance. Only when members of the commission protested did their Polish hosts relent.

At Auschwitz, which the Polish government had established as a "Monument of the Martyrdom of the Polish Nation and of Other Nations," exhibits had been established to commemorate the victims of various nations, including Hungary, Yugoslavia, the German Democratic Republic (East Germany), Belgium, and Denmark. Most omitted any mention of the fact that the vast majority, if not all, of the victims of these countries who were killed at Auschwitz were Jews. Even in the Jewish pavilion, the Jewish identity of the victims and the fact that they were targeted because they were Jews was, rather ludicrously, barely mentioned. By emphasizing Auschwitz's international character and eliminating the fact the victims were Jewish, "the Communists linked

Poland . . . to the other Warsaw Pact countries both as past and potential victims of German aggression and as present beneficiaries of their liberation by the Red Army."[226] Wiesel addressed this issue, passionately if not hyperbolically, when he told the *New York Times:* "They are stealing the Holocaust from us. This is exactly what the Germans wanted to accomplish, to erase the memory of the Jewish people."[227]

Even Pope John Paul II, who had close relations with both individual Jews and the Jewish community, engaged in a form of what has been called Holocaust "de-Judaization" when he visited Auschwitz in 1979. He bemoaned the fact that "there are six million Poles who lost their lives during the Second World War: the fifth of the nation." His suggestion that the Polish Jews who were murdered were murdered because they were Poles ignored historical reality, however.[228] There is a certain irony in the pope's statement because this was precisely what the communist regimes—his mortal enemies—were doing. It was what Wiesel and the other members of the commission had encountered when they visited the communist bloc. It was during this dispute over who should serve on the United States Holocaust Memorial Council, the successor to the commission, that Yitz Greenberg, then the director of the commission, proposed to Wiesel that Father John Pawlikowski be appointed as a member. Before that could happen, however, Pawlikowski had to assure Wiesel that he was not one of those Polish Americans who wished to engage in the de-Judaization of the victims.[229] He would be appointed by Carter and subsequently reappointed by both Presidents Ronald Reagan and Bill Clinton.

It should be noted that this notion that the Holocaust was fundamentally different from other acts of persecution was not something new.[230] In the decades immediately following the war, most scholars who addressed what the Germans had done considered the uniqueness of this effort to be a foregone conclusion. They felt little need to belabor the point. In 1965 German philosopher Karl Jaspers rather matter-of-factly observed, "Anyone who . . . plans the organized slaughter of a people and participates in it does something that is fundamentally different from all crimes that have existed in the past." Other scholars echoed similar views. None of them seemed to think that the point they were making was particularly controversial. Isaac Deutscher, the biographer and admirer of Trotsky and someone who, in the words of Michael Marrus, "could not be accused of Jewish particularism," argued that the murder of the Jews was "absolute[ly] unique." It would, he thought, forever "baffle and terrify mankind."[231] In *Eichmann in Jerusalem,* Arendt declared the Nazis' crimes to be "different not only in degree of seriousness but in essence." What the Nazis tried to do to the Jews constituted a new category of wrongdoing. Their actions were, she argued, "unprecedented" and, though carried out against the Jewish people, they were a "crime against the very nature of mankind."[232]

But what had long been considered self-evident was no longer so in the heat of politics and ideology—certainly not to the White House for whom this was in great measure a matter of politics, and not to the communists for whom ideology reigned supreme. This battle over the Jewish character of the Holocaust and the question of uniqueness would only grow more impassioned and vituperative as the Holocaust came to occupy an increasingly prominent place in the American narrative. Fifteen years would elapse between President Carter's Rose Garden announcement and the day the doors to the USHMM opened. However, many of the questions and debates that began to percolate in those early years illuminated issues that would shape the communal, political, and intellectual discussions about the Holocaust, its meaning and place within American history.

In a New Key

Counting the Victims, Skewing the Numbers

One of the disputes that emerged during the debate with the White House over the establishment of a Holocaust memorial council concerned numbers—big ones. It also became a fight over the identity of the victims, a story I tell in this, the final chapter of the book, because it demonstrates how questions percolating in the 1970s anticipated some of the challenges facing Holocaust commemoration and remembrance in the twenty-first century.

At the initial Rose Garden event, when President Carter first announced the idea for a Holocaust memorial, he referred to "six million" Jewish victims. But a year later, at the first Holocaust Memorial Day to be commemorated in the Capitol Rotunda, he spoke of "eleven million innocent victims exterminated—six million of them Jews."[1] At the same gathering, Vice President Walter Mondale spoke of "eleven million" without even mentioning the word Jew.[2] Six months later the White House issued an executive order mandating the creation of the Holocaust Council as a successor to the commission. The executive order defined the Holocaust as the "systematic and State-sponsored extermination of six million Jews and some five million other peoples by the Nazis and their collaborators." All this raises a question: How did six million Jewish victims become eleven million victims? It was a strange change, particularly since by this point in time "the six million," if not "The Six Million," had become a "rhetorical stand-in" for "the Holocaust." And why did the use of the larger number arouse and continue to arouse such controversy? Would this genocide have been any more tragic if the death toll had been eight million or less tragic if it had been four? Other than to historians, does the exact number really matter? Granted, the White House was not the first to cite the eleven million victim figure. But its use of the number gave it an unprecedented imprimatur that continues until today.[3]

We must begin this discussion by noting that, irrespective of how one defines the Holocaust, the "eleven million" death toll, in the words of historian Peter Novick, makes "no historical sense." If one includes all non-Jewish civilian victims of the Nazis who were killed, the number would be far higher. If one includes only Jews, the number is far too high. Some people, working backward from the number, have proposed that the five million includes three million Soviet POWs and the non-Jewish Poles who were killed. However, if one includes Soviet POWs, then for historical consistency one must include all POWs who were killed in captivity at German hands. Moreover, members of the military, however horribly and illegally they were treated by the Germans, were participants in armed conflict, in contrast to Holocaust victims, who were civilian noncombatants.[4] The Polish non-Jewish civilians who were killed were, for the most part, people whom the Nazis believed—often for the flimsiest, if not imaginary, reasons—were organizing anti-Nazi activity. There was no blanket effort to murder all Poles during the war. And if the five million includes Polish civilians, why not include the civilian casualties of all other nations and ethnicities, as for example Slavs killed by the Germans in noncombat situations?

Elie Wiesel claimed he was blindsided by the White House's mention of eleven million; he balked at this larger figure, arguing that it was an ahistorical accounting.[5] Carter, however, insisted that it be used in all official proclamations and executive orders. Wiesel pushed back, considering it as distasteful and dangerous to the historical integrity of the Holocaust as the White House's previous proposal that the genocide should be "shared," as a White House official put it. The matter became bitter. Presidential staffers accused Wiesel and other survivors of trying to create a "category of second-class victims of the Holocaust." In language that approached antisemitism, they described his insistence on defining the Holocaust as an action against Jews as "narrow, parochial, and indeed, ghetto-like." One White House official declared, with no apparent historical proof, that "all slaves of Eastern Europe and Russia were slated for decimation, degradation, and eventual liquidation" and condemned Wiesel's stance as "morally repugnant."[6] Ironically, an idea created to salve political tensions had spawned its own.

The irony goes deeper if we pursue the source of this fictional number: the revered Holocaust survivor and Nazi hunter Simon Wiesenthal. Wiesenthal had made a career of tracking down Nazi war criminals all over the world, even when the postwar authorities in various countries would have preferred otherwise.[7] He lived in Vienna but visited the United States regularly, where he was depicted as the Nazi hunter who had found Adolf Eichmann. His bravado, derring-do, and insistence that justice be done appealed greatly to American audiences, and he became a much sought-after figure in both Jewish and general settings. In the late 1970s he bragged that during his most recent tour of the United States he had spoken before 28,000 students at twelve universities.[8] Novels and Hollywood films about his exploits, including one film in which he was played by the legendary Laurence Olivier, further enhanced his stature.[9]

Wiesenthal had long faced two problems, one external and one of his own making. Though he was entirely committed to and focused on bringing Nazi war criminals to justice, he needed partners to carry out the task. He might successfully track down fugitives, but then he could not make arrests, conduct legal proceedings, or impose judgments. During the postwar period the Allies, and then the Austrians and Germans, all of whose helped he needed to carry out these tasks, became increasingly less interested in pursuing them. As the Cold War became more heated, Britain and the United States considered winning West Germany's support to be a priority. Tracking down war criminals seemed likely to alienate, not attract, the Germans. West German authorities had a similar attitude toward Nazi war criminals. Already in the early 1950s, less than a decade after the war, they had begun to decry efforts such as Wiesenthal's, a sentiment that emanated from the very top. In 1952 Chancellor Konrad Adenauer, whose government was riddled with former Nazi officials, declared that it was time to stop "sniffing out Nazis." Austrians heartedly agreed. Even the Israelis, beleaguered by all sorts of domestic issues and security challenges, demonstrated, at most, a rather half-hearted devotion to this cause. Wiesenthal increasingly found himself among the lonely few committed to bringing Nazi war criminals to justice.[10] Yet he doggedly persisted.

The other problem Wiesenthal had was his somewhat uneven relationship with the facts. While he deserves great credit for generating media attention to the issue of war criminals, he repeatedly aggrandized his own record by heavily inflating the number of perpetrators he caught.[11] He also claimed credit for actions in which he played little, if any, role. He did not, for example, find Eichmann, though he is often credited with this feat. Tom Segev, author of a very sympathetic biography, remarks that when people thanked Wiesenthal for having caught Eichmann he should have corrected them but did not.[12]

Wiesenthal repeatedly stressed in interviews and speeches that he was different from other Jews. They wanted "vengeance." He wanted "justice." They insisted on dividing the dead and only mourning their own victims. They ignored the "other victims" whom, he claimed, numbered five million. By the end of the 1970s he was peppering his presentations with references to these additional victims. Though he never identified them, he regularly spoke of the "eleven million victims, six million Jews and five million others."[13] How might Wiesenthal's ahistorical figures be explained? Segev suggests that he may have gotten the eleven million from the minutes of the Wannsee Conference, where in 1942 the Nazis planned the murder of European Jewry, listing the number of Jews they planned to kill by country. That total was eleven million.[14] Segev's theory, however, does not explain Wiesenthal's use of the figure, since these eleven million potential victims were all Jews. Rather, Wiesenthal may have created the fraudulent number because he lived in Austria, a country that, for many decades after the war, promulgated the false notion that it, too, had been a victim of Hitler's aggression as the first country invaded by the Germans; in fact, Austrians had enthusiastically welcomed the Germans during the March 1938 Anschluss. Subsequently Austria was a loyal and trusted partner of the Third Reich, engaging in its own spate of vigorous antisemitic actions until the Germans stopped them so that the persecution could proceed in an organized fashion. Wiesenthal, who had a complicated and often strained relationship with Austrian officials, many of whom, as in Germany, were holdovers from the Nazi era, may have wanted to impress upon them that his quest was rooted in a desire to do justice for all people, Austrians included.

But Wiesenthal may have had another motivation for stressing that he thought of the victims in universal, all-inclusive terms. He had a testy, if not competitive, relationship with Wiesel. By the 1970s these two men were probably the best-known survivors in the world. In that light Wiesenthal was intent on differentiating himself from Wiesel. Though he never explicitly said so, there was little doubt that when he contrasted himself to other Jews, those whom he said wanted "vengeance," he meant Wiesel. Wiesel recalled that he once asked Wiesenthal to explain how he reached the number eleven million. According to Wiesel, Wiesenthal responded by accusing him of suffering from "Judeocentrism," being concerned only about Jews. As Wiesel's reputation and clout grew, Wiesenthal became increasingly distressed, if not envious.[15] He was then confronted by Yehuda Bauer and Israel Gutman, two leading Holocaust historians whom he respected; they asked where he had gotten the figure of eleven million. Wiesenthal admitted to having invented it out of whole cloth. He did so, he explained, because he feared that non-Jews would not care about the Holocaust unless they felt that the Germans had targeted them also. He told the two historians that he deliberately chose a smaller number for the non-Jewish death toll so that the Holocaust would remain a predominantly, but not exclusively, Jewish event. The five million number would make "the non-Jews feel like they are part of us." It was, as Bauer observed, "a nice sentiment . . . but ultimately totally counterproductive, not to mention false."[16]

Wiesenthal was not the first survivor to adjust the number of victims for strategic or ideological purposes. In the immediate postwar period, as Timothy Snyder relates in *Bloodlands*, Jakub Berman, who was one of the triumvirate of loyal Stalinist members of the Polish politburo and who had lost much of his immediate family in Treblinka, learned from official documents that far fewer Polish non-Jews had been murdered than Jews. He immediately ordered that the official estimate of non-Jewish Polish dead be increased and that of the Jewish dead be decreased until there was parity between the two (three million each). As Snyder notes, "The Holocaust was already politics of a dangerous and difficult sort. It, like every other historical event, had to be understood . . . in terms that corresponded to Stalin's ideological line." That meant its predominantly Jewish aspect had to be erased. It was transformed into a battle that pitted evil fascists against heroic communists. Even the account of the Warsaw ghetto uprising had to be rewritten so that the Jewish resistance fighters were recast as communists or progressives in a pitched battle against both the Germans as well as Jewish reactionary Zionist forces.[17] The invented Nazi death toll for Poland of three million Jews and three million non-Jews has become "fact."

As with the specious death toll of six million Poles, the eleven million figure has acquired legs that have extended far beyond Wiesenthal's initial claim. Enshrined in presidential orders, Holocaust museums, memorial services, and an array of publications, it is graphic proof of the danger of manipulating the historical record for an ancillary purpose, however well intentioned. Given its dubious origins and fictional status, it is not surprising that those who insist on using it cannot agree on who precisely are these other victims. Yet the number persists.

These machinations have done substantial damage to the historical integrity of the Holocaust.[18] If Wiesenthal can play with the numbers, one might say, why can't Holocaust deniers? However, Wiesenthal's concerns were not entirely illegitimate. Ensuring that the Holocaust not become the province of one group—"it's the Jews' tragedy"—remains an enduring challenge. As the twentieth century drew to a close it would become one of the underlying motifs of the Holocaust narrative.

An Obsession with the Holocaust? A Jewish Critique

At the same time that Wiesenthal worried that non-Jews might not be interested in the Holocaust, some Jewish scholars and leaders worried that Jews were too focused on it. During the 1980s Holocaust commemoration became an increasingly important element of Jewish communal life. It was as if over the past decade gates that had never really been closed were now flung wide open. Programs, memorials, commemorations, and a variety of other projects proliferated. Not everyone saw this as a positive development, however. Some scholars from the burgeoning field of Jewish studies were disturbed by this tragedy's ubiquity and the way many Jews inserted it into every aspect of Jewish life. The critics feared that the lachrymose was becoming the prism through which contemporary Jews were increasingly refracting their history, tradition, and culture. Did this emphasis on the Holocaust, Robert Alter wondered, imbue Jews with a "fearful sense of dread and dislocation"? Did they increasingly perceive of the outside world as a dangerous and threatening place? The Yom Kippur service includes a section known as the Martyrology, which describes the torture and murder of leading rabbis by the Romans during the first and second century. Some synagogues began to discard this traditional liturgy and replace it with readings from Holocaust memoirs. While Alter bemoaned the loss of a liturgy that had been part of the service for centuries, he was more concerned about "the institutional centering of a victimization so unprecedented as to resist meaning." There was certainly a proper place in Jewish liturgy for the memorialization of Holocaust victims, but should it be considered one of the key facets of the holiest service of the Jewish year?[19] Jacob Neusner, never one to mince words, rather provocatively if not distastefully described the phenomenon as "Holocaustomania," complaining that it had become the core component of American Jews' civil religion.[20] Paula Hyman, who would later rank among the premier voices in the field of modern Jewish history, feared that the Holocaust was in the process of being transformed into "the rationale for Jewish survival." She observed that there had been a proliferation of courses on the Holocaust in American universities and that students might not take any other Jewish studies course during their entire academic career.[21] Ismar Schorsch worried that the Holocaust had become the "primary source of fuel to power Jewish life in America," and that an undue emphasis on the Holocaust telegraphed the message that "Jewish survival" was attributable to antisemitism.[22]

It was not by chance that these and other critics all came from the field of Jewish studies. These scholars, who professionally and personally treasured Jewish culture, tradition, and history, feared that the Holocaust might become a convenient replacement for more traditional academic learning. They worried that, in light of the great emphasis on the Holocaust, future generations would only know how Jews died but not how they lived, would only know of Jews as objects, people who have things done to them, and not as subjects, people who do things. Of course, none of these critics could demonstrate that students—Jews and non-Jews—who were drawn to the Holocaust-related courses might not also take a course in rabbinics or some other aspect of Jewish history. Yet their concerns and criticism had an impact in at least one arena. While popular interest in the Holocaust was growing, scholarly interest, at least among Jewish studies scholars, was not. During the 1970s and 1980s, when Jewish studies was blossoming, scholars and graduate students avoided the Holocaust as a field of study. Having a cadre of graduate students is what guarantees that a field will evolve and not become just a matter of passing interest. Even as the number of Jewish students who were pursuing Ph.D.'s in Jewish studies grew during this period, virtually none among them chose to study or to teach the Holocaust. Yet it is important to note that during the early 1970s, when very few of the recently minted Ph.D.'s in Jewish history were selecting the Holocaust as their area of expertise, courses were being offered at Claremont, Marquette, Pacific Lutheran, Temple, Mercy College of Detroit, Wayne State, Catholic Theological Union, Montclair State, Emory School of Theology, and Colgate, among other colleges and universities. The instructors were, by and large, not the newly minted Jewish scholars but some of the non-Jewish scholars and Christian theologians cited in the previous chapter. A number of years would pass before the larger and more prestigious public and private universities would follow the lead of these smaller schools. It is striking that an academic field which has yielded such impressive and extensive work of such high caliber should have had its roots in these smaller, somewhat less prestigious, institutions, "quirky" places, as John Roth, one of the early instructors in the field, has described them.[23]

Historian David Engel attributes the reluctance of the young Jewish scholars to study the Holocaust to their interpretation and application of Salo Baron's 1937 warnings about "the lachrymose conception of Jewish history." Baron had cautioned against the tendency to portray the Jewish experience as a "sheer succession of miseries and persecutions." Doing so would overshadow, if not obliterate, the vast array of positive and laudatory accomplishments that mark Jewish history and culture. The result would be a perception of Jewish experience as but a long chain of persecution and suffering. Engel believes these scholars misinterpreted Baron. While it is true that Baron never retracted his 1937 warning about the lachrymose, neither did he, in the remaining years of his long life, advocate that the study of the Holocaust be marginalized. As we have seen, he organized one of the first conferences in the United States on the topic. He encouraged and enabled Philip Friedman to come to Columbia University as an adjunct professor, where he taught one of the earliest courses on the history of the Holocaust. He found funds to support Friedman's research and wrote the introduction to his major work. In 1948 he invited Friedman to the American Academy of Jewish Research to speak about the study of the Holocaust within the context of Jewish history. As editor of *Jewish Social Studies*, Baron turned the journal into the primary venue for the publication of English-language research on the Holocaust.[24]

But Engel's explanation for the failure of the baby boom generation of Jewish studies scholars to study the Holocaust might be too limited. These critics were not just responding to Baron, but also recoiling from the way the Holocaust was being used to achieve an array of political, religious, philanthropic, and social objectives. Even academics who were devoting their energies to the topic of the Holocaust harbored these concerns. Yaffa Eliach, a Brooklyn College professor, Holocaust survivor, and founder of the first Holocaust center on an American campus, complained that the Holocaust had become, in the hands of certain rabbis and communal leaders, "an instant Judaizer, shocking people back into their Jewishness."[25] I was among those who joined these critics.[26]

Building on Fackenheim's aforementioned dictum of a 614th commandment, Jewish references to the Holocaust proliferated. In the mid-1970s a major Jewish philanthropic organization that raised funds for Israel distributed a poster showing a Jew in Hasidic dress praying before the Western Wall in Jerusalem. The caption read: "Thirty years ago his back was up against a different wall." The message was clear: he survived; now you must give. At the height of the struggle to win rights for Soviet Jews, a Soviet Jewry advocacy group published an ad in newspapers with a Jewish memorial candle in it. The caption read: "This is not the candle Soviet Jews want lit for them."[27] Despite making no mention of the Holocaust, the link in the ad was clear: memorial candles are for the dead. The last time Jews were murdered en masse was the Holocaust, which was being transformed into a tool for inculcating Jewish communal cohesion, philanthropy, and identification. Critics, myself included, feared that such rhetoric reinforced "the historically inaccurate message that anti-Semitism and persecution are the glue that has bound the Jewish people together." We worried that it might transmit a historically invalid message and nurture in post-Holocaust generations "a sense of shame and not of honor." By the early 1980s even Wiesel was expressing his concern that all this focus on the Holocaust, much of which was "trivial and vulgar," had the potential to render "the public insensitive to the tragedy."[28]

But many of the fears about the Holocaust becoming the organizing principle of Jewish communal life did not come to be. It would take a number of years for equilibrium between the lachrymose and the affirmative aspects of Jewish life to be achieved. Eventually it came. In fact, by the 1990s the American Jewish communal leadership had become far more enthralled with the study of Jewish texts and the embrace of Jewish tradition in all its manifestations. The growth of the Jewish women's movement and the creation of nontraditional forms of religious observance injected a sense of affirmation into Jewish communal identity.

It also provided a corrective to the overwhelming weight of Holocaust commemoration. As I argue in the remainder of this book, those who analyzed the Jewish community's remembrance of and identification with the Holocaust without taking into consideration these new developments were bound to get it wrong. Those who relied only on organizational documents and did not go out among the people to see what they were doing were destined to misinterpret what was happening and how it happened.

The Bitburg Affair: The "Watergate of Symbolism"

Historian Charles Maier has observed that historical memory "starts with the dead." This was never truer than in 1985 during what has become known as the "Bitburg Affair." For close to two months this story captured front-page headlines across the United States and was featured on the evening news. On its surface, Bitburg was a debate about the proper way two heads of state—former antagonists and now the closest of allies—should commemorate both World War II and the Holocaust. It became, in the words of Harvard historian and former White House advisor Arthur M. Schlesinger Jr., "one of the most unnecessary embarrassments in the history of American foreign relations." Some analysts have aptly described it as the "Watergate of Symbolism."[29] While the matter may have started with the dead, ultimately it had as much, if not far more, to do with the living.

The affair had its roots in clumsy efforts by President Ronald Reagan and Chancellor Helmut Kohl to celebrate America and Germany's postwar friendship. In the fall of 1984, in a private quiet exchange at the White House, Kohl asked Reagan if, during his forthcoming trip to Germany, he would accompany him to a German military cemetery for a wreath laying ceremony and a symbolic handshake. Kohl had been deeply hurt when Germany had not been included in the fortieth anniversary commemoration of the landing at Normandy. Organizers believed it inappropriate to have the perpetrator of the war present at the commemoration of the deaths of tens of thousands of Allied soldiers. Kohl, however, interpreted this not as a reflection of historical events, but as a snub that indicated that, in the eyes of its Western allies, Germany was still a political and moral outlier. Anxious to counter this notion and demonstrate that Germany was now an equal and full-fledged member of the Western alliance, Kohl asked Reagan, the leader of the free world who had just been reelected president in a landslide, to help him symbolically wipe away any residue of this moral burden. The German chancellor believed that their joint participation in such a ceremony would emphasize the fact that the postwar anticommunist coalition, in which Germany played such a significant role, was as important as the wartime coalition against the fascists, if not more so.[30] Reagan, who needed Kohl's support for his proposed missile defense system, popularly known as "Star Wars," agreed. Planning for the trip was soon underway. And with that the troubles began.

The Germans sent the Americans a list of places the president might visit in addition to the stop at the cemetery. When White House aides selected Dachau from the list, Kohl and his advisors, apparently fearful that pictures of an American president at a concentration camp would only serve to draw attention to Germany's moral turpitude rather than its rehabilitation, reneged. Ignoring the fact that the suggestion of a stop at Dachau had originated with them, German officials announced that the chancellor thought it unwise to include it on the itinerary. The White House agreed. Apparently Reagan, a man who did not like to encounter sorrow, was pleased by the deletion. Administration officials duly informed the press that President Reagan had decided against visiting a concentration camp in West Germany. It was not the decision to avoid the camp that left many people disquieted, however, but the White House's explanation of the president's rationale for not going. White House aides, insisting that Reagan wanted to focus on the future, told reporters: "The Germans of today are not a part of that and shouldn't be made to feel that they are." Then they added a strange statement, given that it came from a president who had shown strong support for the building of a United States Holocaust Museum. "The President now thinks we should try to put this behind us, he thinks that a visit there wouldn't contribute to the theme of reconciliation and friendship."[31]

While this myopic view of history disturbed many people, particularly those concerned about Holocaust commemoration, subsequent events only made matters worse. In February a team of White House and German officials visited the Bitburg military cemetery and chose it as the site for Reagan and Kohl's symbolic handshake. The White House then reiterated its position that the itinerary would not include visits to either an Allied military cemetery or a concentration camp. American veterans' organizations, distressed that the president would honor German but ignore Allied war dead, joined the growing voices of opposition. In March Reagan addressed this issue at a press conference and, once again, managed to further heighten tensions. Glibly severing the past from the present, he told reporters that, while it was important to commemorate the war, he felt "very strongly" that the "memories . . . and passions of the time" should not be "reawakened." Instead, he insisted, his visit should "celebrate" the current "peace . . . and friendship" between the two countries. Then, in an attempt to rationalize his efforts to free

Germany from the yoke of its Nazi past, he added an apparently off-the-cuff explanation as to why a visit to a concentration camp was not sensible: "The German people have very few alive that remember even [*sic*] the war, and certainly none of them were adults and participating in any way." This pronouncement left commentators from across the political spectrum—including some of Reagan's strongest supporters—dumbfounded. It came from a man who had been over thirty years old during World War II and had served in the armed forces. America was home to hundreds of thousands of veterans who had also fought as adults in the war. How could the president of the United States proclaim that there were no veterans alive in Germany when he was a veteran? Reagan hoisted himself even further with his own petard when he asserted that a "guilt feeling . . . [has] been imposed upon them [the German people] and I just think it's unnecessary."[32] The president did not specify who was supposedly responsible for imposing this putative guilt feeling. But those who supported Holocaust commemoration could not help but feel that they were being singled out as this president branded their efforts unnecessary.[33]

It was hard to imagine that the situation could have become even more complicated. But it did when it became public that among those buried in Bitburg were members of the Waffen SS. Though they constituted only a small percentage of the veterans interred in the cemetery, their presence, however small in number, was particularly problematic. In the American popular imagination it was the black-uniformed SS that epitomized the "hard core of Nazism."[34] The SS had hardly acted alone. A broad swath of the German populace had a role in the persecution and extermination programs. However, the SS and its leaders had been among the prime actors in the persecution and annihilation of Jews and Roma. They had run the death camps and engaged in a myriad of lethal exercises against those deemed enemies of the Reich. But there was more. The SS had been the ones who murdered American POWs at Malmedy and massacred the civilian population of the French town of Oradour-sur-Glane. The city of Bitburg had been the staging area for SS's sixth Panzer Army that led the attack in the Battle of the Bulge in which numerous Allied soldiers were killed.[35] Now an American president was going to a cemetery in which SS men were buried. He was not just going there to visit but to engage in a ceremony that SS veterans (the ones Reagan thought were no longer alive) were now asserting honored their contribution to the war.[36]

Reagan, anxious to dispel the notion that those buried in Bitburg were war criminals, added fuel to a blazing public relations fire when he latched on to the fact that, while initially SS members were volunteers who had to be accepted into its ranks, by 1943 a shorthanded Germany was drafting men into the SS. He told reporters that the presence of Waffen SS graves would not deter him from going because the men buried there were "victims of Nazis also." They had been drafted and forced to follow orders, he said. (There is no indication that any research was done on all the Waffen SS members buried there. The White House found one grave of a sixteen-year-old and the president made sure to focus on the soldier's youth.) Lest his point be lost on anyone, Reagan took matters further. He reiterated that they were victims and then equated them with those they had persecuted. These SS men, Reagan declared, "were victims, just as surely as the victims of the concentration camps." With these bizarre and inept statements, Reagan granted these and hundreds of thousands of other Germans who had died fighting for the Third Reich what Raul Hilberg has aptly described as a "nebulous collective innocence."[37]

A firestorm of protest erupted at the remarkable, if not incomprehensible, way in which the president had leveled the distinctions between "those murdered in the camps and the comrade-in-arms of their murderers."[38] Veterans were livid at what they considered a dishonoring of the Americans who had fought. The American Legion, which had close to three million members, reminded the president of the Waffen SS's role in the execution of American POWs. The American Veterans Committee, composed of World War II veterans, contested Reagan's claim that these men were drafted against their will: "Those buried at Bitburg included S.S. active Nazis and not just conscripts."[39] The reaction of German SS veterans was quite different, however, though that was equally troubling. They found nothing objectionable in the president's comments and, even more so, were delighted at the way they felt he had "rehabilitated" their reputations. He had transformed them, they told an American reporter, from feeling like "pariahs" to feeling good, if not proud, of their history.[40] A leading Republican member of Congress aptly described the entire situation as a "moral disaster."[41] In a strange and entirely fortuitous coincidence, on the day after Reagan had united victims and perpetrators by declaring them all "victims," he was scheduled to present Elie Wiesel with the Congressional Gold Medal in a White House ceremony. At that ceremony, Wiesel turned to the president and, with the television cameras from every network recording the event, told him: "That place, Mr. President, is not your place. Your place is with the victims of the SS. . . . The issue here is not politics, but good and evil."[42] That night the clip of Wiesel lecturing the president was among the lead stories on every network newscast. The next day it was a front-page story in virtually every major American newspaper.[43]

In the wake of Wiesel's remarks the criticism escalated. Though Jewish and veteran organizations were among the most vocal, they were hardly alone. Members of Congress voiced their disapproval. Two hundred and fifty-seven representatives and eighty-two senators, including many Republicans who were exceptionally loyal to the president, called for cancellation of the visit. One hundred and forty-three Christian leaders signed an advertisement in the *New York Times* asking the president not to go. Prominent among the signatories were Christian leaders who had devoted their energies, if not their careers, to Christian-Jewish reconciliation in the wake of the Holocaust. They were particularly resentful of the way in which Kohl and Reagan had "marginalized concerns about the Holocaust." They were also disturbed by what they considered, with good reason, the White House's suggestion that it was only Jews who were opposed to the visit. Survivors were left dumbfounded at what they characterized as an "insult" to the victims and a "complete misunderstanding of history." Charles Maier argued that the entire incident constituted far more than a bungled political visit. It was a moment when state leaders trivialized history in the name of contemporary political alignments.[44]

Despite these pleas, the visit proceeded, though not entirely as originally planned. In addition to Bitburg, the president and his entourage visited the Bergen-Belsen concentration camp, which the White House added to the itinerary in an effort to calm the waters.[45] All the networks covered the stop at the cemetery and at Bergen-Belsen live. At the Bitburg visit, which lasted less than ten minutes, Reagan looked stiff and ill at ease. He did not glance at the SS graves, deliver an address, or engage in the symbolic handshake Kohl had wanted so much. His visit to Bergen-Belsen, the supposed antidote to Bitburg, lasted close to an hour. During his various stops, Reagan, clearly anxious to undo some of the damage his verbal gaffes had caused, declared that "the crimes of the SS must rank among the most heinous in human history" and cited the "awful evil" perpetrated by Nazism. Despite Reagan's comments, however, many American editorialists voiced their distress at the muddled way in which the entire event had materialized and the flat-footed fashion in which it had been handled.[46]

While the opposition to and criticism of the visit was forceful, there was another body of reactions that cannot be ignored. A significant proportion of Americans believed that Jewish leaders were "making too big a deal out of Reagan's visit" and that Jews should "stop focusing" on the Holocaust. In some polls as many respondents favored Reagan's visit as opposed it (41 percent on each side).[47] While no one can laud his sense of history, Reagan may have had his finger on the pulse of many Americans who felt it was time to put the past "behind us." As *Time* magazine's Lance Morrow observed after the visit, most Americans had but limited use for history. They might have answered Ralph Waldo Emerson's ironic query: "Why drag about this monstrous corpse of your memory?" by saying there was no reason to do so. Long before the incident, Henry Ford may have expressed this sentiment best when he declared that history "is more or less bunk."[48] Reagan's behavior during the affair had been founded on the notion that a nation could celebrate its positive historical accomplishments and elide the negative. But that was impossible. As Maier observed in his critique of the Bitburg imbroglio, "Insofar as a collection of people wishes to claim existence as a society or nation, it must thereby accept existence as a community through time, hence must acknowledge that acts committed by earlier agents still bind or burden the contemporary community."[49]

Ironically, postwar Germany had, officially at least, accepted this responsibility. Konrad Adenauer, Germany's first postwar chancellor, had instituted an extensive system of reparations. In 1970 Chancellor Willy Brandt had spontaneously fallen to his knees at the site of the Warsaw ghetto memorial. And even Kohl, who was so anxious for this symbolic reconciliation, had noted in a speech he gave at Bergen-Belsen a few weeks before the visit to Bitburg that "reconciliation with the survivors and descendants of the victims is only possible if we accept our history as it really was, if we Germans acknowledge our shame and historical responsibility."[50] The *New York Times*, well aware of the way Kohl and his political compatriots often obfuscated that past, described Kohl's speech as one of the one of "the most forthright and unflinching a West German leader has made about the Hitler era."[51]

One week after the ill-considered Bitburg visit, West German president Richard von Weizsäcker delivered an even more forthright condemnation of not only Hitler, but of the indirect attempt by Kohl and Reagan to rewrite history. Decrying the motivations that gave rise to the Bitburg invitation in the first place, he proclaimed that Germans must have the "strength to look truth straight in the eye—without embellishment and without distortion." Then, in a direct swipe at Kohl, he declared that those born after the war "cannot profess a guilt of their own for crimes that they did not commit." He continued: "All of us, whether guilty or not . . . must accept the past. . . . [The past] cannot be subsequently modified or made not to have happened. . . . However, anyone who closes his eyes to the past, is blind to the present."[52] The power of Weizsäcker's words was immeasurably enhanced by that fact that his father, Ernst, had been Germany's top career diplomat from 1938 to 1943. When Ernst was tried at Nuremberg as a war criminal, his son, the future president of

West Germany, defended him. In the course of so doing he had seen the reams of documents attesting to the horrific and murderous deeds to which his father had willfully blinded himself.

During the Bitburg affair morality, history, and politics violently intersected. None came out the winner. In addition to making an American president look deeply out of touch with history and a German chancellor look manipulative, it set back the public's understanding of what the Holocaust was. While this very public upheaval was precipitated by a series of poorly considered decisions, ludicrously worded statements, maladroit political choreography, and a mangled view of history and historical responsibility, at its heart it was about far more serious matters. Ultimately the incident gave life to William Faulkner's observation that "the past is never dead. It's not even past." Not only was the Holocaust "not even past," it was very much alive and its commemoration was intimately tied up with contemporary politics.

The affair had barely faded from the scene when the past again collided with the present, and the Holocaust with contemporary American foreign policy, despite the best efforts of some of those involved to elide—if not disavow—that past. Kurt Waldheim, who has served as United Nations secretary general from 1972 to 1981, decided in 1985 to run for president of Austria. There had long been rumors about his wartime activities and his association with the Nazis but they had never been pursued. Now, however, when he was running for the presidency, both his political rivals and investigative journalists began to dig into his record to see whether there was truth to the allegations that his version of his war service was not quite accurate. Waldheim had repeatedly asserted, including in his autobiography, that after the Germans incorporated Austria in 1938, he was conscripted against his will into the Wehrmacht army, where he became an officer before being wounded in 1941. Subsequently, according to Waldheim, he returned to Vienna where he spent the rest of the war studying law at the university. Once these oft-made claims were subjected to closer scrutiny it became clear that his rendition was patently false. He had been a member of a Nazi student organization prior to the war and had joined the mounted unit of the SA (storm troopers). He had indeed been wounded in 1941 but, after a few months of recovery, returned to service. He had been in Yugoslavia precisely when brutal operations were underway against partisans. Though he claimed not to have known about any of this and insisted that it was "absolutely absurd" to implicate him, photographs showed him serving as part of a division responsible for some of the most heinous actions against civilians, Jews, and non-Jews. Information also came to light proving that he had, in fact, been stationed in Salonika, Greece, precisely when 42,000 Jews were being deported. The deportations were carried out by his commanding officer, who was executed as a war criminal in 1947. While there was no proof that he had personally participated in these deportations, his claim that he knew nothing about them, despite serving in the very unit responsible, beggared the imagination.

Despite these revelations, Waldheim won the election. That, however, only triggered additional investigations into his war record. The U.S. Department of Justice found documentation that linked Waldheim far more closely to mass deportations of civilians, including Jews and Allied POWs, to concentration and death camps. The Austrian government commissioned an international group of historians to look into the matter. They also found that his claims not to have known anything about the deportations were patently false. Ultimately, Waldheim was deemed a *persona non grata* by the United States and prevented from entering the country.[53] It was the first time the head of government of an American ally had been treated in this fashion. It probably would not have happened two or three decades earlier. A number of the developments we have traced in this book, including research about and public knowledge of the Holocaust, made it harder by the 1980s to bury these lies or explain them away. Survivors and their children, together with many American Jews, felt emboldened enough to challenge Waldheim's claims. Finally, enough Americans understood the nature of the Holocaust to recognize what a record such as Waldheim's meant.

Memory Booms as the World Forgets

During the early 1990s a series of troubling international developments gave the Holocaust an eerie relevance. In Rwanda, the Hutus murdered over 800,000 Tutsis in approximately one hundred days. But it was not just in Africa, where Western commentators seemed to expect such tragedies, that genocide was occurring. Mass murder was also taking place in the heart of Europe. The Yugoslav army and the Bosnian Serb paramilitary forces attacked Bosnia and engaged in a brutal array of atrocities after the Bosnian government declared independence from Yugoslavia. Eventually 250,000 people were killed and millions were left homeless. The fighting in the Balkans gave rise to the term "ethnic cleansing." Introduced by the perpetrators there, it was reminiscent of the Nazi use of euphemism, such as "deportation to the east" or "Final Solution," to linguistically camouflage horrors that included murder, torture, arbitrary arrest and detention, extrajudicial executions, sexual assaults, forcible removal of the civilian population, and wanton destruction of property.[54] These horrors and mass killings occurred in full view of the world's media. For many reporters and observers the Holocaust became, rather than a matter of history, a prism that refracted contemporary events. The image that emerged from that prism suggested that the world in general and Europe in particular had not learned very much. The link to the Holocaust was compounded by the response of much of the rest of the world. Nations that had taken the lead in Holocaust commemoration, including the United States, sat by and ignored pleas for help.

The unprecedented moral and political capital of the Holocaust was nowhere more starkly evident than at the 1993 dedication of the United States Holocaust Memorial Museum, when Elie Wiesel berated President Bill Clinton for not doing more—or anything at all—to halt the slaughter then raging in the former Yugoslavia: "Mr. President, I have been [to the former Yugoslavia]. . . . I cannot sleep since what I've seen. As a Jew, I am saying that we must do something to stop the bloodshed in that country."[55] Wiesel's public challenge to this new president who had been in office less than 100 days did not precipitate an immediate change in American policy. However, according to Roy Gutman, a reporter who covered the conflict for years, it "echoed from that moment on. It rallied people in the Congress and various communities here, in the human rights community, the policy elite in and out of Washington." Remarkably, this was the second president whom Wiesel had publicly called to account in person. Both times he had done so on the foundation of his "authority" as a Holocaust survivor. Regarding Bitburg, however, he had spoken up about an action that had only symbolic implications. In contrast, this time he challenged a foreign policy matter that had no link to the Holocaust or any other direct Jewish interest. Wiesel, standing in front of a museum built on federal land with the support of three presidents and with congressional imprimatur, was using the Holocaust as a moral yardstick with which to assess America's response—or lack thereof—to a contemporary tragedy. If the Holocaust had a mythic element, it was never clearer than at that moment.

There was, however, another message implicit in Wiesel's remarks, a message featured in the newly dedicated museum in an overt and unapologetic fashion. Fifty years earlier America had turned its back on many refugees who might have been saved.[56] This museum concerned an event whose victims and perpetrators were not Americans and which had not happened on American soil. Nonetheless, those most directly involved in constructing it believed it belonged on the Washington Mall because it reminded visitors both of a catastrophe that was contrary to American principles and how the United States had stood by, refusing to engage. It acknowledged America's own failures. Now Wiesel, building on that message, issued a foreign policy challenge: what was happening in Yugoslavia might not be a Holocaust or a genocide, but that did not absolve the United States from acting to halt it. One of the survivors present at the dedication observed: "No one has even entered the place and it's already telegraphing a message America has to hear."[57]

Ironically these events, which so evoked memories of the Holocaust, occurred during what has become known as "the memory boom." Beginning in the 1980s there was a remarkable growth in interest in the link between history and identity. Scholars were beginning to address the issue in earnest. Many academics who had previously eschewed anything that smacked of memory studies were drawn to them. Nations that were newly born or reborn in the wake of communism's fall in Eastern Europe (those whose citizens perpetrated some of the horrors in the former Yugoslavia) "conjure[d] up the past"—often it was more of a constructed past than a genuine one—as part of their engagement in "collective remembrance." There was little doubt that this movement had its roots in the growing concern with and attention to the Holocaust. Pierre Nora, the French political scientist considered to be one of the founding fathers of this boom, posited rather unequivocally: "Whoever says memory, says *Shoah*."[58] While some historians such as Jay Winter believe that the sources of this new engagement with the past were more multifaceted, almost all agree that the interest in the Holocaust was one of the primary motivating factors. By the 1990s the Holocaust was firmly "anchored in Western historical consciousness as never before."[59]

That consciousness was reflected in a spate of Holocaust-related stories that filled media outlets. This time, however, in contrast to previous decades, most of those stories concerned the bystanders rather than the perpetrators or victims. Swiss banks, international corporations, insurance companies, leading museums, the Red Cross, and the Vatican all found themselves under unprecedented pressure to account for their record during the Holocaust. Some opened up their archives in response. Most "discovered" that they had terrible skeletons in their closet, though they may have knowingly kept those skeletons there. Now, however, they could not so easily deny their wartime wrongs and their postwar failings. They had held on to financial assets that rightfully belonged to survivors. These funds sat in their coffers while survivors were rebuffed, often in the most glib and callous fashion. Some heirs were asked to produce death certificates, something the death camps and ghettoes failed to provide. Corporations that had benefitted from slave labor during the war and reaped the benefits of that labor afterward vigorously denied that they were culpable. Now they were called to account. Some of the world's most prominent cultural institutions were forced to admit that they held artwork that they knew had been looted from Jews.[60] Over the four decades since the war, no one, including those within the Jewish community, had paid attention to the grievances of victims and their families.[61]

Nations began, most quite reluctantly, to more honestly confront their history. France had long insisted that Vichy France was not really France so it was not responsible for what happened there. Austria painted itself as a victim. The Swiss had created a myth of neutrality when, in fact, they had often helped the Germans launder their ill-gotten gains.[62] Germany, which prided itself on having paid reparations to victims, had, in fact, placed obstacles in the path of many who sought compensation. The government had helped German corporations shield themselves from potential liability by supporting their claim that they had only been following orders from Berlin. In fact many if not most of these corporate entities had worked closely with the Nazi government and actively sought slave labor because it was cheap and plentiful, thus becoming part of an immense network of exploitation and persecution. Although they were generally motivated more by profits than by genocide, the fact that prisoner-laborers, both Jews and non-Jews, faced horrific work environments resulting in serious injury and death did not seem to trouble the corporations. The postwar efforts of the German government to shield the corporations from direct responsibility, together with the efforts of postwar generations of business leaders to camouflage their corporations' involvement with National Socialism, made it impossible for many survivors of concentration and labor camps to receive any form of settlement before their deaths.[63] But now, as the twentieth century was drawing to a close, the climate was changing. Survivors and their adult children, feeling emboldened by the enhanced attention to the Holocaust, called on corporations to admit their dishonorable role in history. In the United States, class action suits were brought against American subsidiaries of the firms that had benefitted from forced labor or that had retained assets originally belonging to survivors and victims. Several corporations felt compelled to release documents long hidden in company files that made it increasingly clear the Holocaust was not only a genocide of horrendous proportions but also an event of tremendous economic consequences.[64] Most of these cases did not even come to court; companies often settled in order to avoid bad publicity regarding their shameful actions and evasion of all moral imperatives. Some plaintiffs and their lawyers, however, went a step further and accused the corporations of being not just enablers of the Holocaust, but essential perpetrators.

The Red Cross, which had long cast itself as a neutral bastion of goodwill, had to admit it had aided the Nazis. In 1996, after repeated refusals, it released thousands of documents pertaining to its role during the Final Solution. The documents proved what many historians had been saying:

the organization knew precisely what was being done to the Jews and failed to publicize the information. But it had done more than just fail to act. On occasion it provided the Germans' with official cover for their persecution of Jews. Such was the case in 1944 when a Red Cross delegation issued a positive report about Terezin, a ghetto outside of Prague. On other occasions Red Cross officials assisted the Germans in laundering gold looted from Jews. Now, after decades of ignoring demands by survivors and Jewish organizations, the organization released the documents and, of even greater significance, noted that it too had to "share responsibility for the silence of the world community." It placed this admission on its website, where it remains today.[65] When asked why it took so long, the Red Cross response affirmed its complicity: "Because it takes time to face your own history."[66]

Even the Vatican, which for decades had insisted that it had done all it could during the Final Solution, took a small step toward acknowledging its shortcomings. An official Vatican publication, introduced by a statement by Pope John Paul II, noted that a "heavy burden of conscience" should weigh upon Catholics for the "errors and failures" of their brothers and sisters during the Second World War. To this day the Vatican still refuses to release the documents in its archives that would allow scholars to document its precise role. However, when it described its statement as a "call to penitence," it was acknowledging that its record was not pristine.[67]

In 1997 France, the United Kingdom, and the United States convened the London Conference on Nazi Gold. Attended by nations that in the postwar period had received Nazi gold—most of which came from individual victims—the conference established a fund for victims. The fund was financed by the remaining reserves of Nazi gold held by these nations. (Many, if not most, of those who benefited from this were non-Jewish slave laborers.) European nations that had previously denied they had played any role in or profited from the Holocaust now addressed their national myths and agreed it was time to face their actual history. In all these matters, acknowledgment of past wrongs would not have happened without pressure from the highest reaches of the American government, which would not have come without pressure from the leaders of the American Jewish community and, before that, pressure from survivors and their children.[68]

Even as these cases were in the spotlight, another Holocaust-related story grabbed the headlines. In 1997, as President Clinton was about to begin his second term, he nominated Madeleine Albright, the U.S. ambassador to the United Nations, to be secretary of state. Various media outlets began to report that Albright was not telling the truth when she asserted that her parents had fled from Nazi-occupied Czechoslovakia because of their democratic views. In a front-page story, the *Washington Post* reported that the Nazis murdered dozens of her relatives, including three of her grandparents, because they were Jews. Albright steadfastly insisted that she was unaware of her Jewish heritage or the death of her relatives.[69] The public debate surrounding Albright's nomination revolved far less on the policies she might champion and far more about whether she had hidden this information because it might have hindered her professional path. Some critics attributed Albright's silence to the fact that she had begun her scholarly and governmental career decades earlier, when being Jewish and talking about the Holocaust were not convenient. Others agreed that she might not have known but were troubled by, in the words of *New York Times* columnist Frank Rich, "her lack of curiosity" about her background. "What smart, serious, sensitive student of history, let alone Nazi refugee, makes no effort to find out how her grandparents died?"[70] For many American Jews, Albright's personal story intersected with two of their greatest fears: deadly antisemitism, which physically annihilated Jews, and assimilation, as exemplified by her parents' postwar decision to leave the Jewish faith and actively hide that fact from their daughter, colleagues, and friends.[71]

Assaults on the Holocaust: Normalization, Denial, and Trivialization

As international attention to the Holocaust increased, so too did the scholarly battles about its definition and its mythic application to contemporary issues. On its surface this academic discourse concerned the historicization of the Holocaust—placing the Holocaust within the broader social, political, economic, and cultural environment of its times in order to more fully understand its origin. In truth, though they were conducted under the cloak of intellectual discourse, these exchanges were often far more polemical than enlightening, more political than scholarly. Now that the history of the Holocaust was increasingly being written, the fight over how is should be written escalated in tenor and tone.

One of the more debated political-*qua*-academic interchanges began in earnest in the wake of the Bitburg affair. A group of politically conservative German historians challenged the commonly accepted view that the Final Solution was a unique crime. Precipitating what has become known as the *Historikerstreit* (historians' struggle), they posited that if Germany's crimes were compared with wrongdoings of other nations, it would be clear that they were neither "unprecedented" nor "original" but a replica of the "class murder" carried out by the Bolsheviks.[72] Moreover, they contended, not only were the Nazis' crimes not singular, they were legitimate. According to Ernst Nolte, the most prominent of these academics, what happened at Auschwitz was neither the "result of traditional anti-Semitism" nor "genocide" but was rooted in German "anxiety" about what the Soviets might do.[73] Nolte argued that most historical analyses of the Final Solution failed to consider this supposed symmetry between German and Jew. He decried the proliferation of "talk about 'the guilt of the Germans' [which] all too willfully overlooks . . . the guilt of the Jews." According to Nolte, Germany was justified in singling out the Jews as enemies because at the war's outset Zionist leader Chaim Weizmann proclaimed that the Jews would fight the Germans alongside the British. Weizmann's statement rendered the Jews Germany's enemy and also gave Hitler "good reasons to be convinced of this enemy's determination to annihilate him." In suggesting that Jews were fair game for the Nazis, Nolte conveniently excised antisemitism as one of the Holocaust's motivating factors. Though Nolte and his compatriots claimed to be engaged in straightforward historical analysis, they were clearly motivated by the growing attention to the Holocaust and the Bitburg incident. They complained that "crimes" perpetrated against Germany were ignored by the world while the Holocaust was becoming "more alive and powerful."[74] Echoing these views, Martin Walser, one of Germany's best-known writers, complained that the Final Solution was being used as a "moral cudgel" to keep Germany from becoming a "normal" nation.[75]

This was far more than a different approach to history. Critics characterized it a radical attempt to rewrite Germany's past. These German historians essentially repudiated the "historical *nostra culpa* for the Nazi regime" that Germany had given since the end of the war.[76] More than just radically new, it was also deeply flawed. Nolte's use of Weizmann's 1939 statement as a means to justify the Nazi war against the Jews was so farfetched—Charles Maier branded it "tendentious"—that some saw in it deeper, more mendacious, inclinations. It completely elided the Nazis' extreme record of prewar antisemitic acts. Long before Weizmann issued his "declaration of war," Reich Jewry had been ousted from virtually all professions, deprived of their citizenship, pauperized, endured a Reichwide pogrom known as *Kristallnacht*, forced to take overtly Jewish names so that their Jewish identity would be immediately recognizable, removed from schools and universities, and subjected to an array of other degradations. Nolte and his compatriots knew all these facts but ignored them, just as they ignored the way Nazi propaganda had from its founding in the 1920s singled out Jews as Germany's mortal enemy. Moreover, Nolte's contention that the Jews were a legitimate enemy and had to be destroyed by German forces as they pushed eastward ignored the obvious: without a state and an army Jews had no means of waging war. Weizmann's declaration of war on Germany was that of a paper tiger. These efforts to reformulate the historical meaning of the Holocaust so as to lift the burden of history from Germany upset many scholars who discerned a political rather than a scholarly goal.

Nor did this argument resonate among Americans the way it did in Germany. In America there was a different kind of rewriting of history that was of concern to many people: Holocaust denial. At first glance it seemed patently absurd, too absurd to be taken seriously. Since the late 1950s a small but prolific group of individuals, most with overt connections to extremist right-wing and neo-Nazi groups, had been peddling the notion that the Holocaust was a hoax contrived by Jews for their own nefarious purposes. Those promulgating these claims were primarily German expatriates, Nazi loyalists, and others with some connection, however ephemeral, to the Third Reich. The notion that Hitler could have allowed something such as the Final Solution to occur was not only unfathomable to them and their perception of the Fuhrer, but also constituted an obstacle to their dream of resurrecting National Socialism. Though their denial of the Holocaust found a sympathetic reception among far-right groups and individuals, they gained little traction among the general public because those disseminating such polemics were so clearly connected to neo-Nazis.[77]

In the late 1970s deniers changed their tactics. Carefully eschewing any public connection with neo-Nazis, they presented themselves as scholars whose only objective was to correct and revise mistakes in history (hence their self-description as "revisionists"). They created a sham research institute based in California where they held conferences that seemed, at first glance, to be scholarly gatherings. They published an academic-looking publication called the *Journal of Historical Review.* While the externals may have changed, however, their basic claims remained the same. They insisted there had been no genocide of the Jews and that Jews had invented this story to get money and sympathy from the world. Deniers' explanation as to why the Jews created such a massive hoax relied on traditional antisemitic stereotypes: Jews' supposed love of money and their propensity for secret manipulation of the majority population to benefit themselves. Jews, by spreading this "tale," made the world feel guilty about what happened in order to obtain reparations, that is, money, from Germany and to displace another people, the Palestinians, from their land. By relying on these stereotypes the deniers offered the public, at least those with a proclivity toward antisemitism, an explanation that made sense.

The problem for the deniers, of course, is that the Holocaust has the dubious distinction of being the best-documented genocide in the world. The deniers' claims that Jews planted these documents stagger belief.

The mythmakers would have had to sneak documents into myriad files in archives all over Europe. They would have had to make sure that these forged documents had the correct typeface and right printer ribbon so that they matched the documents that preceded and followed them and that they carried the proper and rather complex file numbers that were placed on all official government correspondence. Copies of these bogus documents would need to have been placed in the files of the senders and the originals in the files of the recipients. Further, deniers had to explain where all those Jews went who had not been killed (in their version of events). Most importantly, they would have to explain why postwar Germany not only failed to deny what happened, but took responsibility for this massive crime. Some Nazis on trial contended that they were simply following orders. Others argued that they did not have a direct hand in the criminal actions. None, however, ever said the genocide was a myth.

Many of the deniers' most basic arguments could be refuted with simple logic. Deniers argued that the Nazis were so efficient and successful at achieving their goals that had they wanted to kill all the Jews within their reach they would have done so. Consequently, the fact that there were so many survivors proves that the Nazis did not intend to murder them. This argument can, of course, be refuted by the fact that the Nazis also wished to win the war and did not succeed at that. Hence, the premise that they could succeed at everything they wished is false, as is all that follows from that. Despite the numerous flaws in deniers' arguments, their heightened media presence both in the United States and Europe distressed many people.[78]

The Uniqueness Battle

Even as deniers were attacking the veracity of the Holocaust, other attacks were coming from a different direction. Members of other groups that had suffered discrimination and tragedy began to complain not about the veracity but the attention the Holocaust was receiving. They contended that such attention was preventing their own tragedies from receiving their due. Insisting that the injustices suffered by their groups were the same as or worse than the Holocaust, they began to attack those who argued that the Holocaust was an unprecedented tragedy. In the words of Samantha Power, author of the Pulitzer Prize–winning study *A Problem from Hell: America and the Age of Genocide,* they began to "play and prey upon the moral mileage that the Holocaust has clocked in recent years."[79] Sociologist John Torpey described it as a "contest for the status of worst-victimized." Some of the attacks came from people in the African American community, with whom American Jews now had an increasingly strained relationship. Ali Mazuri, a specialist in African studies, expressed it thus: "Twelve years of Jewish hell—against several centuries of black enslavement."[80] Black Muslim leader Louis Farrakhan attacked Jews for demanding that so much attention be paid to the Holocaust: "Don't push your six million down our throats, when we lost 100 million."[81] Few could claim to be surprised to hear this from Farrakhan, who had a well-documented record of using antisemitic rhetoric. It was more disturbing when the respected novelist Toni Morrison, certainly no ally of Farrakhan, engaged in the same kind of creative accounting. She dedicated her acclaimed 1987 novel *Beloved* to "Sixty Million and More," later explaining that sixty million was the death toll for the Africans forcibly taken from their homes but who died even before reaching these shores. Peter Novick, no fan of Holocaust commemoration, described these figures as "off the wall" and noted that they bore "no relation to any scholarly estimate" except for the fact, he wryly observed, that sixty million "is, of course, ten times six million."[82]

While there are legitimate grounds to compare and contrast slavery with the Holocaust, other comparisons strained credibility beyond recognition. Groups whose causes bore no resemblance to slavery, mass killings, or genocide appropriated the Holocaust also. Evangelist Pat Robertson, preaching on his Christian Broadcasting Network, declared, "Just what Nazi Germany did to the Jews, so liberal America is now doing to evangelical Christians. . . . It's no different. It is . . . the homosexuals who want to destroy all Christians," accompanying his tirade with images of Nazi horrors. C. Everett Koop, who served as surgeon general under President Reagan, used the same analogy in relation to abortions. There is a progression, he warned, from "liberalized abortion . . . to active euthanasia . . . to the very beginnings of the political climate that led to Auschwitz, Dachau, and Belsen."[83] This kind of trivialization did not stop with human victims. Activists on behalf of animal rights also framed their efforts in Holocaust-related terms. The organization People for the Ethical Treatment of Animals (PETA) mounted an exhibition, "Holocaust on your Plate," which juxtaposed images of people in concentration camps with those of farm animals: an emaciated man next to a starving cow. One PETA leader declared "six million people died in concentration camps, but six billion broiler chickens will die this year in slaughterhouses."[84] Senator Al Gore compared the contemporary ecological situation facing the world to *Kristallnacht,* which in 1938 presaged a terrible tragedy that was soon to come.[85] By the end of the 1980s the director of Yad Vashem noted the American tendency toward "faddism, trivialization, [and] oversimplification" regarding the Holocaust. It had become, he said, a "metaphor for all of society's ills."[86]

Even as this jockeying over Holocaust analogies was taking place, another related imbroglio was brewing. The notion that there was something unprecedented about the Holocaust prompted a barrage of attacks. In an attempt to explain why he saw this as a particularly Jewish tragedy, Wiesel had said, "Not all victims were Jews but all Jews were victims." Sociologist John Murray Cuddihy dismissed this statement as a form of triumphalism and a secular reformulation of the concept of "chosen people" that gave voice to Jews' intention to "exclude all other groups besides" themselves.[87] As these types of attacks grew in intensity some Holocaust scholars, including Yehuda Bauer, Raul Hilberg, Lucy Dawidowicz, Michael Marrus, and Saul Friedlander, responded by asserting even more strongly that this event differed from other genocides and from previous acts of persecution visited upon the Jews. In other words, it had no historical precedent. Dawidowicz described the Holocaust as "unparalleled [in its] scope, devastating effect, and incomprehensible intent." It was the "quintessential epitome of evil."[88] Bauer wrote: "Holocaust was the policy of the total, sacral Nazi act of mass murder of all Jews they could lay hands on. Genocide was horrible enough, but it did not entail total murder if only because the subject peoples were needed as slaves. They were, indeed, 'subhumans' in Nazi terminology. The Jews were not human at all."[89] For Marrus the uniqueness was not a matter of numbers or even barbarity. It was the fact that only in the case of the Jews and not Jehovah's Witnesses, homosexuals, or Poles did "Nazi ideology require their total disappearance." Raul Hilberg labeled the Holocaust "the benchmark, the defining moment in the drama of good and evil."[90]

Wiesel took matters even further. Expressing himself in a register that was both theological, mystical, and anathema to most scholars, he insisted on uniqueness. "The Holocaust is unique; not just another event. . . . The Holocaust transcends history. . . . The dead are in possession of a secret that we, the living, are neither worthy of nor capable of recovering. . . . The Holocaust [is] the ultimate event, the ultimate mystery, never to be comprehended or transmitted. Only those who were there know what it was; the others will never know." Among theologians the response was similar. Roy and Alice Eckardt called the Holocaust "uniquely unique."[91] Emil Fackenheim, a bit more ambiguously, described it as "epoch making."

Not surprisingly, historians, including those who believed the event was unprecedented, were decidedly uncomfortable with these kinds of constructs. Bauer decried the notion that the Holocaust could not be "comprehended or transmitted." "If it took place outside of history . . . it becomes a mysterious event, an upside-down miracle, so to speak, an event of religious significance, in the sense that it is not man-made as the term is normally understood." He added an important caveat, which made his stance on uniqueness far more nuanced and less absolutist than Wiesel's: "To declare that there are no parallels, and that the whole phenomenon is inexplicable is equally a mystification. . . . Once an event has happened, it can happen again, not in precisely the same form, but in one of an infinite number of variations."[92] While it may be without parallels or precedents, the Holocaust was not a mystical event:

> If what happens to the Jews is unique, then by definition it doesn't concern us, beyond our pity and commiseration for the victims. If the Holocaust is not a universal problem then why should a public school system in Philadelphia, New York, or Timbuktu teach it? Well, the answer is that there is no uniqueness, not even of a unique event. Anything that happens once, can happen again: not quite in the same way, perhaps, but in an equivalent form.[93]

As the notion of the Holocaust's incomprehensibility grew more ubiquitous, he reiterated his differences with the theological and mystical position even more directly. "I disagree with writers, philosophers, and theologians who try to remove the Holocaust into some abstract sphere of mystification, and tell us 'we shall never know.' If they mean knowledge equal to the actual experience, obviously not—but then neither can they experience the pin prick of their little child's finger."[94]

Bauer was hardly alone. Other scholars, including those sympathetic to Wiesel as a witness, took sharp issue with his assertion that "we shall never understand how Auschwitz was possible" and that Auschwitz was an "unintelligible anomaly."[95] These scholars were spending their time, intellect, and energy trying to make what happened at Auschwitz intelligible. Some recognized the problematic nature of this discussion. Ismar Schorsch believed the emphasis on uniqueness, though not the idea itself, was "counterproductive." Yet at the same time he wondered whether forgoing the claim of uniqueness somehow "diminish[ed] the horror of the crime."[96]

The most exhaustive response to these attacks came from Jewish philosopher and scholar Steven Katz, who in 1994 published the first of a proposed three-volume study entitled *The Holocaust in Historical Context*. While other scholars had posited that the Holocaust was a unique type of genocide, Katz took matters further and compared and contrasted the Holocaust to virtually every instance of mass murder. He argued that none of them—with the exception of the Holocaust—fell into the category of genocide.[97] There were historians of the Holocaust, including those who believed the Holocaust was unique, who felt Katz was taking too absolutist a position. Some began to echo Schorsch's observation that there was something counterproductive about this debate.

But that was not the only Holocaust-related fight that began in the academic world and spilled over into the more general arena. In 1996 a newly minted Harvard Ph.D., Daniel Jonah Goldhagen, published his revised dissertation as *Hitler's Willing Executioners: Ordinary Germans and the Holocaust*, the central thesis of which was that for well over a century Germany had been home to a unique and virulent form of antisemitism that was "eliminationist" in nature, that is, it espoused killing Jews. Though it had long preceded the Nazis, only during the Third Reich were all the pieces in place for its genocidal goals to be realized. The book prompted a firestorm of criticism in the academic world and praise outside of it. Scholars dismissed it as a "sweeping polemic," "mono-causal," and "radically incomplete."[98] Critics wondered how Goldhagen might explain the fact that a thriving Jewish community had existed in Germany for centuries despite the existence of this so-called eliminationist anti-semitism. Were those Jews blind to these desires to murder them?[99] Even those scholars who agreed with him that antisemitism was the Nazis' prime motivator were troubled by his sweeping argument and his failure to consider the fact that other countries with long records of antisemi-tism had never engaged in or considered engaging in genocide against the Jews. Despite the fault most Holocaust historians found with his argu-ment, the broader public embraced it with enough vigor to keep it on the *New York Times* bestseller list for weeks. How might we explain this stark difference in popular and academic reception? Some attributed the book's popularity, not only in America but also, to the surprise of many critics, in Germany, to its straightforward and relatively uncomplicated thesis for the origins of the Holocaust. As one critic observed: "The Germans killed the Jews because they wanted to; they wanted to since the mid-nineteenth century."[100]

At the same time that scholars were struggling over Katz and Goldhagen, another area of inquiry was emerging. Increasing numbers of scholars began to question whether men's and women's experiences during the Holocaust had been entirely similar. This issue had first been addressed in the early 1980s when Joan Ringelheim convened a confer-ence and authored some of the earliest articles on the topic. It was, how-ever a decade later, after a conference in Israel and the publication of a book on the topic by Yale University Press, that these disparate inquiries coalesced as an emerging field. Dalia Ofer and Lenore Weitzman, the editors of the book, and virtually all of the contributors to it insisted that they were not arguing that women's experiences during the Holocaust were totally different from those of men: "That would be as false and misleading as to argue that their experiences were identical to those of men." However, there were differences based on gender: rape, sexual abuse, the danger of pregnancy, and the illusion harbored by many Jews that the Nazis would leave women alone, hence there was no need for women to escape. Ofer, Weitzman, and other scholars argued that without accounting for gender differences one could not gain a comprehensive account of the Holocaust.[101]

But here too there was controversy. Shortly after the book appeared it was subjected to a scathing attack in *Commentary* by Gabriel Schoenfeld, who accused the editors and contributors of more than just trivializing the Holocaust. He contended that they had a "naked ideological agenda" whose objective was to engage in "propaganda" and to "sever Jewish women, in their own minds, from their families as well as from the larger Jewish community."[102] Most of the scholars whom Schoenfeld attacked accused him of distorting their words and ideas. Soon, as is often the case in scholarship, the law of unintended consequences prevailed. If this line of inquiry had been a fledgling field before Schoenfeld's attack, by the second decade of the twenty-first century it had become a respected, nuanced, and well-researched area. By that point in time Schoenfeld's criticism sounded strangely dated.

Impassioned Attacks

In the late 1990s an even more vituperative series of attacks on Holocaust studies emerged. Some of the most vigorous came from David Stannard and Ward Churchill, specialists in Native American history. They argued that the treatment of Native Americans by European settlers qualified as a genocide and surpassed in horror what was done to the Jews. Churchill, ignoring the way in which the Nazis had specifically targeted Jews, redefined the Holocaust to include all those killed by the Germans: Sinti and Roma, Soviet POWs, Eastern European civilians, Slavs, and millions of others. There are certainly legitimate historical grounds on which to debate whether the terrible treatment of Native Americans by the American government and its citizens was the same as or distinct from the Final Solution. What raised the ire of many people, however, was the way Churchill and Stannard relied on language that contained echoes of antisemitism. Churchill, who was eventually dismissed from his university position for falsification of his research and plagiarism, labeled those who argued for uniqueness as "racists," "violence provoking," and "conspiracy theorists" who were part of a "cult" that promulgated a "religious dogma." He even attributed America's refusal to pay proper attention to the destruction of Native Americas to supporters of "Zionism" who wished to maintain the "privileged political status of Israel." Stannard also accused "Jewish uniqueness advocates . . . [of] denial of the [geno-cidal] experience of others."[103]

A far less vociferous and polemical attack on Holocaust commemora-tion, remembrance, and study came from historian Peter Novick. His book *The Holocaust in American Life* (1999) was part of a small but widely discussed body of literature that appeared at the turn of the millennium. In it he faulted Jews and Holocaust scholars for using the Holocaust for ulterior purposes. He seemed unsettled—if not angry—by the surge of attention to the Holocaust, particularly in the wake of the opening of the United States Holocaust Memorial Museum in 1993 and the release that same year of Steven Spielberg's film *Schindler's List*. For Novick, this rise in interest in the Holocaust was due to the machinations of Jewish com-munal leaders beginning in the 1970s. He maintained that these leaders, anxious to generate support for Israel and to fight against assimilation and intermarriage, were convinced that only one thing could motivate Jews to maintain their Jewish identity: fear. They lit upon the Holocaust, the exemplar of Jewish suffering, and determined that it was a perfect tool with which to frighten Jews. Consequently they decided to put the Holocaust, in Novick's words, "at the center of how Jews understood themselves and wanted others to understand them."[104] He based this on an assertion that "historical events are most talked about shortly after their occurrence." Given that the Holocaust did not emerge as "the Holocaust" until two to three decades after 1945, he contended, its emer-gence could not have happened naturally: "Without official sanction, it could not [have] become a public communal emblem." He found this sanction in the activities of the organized Jewish community and the work of those he called a "cadre of Holocaust memory professionals."[105]

There are fundamental flaws in Novick's argument. While he is cer-tainly correct that there was a substantial surge of interest in the Jewish community in the 1970s, he ignored the attention to the Holocaust which preceded that surge.[106] As we have repeatedly seen, the topic was decid-edly not absent from either the popular or scholarly arena in those years. Furthermore, Novick ignored the fact that there are often historical inci-dents, particularly involving great national or communal traumas, which must wait years, if not generations, to be explored in depth. Most strik-ingly, Novick elided or discounted many of the explanations for the increased interest, including the traumatic fears that beset many Jews in May 1967 and the joyous relief that followed in June with the outcome of the Six Day War. Jewish organizations responded to this surge of inter-est; they did not generate it. American Jews had feared another Holocaust. History, however, did not to repeat itself, in part, American Jews told themselves, because this time they did not remain silent.

The world might have been willing to sit idly by, but they were not. They had raised funds that they felt would help Israel defend itself before the war and recover after the war. Many had volunteered to go and help. Most of all, they had been unequivocally outspoken in their support. They had not felt, as might have been the case in the 1930s and 1940s, that they had to temper their public calls for support of a Jewish cause. They had not fought on the battlefield but felt as if they had fought on its periphery. In the wake of Israel's unexpected victory, American Jews may have found it more bearable to look back at an unbearable past. It is easier to grapple with horrific tragedy after the dissipation of another threat provides some semblance of closure. That contemporary events did not result in another Holocaust made it possible to reconsider the Nazi genocide as part of history rather than as the living present, and thus easier to face. (One might argue that this, in fact, was the reason for the great popularity of Leon Uris's novel *Exodus* and its subsequent film adaptation. It began with tragedy but ended with victory. It gave the Holocaust a happy, or at least bearable, ending.) This was especially so in an America in which numerous groups—ethnic, political, religious, and gender—began in the 1970s to celebrate their victimhood, not as a badge of honor, but as something that was being overcome.

While the evidence does not support Novick's claim that interest in the Holocaust was created ex nihilo by Jewish communal organizations, he is certainly correct that the response of Jewish organizations to this surge of interest in the Holocaust often was exploitative and simply in bad taste. But, as we have also seen, there already was a critique about "the use and abuse" of the Holocaust in the 1980s by Jewish scholars, including those who studied the Holocaust.[107] I wrote that making the Holocaust the linchpin of Jewish life was "not only . . . exploitative of both victims and the Jew whose 'conscience is being raised,' but it reinforces the historically inaccurate message that anti-Semitism and persecution are the glue that has bound the Jewish people together, and it is because of the ever-present threat of anti-Semitism that Jews must remain Jews."[108] The critique from Jewish studies scholars in the 1980s and Novick's subsequent comments may sound the same, but they are not. First of all, nearly two decades separated them. The concerns of the early critics was that there was too much focus on the Holocaust, not that this interest had been created out of whole cloth by communal organizers. Second, the early critics were people with a personal commitment to Jewish scholarship and to Jewish tradition. This affords their critique added gravitas. They were part of this world, were disturbed by what they saw, and criticized it in the strongest terms. It is, however, equally striking that by the late 1990s these scholars had abandoned this trope—though they still cautioned about instrumentalization of the topic—because they recognized that Jewish life and scholarship had not become totally subsumed by the Holocaust as they had feared.

Much of Novick's reputation in the scholarly world rests on his book *That Noble Dream*, an insightful and intellectually provocative exploration of the way historians have shaped our notion of history. It is strange, therefore, that he, a man whose professional persona was linked to scholarship and the academy, simply ignored the role that scholars—Novick's professional colleagues—played in creating an academically vibrant, groundbreaking, and impressive field. While scholarly works may not necessarily spawn popular interest, they certainly have a trickle-down effect on the broader public. Moreover, irrespective of the impact of scholarship on popular culture, the creation of such a vibrant field of study should have been of value to a historian such as Novick.[109] Novick reached his mistaken conclusions about the engineering of interest in the Holocaust because he focused on the actions of organizations. He failed to give sufficient weight to—or, in certain cases, even acknowledge— other developments in the Jewish community during the last two decades of the twentieth century. He paid little attention to the events on the ground, the activities of Jewish baby boomers who were then coming of age and were part of a "protest generation." The students of Heschel, Rubenstein, Greenberg, Fackenheim, and others, whose rebellions and revolutions I have addressed in these pages, were highly unlikely to respond to exhortations from the very organizations they were vilifying. In fact, they paid little attention, almost on principle, to organized Jewish community life except to attack and challenge it. They were intent on making Judaism a celebratory matter.[110] Furthermore, as Hasia Diner has shown, many of these young people came from the very circles—camps, youth groups, day schools—where the Holocaust was already commemorated. They did not need the establishment's exhortations or machinations. Interest in the Holocaust emerged as part of this Jewish renaissance, one based far more on pulls (a desire to affiliate for positive reasons) than, as Novick posited, on pushes (fears of antisemitism).

Novick also gave far too little credit to the critical role of non-Jewish scholars in developing the field. Littell, Cargas, Locke, Rittner, Fleischner, the Eckardts, and other theologians were not responding to Jewish organizations. The baby boom scholars, including Browning, Hayes, Roth, Schleunes, and others saw Vietnam, civil rights, and Watergate as their personal impetus into the field. They certainly were not motivated to act by what took place in the boardrooms of Jewish organizations. Both Hayes and Browning recalled reading Novick's book when it first appeared and failing to find any explanation for their interest in the field, or that of their non-Jewish colleagues. Novick had written as if this large body of important and productive scholars simply did not exist. As Browning noted: "I certainly did not see myself in those pages."[111] Whatever their motivations, none of these scholars came to study the Holocaust because of machinations of Jewish leaders and organizations as Novick imagined. It seems fitting to note here that, while I have repeatedly pointed to the ethnic or religious identity of many of the scholars in the field, I have done so not to suggest that their personal backgrounds ultimately shaped or influenced their perspectives on the topic or the quality of their research. Doris Bergen, an expert on the German church during the Holocaust, recalls that when in the very early 1990s she gave her first paper on the German Christian Movement (*Glaubensbewegung 'Deutsche Christen'*), a prominent historian of Nazi Germany introduced her as "a Mennonite farm girl from Saskatchewan." While he may have considered the remark humorous, Bergen interpreted his comment to mean that she was "sincere, earnest, an outsider and therefore capable of original or at least objective insights." Most significantly, it was intended "to signal unmistakably that I am not Jewish." For this senior historian, who Bergen was or whom "he perceived [her] to be—was inseparable from [her] scholarship."[112] In fact, as Saul Friedlander has observed, "no distinction was warranted among historians of various backgrounds in their professional approach to the Third Reich, that *all* historians dealing with this theme had to be aware of their unavoidably subjective approach, and that all could muster enough self-critical insight to restrain this subjectivity."[113] While these scholars' biographies might have led them to the field in general and to particular issues within it, they had enough scholarly self-awareness to avoid letting the "personal" corrupt or compromise their analysis. Their past may dictate what they think about but not what they think.[114] I am fully aware that, as the Freudians have taught us, one can never fully shed one's autobiography. However, it is the responsibility of scholars to acknowledge that fact and then aim, as best they can, at objective analysis. The work of those who have been unable to make this delineation has, by and large, been left by the wayside. Evidence of Novick's complicated relationship with this topic can be found in his comments regarding Wiesenthal's eleven million figure. As noted, Novick unequivocally dismissed the number as entirely baseless. Yet he took Wiesel and Jewish leaders to task for their adamant refusal to accept the eleven million number as historically valid, describing their behavior as akin to the way "devout Christians would respond to the expansion of the victims of the Crucifixion to three—the Son of God and two thieves."[115] Considering that the Crucifixion has for millennia served as the root source of the antisemitic sentiment that, following numerous iterations and millennia of evolution, resulted in the Holocaust, this is a strange analogy indeed.

Novick's book appeared at the same time as Tim Cole's *Selling the Holocaust*, which set out to determine whether the focus on, in Cole's words, "the myth of the 'Holocaust' at the end of the twentieth century is a good or bad thing." (Cole's use of the term "myth," is not, of course, meant to suggest that the Holocaust did not happen, as deniers would have it. He is referring to the layers of meaning, many of which have been addressed in these pages, that have come to be associated with this event.) Cole begins his book by quoting an oft-cited complaint of Rabbi Arnold Wolf, made in 1980, that the Jewish community in New Haven spent ten times more money on a Holocaust memorial than it does on "all the college students" there. Wolf found this "shocking" and declared that the "Holocaust is being sold."[116] Since the only college in New Haven with a substantial Jewish population is Yale, where Wolf was head of the Hillel chapter, one can assume that this university was his main area of concern. While his charge may have contained some truth at that time, matters changed considerably between 1980 and the publication of Cole's book, something to which Cole (and Novick) paid little, if any, heed. In fact, the situation changed within a year or two of Wolf's statement, and by the late 1990s the Yale campus was home to a magnificent new Hillel building. In addition, Yale students had access to a vibrant Jewish studies program and an array of courses on rabbinics, history, and literature. While there were courses on the Holocaust as well, far more dealt with how Jews lived, not how they died. In fact, when both Cole and Novick were writing their books, Yale had a number of endowed chairs in different areas of Jewish studies but none in the Holocaust. (By 2015 there were even more endowed chairs but still none in the Holocaust.) Wolf's critique may have pertained to a brief moment in the late 1970s, but certainly not to the late 1990s. In fact, during the mid- to late 1990s the USHMM, concerned that there was not enough serious research and training of scholars in Holocaust studies, began to fund chairs to address the lack, though these new positions remained far outnumbered by the dozens of chairs in other areas of Jewish studies.

Cole joined Novick in arguing that the Holocaust was being packaged and distorted. One of Cole's prime examples of "Holocaust kitsch" was the publication of what he describes as a "Holocaust cookbook." Since it is hard to believe that Cole would have deliberately distorted the substance of the book in question, one must assume he never actually saw it.[117] The book was from Terezin, compiled by women inmates who tried to overcome their hunger pangs by reminiscing about the delicacies they used to prepare. (According to Michael Berenbaum, who as the director of the USHMM's Holocaust Research Institute wrote the cookbook's introduction, historians have since learned of similar efforts in other camps and ghettoes.)[118] Cole also contended that the USHMM tried to give the Holocaust a "suitably upbeat ending," organizing the exhibits so that the last section visitors see concerns the camps' liberation by American forces and the immigration of many survivors to Israel. But in fact, the final part of the exhibit is a movie of interviews with survivors; while they do speak of their liberation by American soldiers, their message is hardly upbeat. In fact, some influential lay leaders—the people giving and raising much of the money needed to build the museum—wanted a more affirming ending. The professional leaders of the museum fought that notion, however.[119]

Both Novick and Cole were highly critical of Steven Spielberg's *Schindler's List*, which premiered a few months after the opening of the USHMM. The film, cited by the American Film Institute as one of the ten best American motion pictures ever made, was seen by 25 million people in the theaters and another 65 million when it was shown on broadcast television—without commercials.[120] Both Cole and Novick took Spielberg to task, with some justification, for choosing to tell a heroic story in which people were saved and not murdered. There is certainly much to critique about this movie, particularly its melodramatic ending in which Schindler gives a redemptive speech to the German guards, and then, weeping and contrite, begs the survivors' forgiveness for not having saved more Jews. The scene is completely invented.

Novick concedes that, despite the film being a heroic story, it nonetheless left viewers—including him—"overwhelmed by the horror of the events and deeply moved." Possibly somewhat unnerved by his emotional response, he wonders why the "eliciting of these responses . . . is seen as so urgently important a task."[121] One could ask the same question, however, of productions such as *Roots* (1977), *Amistad* (1997), *12 Years a Slave* (2014), and others that address the slavery and abuse of African Americans. I would argue that works of this genre, however flawed, are profoundly important, particularly for Americans whose families have not been directly impacted by the events depicted therein. These works serve as vehicles for transforming abstract distant knowledge into something far more concrete. They provide a broad swath of Americans with graphic representation of the horrors of a specific tragedy, representations that many had managed to conveniently relegate to the distant past. Nevertheless, Novick and Cole are certainly correct that some of the ways in which the Holocaust has been remembered are both distasteful and distorted. For example, Cole addressed what he claimed was an assertion by tour organizers that a visit to Auschwitz or other camps gives one a sense of the Holocaust experience. As he noted, nothing could be further from the truth. The piles of rotting cadavers and their attendant odors are absent, as is the all-prevailing fear that beset every inmate. Such trips, situated so far in time from the events commemorated, cannot constitute anything but a visit to a historic site. This is also true regarding pilgrimages to Gettysburg. Its rolling green fields evoke no comparison to the bloody carnage that occurred there. That does not mean, however, that visits to such places should be avoided or denigrated. It is simply the nature of tourism that historical sites are for many people nothing more than places to be checked off a personal vacation list. But for Cole to speak of "Auschwitz-land"—akin to Elvis's Graceland or Disneyland—is itself of questionable taste and raises questions about the validity of his critique.[122]

Since both Cole and Novick contend that the Holocaust has been memorialized in such a way as to foster a fortress mentality in American Jews—making them view the outside world as a dangerous and threatening place—one might have thought the historians would have approved of Spielberg's movie in which a Gentile rescues Jews. The story helps give the lie to the notion that Jews were all but abandoned by non-Jews during the war. But this did not temper their clear dislike of the film. Cole was also contemptuous of Spielberg's decision to use the considerable profits from the film to gather testimonies from Holocaust survivors. To Cole, the filmmaker was merely trying to establish a parallel between Schindler and himself. One rescued victims; the other rescued testimonies.[123] (One wonders if Cole would have been happier if Spielberg had pocketed the profits instead.) Novick, with a measure of what seemed to be muted glee, exposed what in his mind was Spielberg's attempt to dupe his audience. One might describe it as Novick's "gotcha" moment. He noted that the movie concludes with a talmudic dictum—"Whoever saves one life it is as if he saved the world entire"—and that this aphorism appears in Jewish texts in two versions. The other reads, "One who saves one life *in Israel* it is as if he saved the world entire," which Novick claims is the older and more authentic of the two. His suggestion was that Spielberg used the one without the phrase "in Israel," despite being less authoritative, because the director wanted viewers to think that Judaism has a universal commitment to saving the downtrodden, and thus universalize the message of his film and, perhaps, of the Holocaust itself. In this, however, Novick was mistaken. Talmud scholars who have examined the manuscripts in which these teachings are found are convinced that the version without the added phrase is in fact older and, therefore, authoritative.[124]

Novick's critique of Holocaust memorialization is particularly severe. His references to the "sacralization" of the Holocaust; his depiction of the USHMM as an "epistle to the Gentiles" and the "central address for American Jewry" to learn about what it means to be Jewish; and, even more distastefully, his claim that Jews are intent on "permanent possession of the gold medal in the Victimization Olympics" are, at best, discordant coming from a man whose life had been one of scholarship. Moreover, here too he proved to be wrong. The museum has won praise from many people, including scholars who were dubious about the entire enterprise while it was being built. It has in fact become one of the primary sources of serious scholarship on the Holocaust and an important voice in calling attention to other genocides worldwide. What it has not become is the central address of American Jewry.

Cole also used questionable language to describe aspects of the USHMM, calling its installation of photographs depicting Nazi medical experiments as "peepshow Holocaust," because the designers placed a wall around the exhibit compelling visitors to peer over it in order to view the images. But he failed to note that educational specialists who reviewed the plans for the permanent exhibition feared that pictures of the experiments might disturb children who visited the museum. Convinced that these medical experiments were a prime example of the nature of the Holocaust and must be included in the exhibit, museum designers grappled with a number of alternatives and chose this one.[125] While the solution may not be ideal, it is hardly a "peepshow."

At the conclusion of his book Cole returned to the question he posed at its beginning. Is attention to the Holocaust doing harm or good?[126] Lest his readers have any doubt about what he thinks—one is hard-pressed to imagine that they would—he concluded: "It may actually be doing us harm."[127] It is "the myth of the Holocaust," not the history itself but the layers of meaning that have been appended to it, that Cole fears. His fears are not, as I have noted and will return to below, completely unfounded. He is right that the Holocaust has been and continues to be used for ancillary and often political purposes. However, it cannot be ignored that this selfsame "myth" is responsible for the emergence of an impressive academic field of study. Second and more significantly, it was inevitable that an event as traumatic as the Holocaust would have layers of meaning appended to it and would give rise to such a "myth." The point, particularly for scholars and especially historians, is not to condemn the attention paid to it and the way that it is remembered in a wholesale and often incorrect fashion but to fight to ensure that the lessons individuals draw from this event do not distort the truth. For example, there is a well-known story about ninety-three young girls (virgins) in a ghetto who took poison rather than submit to being raped by the Nazis. They were all students at an ultra-Orthodox *Bais Yaakov* seminary. Long a staple in the Haredi (ultra-Orthodox) community, the story was seen as a way of demonstrating that resistors and resistance came in many forms. Despite the fact that many historians question whether this story could be true—even some Haredi educators have begun to urge that it be dropped from the community's curriculum because of its dubious historicity—Haredim have embraced it as an example of how Orthodox Jews died for their faith, and it maintains a mythic hold on the community's imagination.[128]

In his final paragraph, Cole offers attempts yet again to prove his thesis that attention to the Holocaust has done more harm than good. He attributes the rise of Holocaust denial to all the attention the Holocaust and its "mythic" elements have received.[129] Here Cole is partially correct. As we have noted, deniers did become more active during the 1970s and 1980s. Their attacks were certainly stimulated by the rise in attention to the Holocaust. But his suggestion that, had there been less attention paid to the Holocaust, denial would not have emerged is somewhat akin to blaming the rise of the racist White Citizens' Councils in the American South on the growing presence of the civil rights movement. In fact, the impact that deniers wield has diminished in recent years even as attention to the Holocaust has further increased. That decrease can be traced to the precise and detailed scholarship entailed in Holocaust studies, the very scholarship that both Cole and Novick ignore.

Ironically, a portion of that scholarship was prompted by the deniers themselves and a gamble they took that backfired on them. In 2000 David Irving, then the world's best-known Holocaust denier, sued me for libel for calling him a denier and an antisemite. With support and encouragement from deniers worldwide, he brought the case in the United Kingdom, where the legal system placed the burden of proof on me, as the defendant, to demonstrate the truth of what I had written. (Had he brought the case in the United States the burden would have been on him to prove the alleged falsehood. He would have been precluded from bringing such a case in the United States, however, because of the "public figure" ruling with regard to defamation cases.)[130] Though a number of leading Holocaust scholars suggested I just ignore his accusations—something that is not so simply done—I knew that if I did not defend myself he would win by default. He could then legitimately say he was not a Holocaust denier because the court had found me guilty of libel for calling him one. Though I do not believe history should be adjudicated in the courtroom, I felt I had no choice but to contest his charges.

My lawyers and I were intent on making sure the trial did not center on proving if the Holocaust had actually happened, as had occurred in other cases where deniers were on trial. In those cases, of course, the denier was always the defendant. This case was the first and, thus far, the only time that a denier was the claimant and the historian the defendant. As someone pointed out to me as the trial was about to begin, it was the twenty-first-century equivalent of a war crimes trial in which the perpetrator sues the survivor.[131] Our strategy was merely to prove the "sting of the libel," that is, that my words were true. We focused on proving that Irving was a denier who knowingly invented and distorted evidence about the Final Solution. We tracked each of his assertions about the Holocaust and demonstrated that his claims were naught but a tissue of lies. While Irving was the one we had to prove a liar, by exposing his lies we also did significant damage to Holocaust denial in general. Other deniers had adopted his claims and he, in turn, reiterated theirs. It was a merry-go-round of citations and arguments.

We made another decision that significantly enhanced the impact of the trial. We chose not to call survivors to testify, for they would have been "witnesses of fact" and in our estimation we did not need to assert the facts of this genocide. Rather, we relied on a small group of "expert witnesses," all of them outstanding historians. Richard Evans, Robert Jan van Pelt, Christopher Browning, and Peter Longerich followed Irving's footnotes back to his sources and showed that every time he cited a document or an event to prove his claims, he distorted, invented, or fabricated evidence. Not only were their findings devastating to Irving, but by extension they also pulled out any semblance of credibility from other deniers. The judge found that my critique of Irving was justified. The words he chose to describe Irving's writings about the Holocaust were unambiguous: "distorts," "perverts," "misleading," "unjustified," "travesty," and "unreal." These historians' meticulous and detailed findings are a legacy of the trial and another demonstration of the impressive growth in the field of Holocaust studies. They constitute a stunning example of the proper way to fight Holocaust denial: with facts and evidence rather than emotions or law. One is hard-pressed to find another field that has emerged so rapidly and produced such an array of scholarship.

Competitive Genocides? The Holocaust versus All Others

Another substantial complaint about attention paid to the Holocaust, voiced by Peter Novick and others, is that the Holocaust constitutes "a sponge of historical memory that sucks the juices out of alternative commemorative and reparation projects."[132] Historian A. Dirk Moses contends that making the Holocaust a "template against which other genocides can be measured" has served to "occlude . . . other genocides," because if the newer event is judged not to be akin to the Holocaust it is duly ignored.[133] According to these critics, policy makers either pay so much attention to the Holocaust that they disregard contemporary acts of genocide, or they assert that since another event is not as bad as the Holocaust, no action is necessary. Novick made this one of his primary arguments, placing it in the introduction where it was bound to be noticed. He wrote that during the Bosnian conflict in the 1990s the debate on whether the United States should intervene focused on judging if what was going on there was "'truly holocaustal or merely genocidal'; 'truly genocidal or merely atrocious.'" Novick rightfully condemned these "truly disgusting modes of speaking and decision making," and argued that America's obsession with the Holocaust was responsible for preventing the United States and other Western nations from intervening. There are problems with this assertion. As Berel Lang observed in his critique of Novick's thesis, it is strange that in an impressively sourced book—there are sixty-six pages of notes—this provocative quote ("truly holocaustal"), for which Novick rightfully expresses contempt, is made without attribution.[134] Given Novick's legitimate contempt for these noxious words, it is hard to explain how he could have failed to cite who spoke them.

More important, however, is that Novick's assertions are simply incorrect. Holocaust analogies do not draw attention away from other tragedies—quite the opposite, in fact. Such comparisons have, by and large, effectively drawn attention to more recent atrocities, particularly during the Bosnian crisis, certainly the worst conflagration on the European continent since World War II.[135] During this and other terrible conflicts, journalists, pundits, intellectuals, activists, and policy makers quickly learned that comparison to the Holocaust was often the only thing that aroused the western world from indifference. Television stations repeatedly interspersed footage of atrocities in Bosnia with images of the Holocaust. The message was clear: what is happening in the region is akin to what happened in that same part of the world less than five decades earlier. Roy Gutman, who eventually won a Pulitzer Prize for his coverage of this war, recalled that his early reports from Bosnia in August 1992 generated little public response. That changed dramatically when his editors appended to a subsequent story a dramatic banner headline: "The Death Camps of Bosnia." Unlike his previous reports, this one was picked up and reprinted by media outlets worldwide.[136] Activists discovered the same thing. A newly formed organization "Jews Against Genocide" (JAG), dedicated to arousing opposition to the atrocities in Bosnia, conducted rallies, protests, and vigils. Most of them garnered little attention. Things changed, however, on the day they switched not their tactics, but their rhetoric. At one protest they began to chant: "You've seen *Schindler's List*; now look at Bosnia." People stopped, took the proffered leaflets, and asked questions. As one of the organizers recalls, "We felt vulgar using the analogy but it worked."[137]

Of course, sometimes analogies, including to the Holocaust, don't work. For example, Secretary of State Warren Christopher insisted, as President Clinton did initially, that what was happening in Bosnia was the result of age-old rivalries. Depicting events there as just another link in a chain of a centuries-old tit-for-tat, the Clinton administration argued that American intervention would be futile. Christopher, concerned that the Holocaust analogy might push the United States into getting involved, dismissed its appropriateness: "I never heard of any genocide by the Jews against the German people."[138] The fact that Christopher and other American policy makers felt that they had to contrast events in the former Yugoslavia with the Holocaust shows the power of the analogy. They were afraid of it.

Eventually the attention brought to Bosnia via the Holocaust analogy led in the other direction, toward American intervention. In her book Samantha Power credits it with being one of the things that helped "stir the conscience" of the world. "Holocaust-based lobbying" was among the factors "behind the large American contributions to UN relief and peace-keeping missions." When Wiesel challenged State Department officials about liberating some of the prisoner camps in the former Yugoslavia, he was told that officials feared that if they did, "there would be retaliation and prisoners would be killed." Wiesel, "eyes flashing," responded: "Do you realize that that is precisely what the State Department said during World War II?"[139] When America and NATO finally did intervene in Kosovo in 1998, historian Alan Steinweis notes that Clinton used the example of the Holocaust to explain, if not justify, his decision. In fact, once again it was Wiesel whom he cited in his decision. "Elie has said," the president noted in a speech, "that Kosovo is not the Holocaust, but that distinction should not deter us from doing what is right."[140]

The Holocaust analogy also served to help set up an international criminal court. Madeleine Albright, who was involved in this process both as ambassador to the United Nations and as Christopher's successor as secretary of state, repeatedly wove Holocaust references into her public comments. After her tenure she acknowledged that her awareness of the Holocaust on both the historical and personal levels helped shape her policies in Bosnia and Kosovo.[141] Accordingly, sociologist John Torpey has argued that the Holocaust does not draw attention away from the suffering of others; in fact, it does the exact opposite: "The emblematic status . . . [of the] Jewish Holocaust has helped others who have been subjected to state-sponsored atrocities to gain attention for those calamities." Among those who have cited the Holocaust as a means of buttressing the legitimacy of their demands for reparation are African and aboriginal groups subjected to slavery and colonialism.[142] Wole Soyinka, the Nigerian winner of the Nobel Prize in literature, has acknowledged that those who wish to secure reparations for what Africans suffered under colonialism see a model for them in the "example of the Jews and the obsessed commitment of survivors of the Holocaust, and their descendants, to recover both their material patrimony and the humanity of which they were brutally deprived."[143] That is exactly what happened in the early 1990s when the Organization of African Unity instructed a committee to "explore the modalities and strategies of an African campaign of restitution similar to the compensation paid by Germany to Israel and the survivors of the Holocaust."[144] However imperfect these analogies, they do not divert attention away from other genocides. In the United States such comparisons have rarely been strong enough to change foreign policy, with the State Department consistently reluctant to intervene militarily in order to stop genocide. If policy makers are averse to getting involved, they will simply ignore the analogy. If they are inclined to action, the analogy gives them moral and historic cover. The missing ingredient has not been a proper analogy; it has been the will to try to stop genocide.[145]

Though admittedly anecdotal, the repeated experiences of Father John Pawlikowski bear noting. Part of his course at Catholic Theological Union on "Ethics in the Light of Holocaust and Genocide" entails a visit to the Holocaust museum in Illinois or Washington. He has repeatedly been struck by students' comments that they planned to visit for an hour and instead stayed for four, or that they returned for additional visits. It was not the students' interest that Pawlikowski found remarkable but the fact that so many of them were from African countries and other parts of the world that have been the site of post-Holocaust genocidal actions. He believes the Holocaust, rather than "competing" with what happened in their countries and on their continents, provides a framework within which they can contextualize their experiences.[146]

There is a certain irony to the fact that those who consider the Holocaust if not unique than at least unprecedented have proposed many of these analogies. (Otherwise, why would they choose this particular example and not some other tragedy?) The irony lies in the fact that, as both Jeffrey Alexander and Gavriel Rosenfeld have noted, this frequent reliance on the Holocaust as an analogy has promoted its universalization. Because it is so frequently cited as a benchmark—even when the comparison is wrong—the notion of uniqueness has been "neutralized."[147] More than just neutralized or rendered irrelevant, the debate about uniqueness has itself has run out of steam. As one researcher has noted, it has "lost its intellectual and emotional power . . . among scholars." The consensus among most Holocaust academics is that there is little more to say that could possibly enlighten either this topic or the field itself. David Cesarani criticized those who remained ensnared in the fight against the concept of uniqueness as "re-fight[ing] an old battle and . . . hardly representative of historical scholarship today." Jürgen Matthäus dismissed the debate as "analytically sterile." It remains to be seen whether those who are still disturbed by the notion will revive the battle with their attacks on it.[148]

As the debate over uniqueness runs its course, another far more illuminating trend in Holocaust studies is emerging. It is one that in the 1970s and 1980s many Holocaust scholars instinctively eschewed. Typified by the work of historian Timothy Snyder, whose aforementioned *Bloodlands* analyzes and compares Nazi and Stalinist crimes in Europe, there have been attempts to situate the Holocaust in many different contexts, including world wars, totalitarian systems, nationalism, and more. As historian Doris Bergen observes, "Such contextualization speaks to the maturity of a dynamic field that opens out in every direction."[149] Snyder explores in excruciating detail the horrors perpetrated by both systems. Ultimately, without entering into a debate or competition, he posits that the Holocaust was different because of the Nazi intent to wipe out an entire people.[150] But by the time he reaches that conclusion, it seems strangely irrelevant, certainly regarding the personal suffering endured by victims of both Hitler and Stalin. Invariably, much future research and teaching about the Holocaust will compare and contrast genocides rather than evade them on principle. This will be far more intellectually illuminating than the competitive atmosphere that prevailed during much of the 1980s and 1990s.

There are other trends emerging in Holocaust studies that should be acknowledged. A new generation of scholars is shedding light on narrowly defined but exceptionally important aspects of the Holocaust, filling in important lacunae now that the bigger picture has been clearly drawn. To do so they are relying on newly released archives, in the process exemplifying scholarship of the highest level and demonstrating that there is far more to know about this genocide. But there is another area that is emerging as well, reflecting that the generation of victims and personal witnesses is slowly vanishing. This new group of scholars is stepping back and asking how Holocaust memory has been and is being formed. James Young pioneered this work a number of decades ago, but younger scholars such as Oren Stier and Noah Shenker are pushing it further.[151]

Scaring the People: On How Not to Proceed

I end this excursion through the history of the Holocaust narrative in American life with a cautionary note. It is not the scholarship about which I am concerned. That is proceeding at an unprecedentedly high level. It is what is going on outside the scholarly arena that gives me pause. I turn to two phenomena that are extensions of each other.

Since the beginning of the twenty-first century there has been a marked revival of antisemitism. There have been an increasing number of physical and verbal attacks on Jews, particularly in Europe. Jews have been murdered in museums, schools, kosher markets, and on the street in Paris (2006, 2015), Toulouse (2012), Brussels (2014), and Copenhagen (2015). Jews have been entrapped in synagogues and have had to call for police aid in order to be extricated. There have been assaults on Jews' homes. The home invaders have made it explicitly clear that they chose these homes because Jews lived in them. Synagogues and Jewish institutions regularly have guards posted at the entrance. Some Jews in France have removed the mezzuzot from the doorposts of their homes and have urged their Jewish neighbors to do the same, lest antisemites be attracted to the neighborhood. Jews are urging Jews to go underground.[152] In virtually every large city in Europe one need not know the precise address of a synagogue. Once one arrives on the street, the presence of armed guards or a police car indicates its location. Visitors to European synagogues are told to bring their passports or other forms of identification in order to gain entry. In many European countries, Jewish leaders urge both the locals and visitors to avoid wearing or carrying anything that will mark them as Jews. Kippot should be replaced with baseball caps. Shirts or anything that sports a Jewish-looking logo should be avoided. Parents who bring their children to Jewish schools are reassured by the fact that the grounds are patrolled by armed guards—sometimes carrying submachine guns—and distressed that they have placed their children in a setting that calls for that precaution.

As the situation has escalated over the past decade many people have asked: "Is this the 1930s? Is this a Holocaust redux?" The situation is certainly troubling, but the analogy is wrong. What is happening today bears no historical resonance to the Nazi period, for multiple reasons. First, in the 1930s Jews in Germany and other parts of the ever-expanding Reich faced state-sponsored antisemitism. What Jews face today is violence that comes in part from radical Muslim extremists. They hate not only Jews but the state and its secular culture as well. This was strikingly evident to those who still needed additional proof from the simultaneous attacks in Paris and Copenhagen (2015) on secular and Jewish institutions. Furthermore, as immigrants or the children of immigrants from a variety of Muslim countries, they themselves face opposition from extreme right-wing groups, most of whom currently have little political clout. In contrast to the 1930s, today government leaders roundly and immediately condemn these attacks. They attempt to reassure the Jewish community that it is safe. They properly rely on government resources to protect Jews and Jewish institutions. Second, most of the recent attacks—with the exception, of course, of murder—are mild in comparison to what Jews faced under Nazi rule in the 1930s. To draw comparisons to the Holocaust is to elevate in intensity today's actions and diminish the ones from the 1930s. Third, Jews today have an option that they did not have in the 1930s: someplace to go. Small but increasingly significant numbers of European Jews are voting with their feet. Finally, there is one other intangible but crucially important element that differentiates the Holocaust from today. It is, in many respects, the binding theme of this book: memory. In the 1930s Jews could not imagine, understandably so, the tragedy that would ensue. Today we know that "Never Again" in truth has become "Again and Again." Nonetheless, while today's tragedies are not akin to the dawn of a new Holocaust, it is fitting to recall what Elie Wiesel told President Clinton regarding the former Yugoslavia: just because something is not akin to the Holocaust does not mean it is not disturbing and worthy of action.

The rise in antisemitism has frightened many Jews. Those threats and fears are real. The non-Jewish majority in whose midst Jews live must take these attacks seriously, something which they seem a bit more inclined to do now that their security has been threatened. At the same time, these fears must not be instrumentalized or aggrandized in order to strengthen Jewish identity. The current situation, though often disturbing and terribly frightening, must not be compared to the Holocaust because it is not comparable to the Holocaust. Nor is every critique of a Jew or of Israel necessarily antisemitic. To glibly label each as such is both wrong and manipulative. Jewish communal leaders and Israeli politicians have often been guilty of using the Holocaust in an inappropriate and exaggerated fashion in order to arouse people's fears or to generate support for the Jewish state. They thus turn the Holocaust into a political tool. This cheapens it and is wrong both morally and strategically. Eventually people become inured to the threat of another Holocaust. They dismiss the warnings and they dismiss the Holocaust's historical and moral importance. The Holocaust should not serve as a tool for ensuring generosity, promoting vigilance, or winning support for a particular political position. Its distortion exploits both the memory of the genocide itself and the people it is intended to arouse or scare. It turns the Holocaust into a cudgel.

It would be easy to end here, but there is another, equally distasteful aspect to this use and abuse of the Holocaust, if not more so. It comes from the other side, if you will. There are those who rely on the Holocaust in the interest of pursuing an anti-Israel or a pro-Palestinian agenda (they are not always one and the same). Irrespective of how one feels about the situation in the Middle East in general and Israel's policies in particular, to speak of a genocide of the Palestinians or "Nazi-like" tactics of the Israeli army is to both exaggerate what is taking place today and to diminish the horrors of the Final Solution. These frequently vituperative attacks come, in the main, from the political left, which has shown an increased tolerance, if not more than that, for antisemitic expression. Above I addressed the Holocaust denial that I encountered in court—what I call hard-core Holocaust denial. It denies the facts of the Holocaust: the gas chambers, the deportations, the death camps, and the Nazi plan to annihilate European Jewry. The analogies between Israel today and Nazi Germany of the 1930s and 1940s are a form of what I call soft-core Holocaust denial. By making false comparisons, politically motivated individuals deny the severity of the past while exaggerating the severity of the present.

I cannot predict what the future will hold for Holocaust research or commemoration. Nonetheless, certain cautions seem appropriate. Comparisons are tempting: they help us understand how something is akin to and different from something else. But comparisons, particularly when used for unrelated objectives, can also become a form of distortion. This is true for both those in the scholarly world and those outside of it. In short, neither contemporary antisemitism nor anything else happening today bears any resemblance to the harbingers or events of the Holocaust. They may be quite bad but they are not a Holocaust. The Holocaust was a crucial moment in Jewish and world history. The way it is remembered, inevitably, will continue to evolve. Such is the case with all of history. The particular prism through which we view an event will shape our memories of it. But even as memory is refracted by time, place, and context, it must not be distorted to fit ancillary aims.

Forgetting would be a tragedy. Making too easy comparisons, even when they serve worthy goals, equally so.

Notes

INTRODUCTION

1. The subtitle the show carried was *The Story of Family Weiss.* But this offered no indication of who this family was and when they lived.

2. Samuel G. Freedman, "Laying Claim to Sorrow Beyond Words," *New York Times,* December 13, 1997.

3. Edward Anthony de Marco Jr., "Asian Holocaust: Coverage of the Khmer Rouge by Three U.S. News Organizations, 1974–1979" (Ph.D. diss., University of Georgia, 1988); Sheng-Mei Ma, "Contrasting Two Survival Literatures: On the Jewish Holocaust and the Chinese Cultural Revolution," *Holocaust and Genocide Studies* 2, no. 1 (1987): 81; Gruver Eric Lane, "Surviving the Agricultural Holocaust: A Texas Tenant Stays on the Land, 1928–1940" (Ph.D. diss., East Texas State University, 1995).

4. Chris Cottrell, "Memorial to Roma Holocaust Victims Opens in Berlin," *New York Times,* October 24, 2012.

5. Raul Hilberg, "Developments in the Historiography of the Holocaust," in *Comprehending the Holocaust: Historical and Literary Research,* ed. Asher Cohen, Joav Gelber, and Charlotte Wardi (Frankfurt am Main: Peter Lang, 1988), 21.

6. Hasia Diner, *We Remember with Reverence and Love: American Jews and the Myth of Silence after the Holocaust, 1945–1962* (New York: New York University Press, 2009).

7. For a full discussion of how the Holocaust was treated on television see Jeffrey Shandler, *While America Watches: Televising the Holocaust* (New York: Oxford University Press, 1999).

8. Nathan Glazer, *American Judaism* (Chicago: University of Chicago Press, 1957), 114–115; Stephen Whitfield, "The Holocaust and the American Jewish Intellectual," *Judaism* 28, no. 4 (1979): 394–395.

9. By the early 1950s Prime Minister David Ben-Gurion was negotiating with the Germans regarding reparations for the Holocaust. Jewish leaders may have been concerned this effort would call public attention to Germany's crimes and jeopardize these negotiations. Rochelle G. Saidel, *Never Too Late to Remember: The Politics Behind New York City's Holocaust Museum* (New York: Holmes and Meier, 1996), 51–52.

10. David de Sola Pool, "Proposed Memorial Upheld: Letters to the Editor," *New York Times,* June 20, 1952.

11. Saidel, *Never Too Late*, 54, 60; William E. Farrell, "City Rejects Park Memorials to Slain Jews; Art Board Member Calls One Too Big, One Too Tragic," *New York Times*, February 11, 1965; James E. Young, "America's Holocaust: Memory and the Politics of Identity," in *The Americanization of the Holocaust*, ed. Hilene Flanzbaum (Baltimore: Johns Hopkins University Press, 1999), 70.

12. Steven Bayme, "Dr. Irving Greenberg: A Biographical Introduction," in *Continuity and Change: A Festschrift in Honor of Irving Greenberg's 75th Birthday*, ed. Steven T. Katz and Steven Bayme (Lanham, Md.: University Press of America, 2010), 4.

13. Edward T. Linenthal, *Preserving Memory: The Struggle to Create America's Holocaust Museum* (New York: Viking, 1995), 6ff.; Alan E. Steinweis, "The Auschwitz Analogy: Holocaust Memory and American Debates over Intervention in Bosnia and Kosovo in the 1990s," *Holocaust and Genocide Studies* 19, no. 2 (2005): 276–289.

CHAPTER 1 — TERMS OF DEBATE

1. Jacob Robinson, "Holocaust," in *Encyclopedia Judaica*, ed. Cecil Roth (Jerusalem: Keter, 1972), 890.

2. Allen Rosen, *The Wonder of Their Voices: The 1946 Holocaust Interviews of David Boder* (New York: Oxford, 2010), 19, 78.

3. David P. Boder, *I Did Not Interview the Dead* (Urbana: University of Illinois Press, 1949).

4. Carl Marziali and Ira Glass, "Before It Had a Name: Mr. Boder Vanishes," *This American Life*, October 26, 2001, http://www.thisamericanlife.org/radio-archives/episode/197/transcript, accessed March 25, 2015.

5. Michael Marrus, "Lessons of the Holocaust," unpublished manuscript, 68. Telford Taylor, *Anatomy of the Nuremberg Trials: A Personal Memoir* (Boston: Little, Brown, 1992), xi.

6. Jeffrey Alexander, "On the Social Construction of Moral Universals: The 'Holocaust' from War Crime to Trauma Drama," *European Journal of Social Theory* 5, no. 1 (2002): 6.

7. Salo W. Baron, "Foreword," in *Guide to Jewish History under Nazi Impact*, ed. Jacob Robinson and Philip Friedman (New York: YIVO Institute for Jewish Research, 1960), xix–xx, as cited in Orna Kenan, *Between Memory and History: The Evolution of Israeli Historiography of the Holocaust, 1945–1961* (New York: Peter Lang, 2003), 8.

8. Gershom Scholem, "Judaic Studies" [Hebrew], in *Od Davar* (Explications and Implications), 8–9, as cited in Kenan, *Between Memory and History*, 9.

9. Elliot E. Cohen, "An Act of Affirmation," *Commentary*, November 1, 1945.

10. The Jewish calendar marks off a three-week period to commemorate the destruction of the Temple.

11. Jeffrey Shandler, "Jewish Culture," in *Oxford Handbook of Holocaust Studies*, ed. Peter Hayes and John Roth (New York: Oxford University Press, 2010), 593 (hereafter *Oxford Handbook*); Hasia Diner, *We Remember* (New York: New York University Press, 2010), 22.

12. For example, the Hebrew word for sword is *herev*, from the same root.

13. Adolf Eichmann, *The Trial of Adolf Eichmann: Record of Proceedings in the District Court of Jerusalem* (Jerusalem: Trust for the Publication of the Proceedings of the Eichmann Trial, in cooperation with the Israel State Archives and Yad Vashem, the Holocaust Martyrs' and Heroes' Remembrance Authority, 1992), 183 (hereafter *TAE*).

14. Jeffrey Shandler, *While America Watches: Televising the Holocaust* (New York: Oxford University Press, 1999), 116.

15. See Isaiah 47:11; Psalms 35:3; Job 30:3, 30:14, 38:27.

16. Jon Petrie, "The Secular Word Holocaust: Scholarly Myths, History, and 20th Century Meanings," *Journal of Genocide Research* 2, no. 1 (2000): 63.

17. Dalia Ofer, "Linguistic Conceptualization of the Holocaust in Palestine and Israel, 1942–53," *Journal of Contemporary History* 31, no. 3 (1996): 568–571. The protest statement issued by the Jewish Agency for Palestine in 1942 used this term. Uriel Tal, "Holocaust," in *Encyclopedia of the Holocaust*, ed. Israel Gutman (New York: Macmillan Library Reference, 1995), 681.

18. Diner, *We Remember*, 366.

19. Chaim Weizmann, letter to Israel Goldstein, December 24, 1942, http://www .balashon.com/2008/04/shoah-and-holocaust.html, accessed March 4, 2015.

20. Zachariah Shuster, "Must the Jews Quit Europe?" *Commentary*, December 1945; "Birth of the State of Israel: Act of Provisional Council," *Palestine Post* (Jerusalem), May 30, 1948, 4; Diner, *We Remember*, 125.

21. Franklin H. Littell, "Inventing the Holocaust: A Christian's Retrospect," *Holocaust and Genocide Studies* 9, no. 2 (1995): 173–174.

22. Salo W. Baron, "Opening Remarks," *Jewish Social Studies* 12, no. 1 (1950): 13–16, http://www.jstor.org.proxy.library.emory.edu/stable/4464853. Another participant at the conference was Hannah Arendt. Arendt, "Social Science Techniques and the Study of Concentration Camps," *Jewish Social Studies* 12, no. 1 (1950): 49–63, http://www.jstor .org/stable/4464856; YIVO also used "Catastrophe" during the early 1950s. See, for example, YIVO Institute for Jewish Research, *YIVO Annual of Jewish Social Science 8: Studies on the Epoch of the Jewish Catastrophe* (New York: Yiddish Scientific Institute, 1953).

23. Gerd Korman, "The Holocaust in American Historical Writing," *Societas* 2, no. 3 (1972): 261; Leon A. Jick, "The Holocaust: Its Use and Abuse within the American Public," *Yad Vashem Studies* 14 (1981): 307.

24. Petrie, *The Secular Word Holocaust*, 9–10.

25. Ibid., 9–10, 11.

26. *Oxford Dictionaries*, s.v. "holocaust," http://oxforddictionaries.com/definition/ holocaust?view=uk, accessed March 2, 2015.

27. Franklin H. Littell, *The Crucifixion of the Jews* (New York: Harper & Row, 1975); Arthur Roy and Alice Eckardt, *Long Night's Journey into Day: Life and Faith after the*

Holocaust (Detroit: Wayne State University Press, 1982); Rosemary Radford Ruether, *Faith and Fratricide: The Theological Roots of Anti-Semitism* (New York: Seabury Press, 1974).

28. "Merchants Urge New Court Building: Association Publishes Corrigan Attack on 'Fire Trap' Structure at 300 Mulberry Street," *New York Times*, November 30, 1928.

29. Harold Denny, "Russians Predict War and Revolts: Assert Sarajevo Anniversary Finds World Preparing Another Holocaust," *New York Times*, June 29, 1934.

30. "Talk for Junior League," *New York Times*, December 8, 1936.

31. "500 Die in Holocaust: Thousands Flee Blazing Forests in Wisconsin and Minnesota," *Washington Post*, October 14, 1918.

32. Charles Fishman, "Earliest Reference to Holocaust," Humanities and Social Sciences Online: H-Holocaust, April 29, 1995, http://h-net.msu.edu/cgi-bin/logbrowse.pl?trx=vx&list=H-Holocaust&month=9504&week=e&msg=QAS8vu3Q8muocP/Eh/DJGA&user=&pw=, accessed March 6, 2014.

33. "The Holland Holocaust: Beppi Keeps Bep from Becoming Too Lonesome," *Los Angeles Times*, October 24, 1934.

34. Petrie, *The Secular Word Holocaust*, 5.

35. Alan Rosenberg and Evelyn Silverman, "The Issue of the Holocaust as a Unique Event," in *Genocide in Our Time: An Annotated Bibliography with Analytical Introductions*, ed. Michael N. Dobkowski and Isidor Wallimann (Ann Arbor, MI: Pieran Press, 1992), 49.

36. Samuel D. Kassow, *Who Will Write Our History: Emanuel Ringelblum, the Warsaw Ghetto, and the Oyneg Shabes Archive* (Bloomington: Indiana University Press, 2007).

37. See for example David A. Hackett, trans. and ed., *The Buchenwald Report* (Boulder, CO: Westview, 1995). The American liberators of Buchenwald played a pivotal role in facilitating the collection of this documentation. Dan Mikhman, "Introduction," in *Holocaust Historiography: Emergence, Challenges, Polemic, and Achievements*, ed. David Bankier and Dan Mikhman (Jerusalem: Yad Vashem, 2008), 11–12 (hereafter *Holocaust Historiography*).

38. Roni Stauber, "Laying the Foundations for Holocaust Studies: The Impact of Philip Friedman," *Search and Research: Lectures and Papers* 15 (Jerusalem: Yad Vashem, 2009), 19.

39. Kenan, *Between Memory and History*, 101, 104; Laura Jockusch, "Chroniclers of Catastrophe: History Writing as a Jewish Response to Persecutions before and after the Holocaust," in *Holocaust Historiography*, 136.

40. Peter Hayes, "Holocaust Studies: Reflections and Predictions" (Joseph and Rebecca Meyerhoff Annual Lecture, Center for Advanced Holocaust Studies, United States Holocaust Memorial Museum, Washington, D.C., November 15, 2013), 4.

41. Philip Friedman, *This Was Oswiecim: The Story of a Murder Camp* (London: United Jewish Relief Appeal, 1946). That Friedman was able to compile all this information

about Auschwitz by November 1945 is, despite certain mistakes in the book, an impressive accomplishment.

42. Roni Stauber, *The Holocaust in Israeli Public Debate in the 1950s: Ideology and Memory* (London: Vallentine Mitchell, 2007), chapters 9–11; Stauber, "Laying the Foundations," 31–33.

43. Philip Friedman, "Preliminary Problems and Methodologies: Problems of Research on the Jewish Catastrophe in the Nazi Period," *Yad Vashem Studies* 2 (1958): 116, 119–121; Friedman, "Jewish Resistance to Nazism," in *Roads to Extinction: Essays on the Holocaust*, ed. Ada June Friedman (New York: Jewish Publication Society of America, 1980), 387–408 (hereafter *Roads to Extinction*); Stauber, "Laying the Foundations," 52.

44. Philip Friedman, "Social Conflict in the Ghetto," in *Roads to Extinction*, 149; Friedman, "The Destruction of the Jews of Lwow, 1941–1944," in *Roads to Extinction*, 252; Friedman, "Preliminary Problems and Methodological Aspects of Research on the Judenrat," in *Roads to Extinction*, 539–551.

45. See for example the heated debate about Claude Lanzmann's film *The Last of the Unjust* (2013), in which Benjamin Murmelstein, the elder of the Terezin council and the only one to survive, defends himself against all criticisms of his work. *The Last of the Unjust* (*Le dernier des injustes*), directed by Claude Lanzmann (2013; New York: Cohen Media Group, 2014), DVD; Richard Brody, "Claude Lanzmann's *The Last of the Unjust*," *New Yorker*, September 27, 2013, http://www.newyorker.com/online/blogs/movies/2013/09/claude-lanzmann-the-last-of-the-unjust-review.html, accessed September 27, 2014; J. Hoberman, "'The Last of the Unjust,' the New Film by the Director of 'Shoah,' Is a Moral and Aesthetic Blunder," *Tablet Magazine*, February 5, 2014, http://www.tabletmag.com/jewish-arts-and-culture/161448/last-of-the-unjust-lanzmann-hoberman, accessed February 5, 2014.

46. Philip Friedman, "The Extermination of the Polish Jews," in *Roads to Extinction*, 238; Friedman, "The Extermination of the Gypsies," in *Roads to Extinction*, 381–386.

47. Philip Friedman, "American Jewish Research and Literature on the Holocaust," in *Roads to Extinction*, 525, 533; Roni Stauber, "Philip Friedman and the Beginnings of Holocaust Studies," in *Holocaust Historiography*, 91–95.

48. Friedman, "Research on the Recent Jewish Tragedy," *Jewish Social Studies* 12, no. 1 (1950): 25, http://www.jstor.org/stable/4464854, accessed March 12, 2014.

49. Friedman, "European Jewish Research on the Holocaust," in *Roads to Extinction*, 503, 505.

50. Donald Bloxham, "Jewish Witnesses in War Crimes Trials of the Postwar Era," in *Holocaust Historiography*, 542–543, 548–549.

51. David Engel, *Historians of the Jews and the Holocaust* (Stanford, CA: Stanford University Press, 2010), 134; Yehuda Bauer, *Rethinking the Holocaust* (New Haven, CT: Yale University Press, 2001), 55.

52. Hilberg's book was not the first history of the Holocaust to appear in English. It was preceded by Gerald Reitlinger, *The Final Solution: The Attempt to Exterminate the Jews of Europe, 1939–1945* (New York: Beechhurst Press, 1953), and Leon Poliakov, *Harvest of Hate: The Nazi Program for the Destruction of the Jews of Europe* (Syracuse, NY: Syracuse University Press, 1954). Neither had the sweep or documentary evidence marshaled by Hilberg.

53. Raul Hilberg, *The Politics of Memory: The Journey of a Holocaust Historian* (Chicago: Ivan R. Dee, 1996), 66.

54. Raul Hilberg, "Working on the Holocaust," *Psychohistory Review* 14, no. 3 (1986): 8.

55. Samuel Eliot Morison and Henry Steele Commager, *The Growth of the American Republic*, vol. 2 (New York: Oxford University Press, 1962), 605–606; Gerd Korman, "Silence in American Textbooks," *Yad Vashem Studies* 8 (1970): 183, 190.

56. For change in Anne's "identity" see Morison and Commager, *The Growth of the American Republic*, 6th rev. ed. (New York: Oxford University Press, 1969), 609–610; Korman, "Silence," 270.

57. The historian A.J.P. Taylor made a similar argument. He blamed the war on the Allies who had failed to recognize that Hitler was, in fact, "no more wicked" than the leaders of those European nations that would fight him. Though popular with many Americans, these views were generally excoriated by mainstream historians and dismissed as being on the fringe. A.J.P. Taylor, *The Origins of the Second World War* (London: Hamish Hamilton, 1961).

58. Mikhman, "Is There an Israeli School of Holocaust Studies?" in *Holocaust Historiography*, 51.

59. Saul Friedlander, "The Extermination of the European Jews in Historiography: Fifty Years Later," in *Thinking about the Holocaust: After Half a Century*, ed. Alvin H. Rosenfeld (Bloomington: Indiana University Press, 1997), 9.

60. Jürgen Matthäus, "Agents of the Final Solution," in *Holocaust Historiography*, 327–337.

61. Raul Hilberg, *The Destruction of the European Jews* (Chicago: Quadrangle Books, 1967), v. This distrust persisted for a number of decades. Lucy Dawidowicz, whose more popular book on the Final Solution would become a big seller in the 1980s, also avoided testimonies because, she claimed, they were so full of mistakes that for the unwary researcher they could be "more hazard than help." Lucy Dawidowicz, *The Holocaust and the Historians* (Cambridge, MA: Harvard University Press, 1981), 177; Annette Wieviorka, *The Era of the Witness* (Ithaca, NY: Cornell University Press, 2006), xiii.

62. Hilberg, *Destruction*, 663–666, 667, 669.

63. Stauber, "The Holocaust in Israeli Public Debate," 140.

64. Hilberg, *Politics of Memory*, 109–111.

65. Joseph Melkman, "Review of Hilberg's *The Destruction of European Jewry*," as cited in Stauber, "The Holocaust in Israeli Public Debate," 141.

66. Stauber, "The Holocaust in Israeli Public Debate," 142.

67. Hilberg, *Politics of Memory*, 111.

68. H. R. Trevor-Roper, "*The Destruction of European Jews*, by Raul Hilberg," *Commentary*, April 1, 1962.

69. Andreas Dorpalen, "*The Destruction of European Jews* (Book Review)," *Journal of Modern History* 34, no. 2 (1962): 226.

70. A. A. Roback, "A Modern Balaam in Reverse: The Hilberg-Trevor-Roper Slur on Jewish Courage," *Jewish Quarterly* 9, no. 3 (1962): 6–8.

71. "Letters to the Editor: Jewish Resistance," *Commentary*, August 1, 1962.

72. Gordon Wright, *The Ordeal of Total War, 1939–1945* (New York: Harper & Row, 1968), as quoted in Korman, "Silence," 265.

73. Bruno Bettelheim, "The Ignored Lesson of Anne Frank," *Harper's Magazine*, November 1960, 45–50. While no stay in a Nazi-run camp was ever easy, there is no comparison between the conditions he faced in a camp in 1938 and those faced by inmates in death camps.

74. Bruno Bettelheim, *The Informed Heart: Autonomy in a Mass Age* (Glencoe, IL: Free Press, 1960), as quoted in Engel, *Historians*, 145; Bettelheim, "The Holocaust— One Generation Later," in *Surviving and Other Essays* (New York: Knopf, 1979), 101. For Bettelheim's views on the impact of a diaspora existence see his "Freedom from Ghetto Thinking," *Midstream: A Monthly Jewish Review* 8, no. 2 (1962): 17, 18, 20.

75. Dan Michman, "Jews," in *The Oxford Handbook of Holocaust Studies* (Oxford: Oxford University Press, 2010), 189–190.

76. Donald Bloxham and Tony Kushner, *The Holocaust: Critical Historical Approaches* (Manchester: Manchester University Press; New York: Palgrave Macmillan, 2005), 19.

77. Diner, *We Remember*, 150ff., 160ff.

78. Leonard Dinnerstein, *America and the Survivors of the Holocaust: The Evolution of a United States Displaced Persons Policy, 1945–1950* (New York: Columbia University Press, 1982); Diner, *We Remember*, 154–158.

79. Diner, *We Remember*, 162.

80. Beth Cohen, *Case Closed: Holocaust Survivors in Postwar America* (New Brunswick, NJ: Rutgers University Press, 2007), 2.

81. Hannah Arendt, "We Refugees," in *The Jewish Writings*, ed. Jerome Kohn and Ron H. Feldman (New York: Schocken Books, 2007), 264.

82. Henry Greenspan, *On Listening to Holocaust Survivors: Recounting and Life History* (Westport, CT: Praeger, 1998), 34.

83. Elie Wiesel, *A Jew Today*, 193–194, as quoted in Greenspan, *On Listening*, 34.

84. Dorothy Rabinowitz, *New Lives: Survivors of the Holocaust Living in America* (New York: Random House, 1996), 92; Edward Linenthal, *Preserving Memory* (New York: Viking Press, 1999), 6.

85. William G. Niederland, "Psychiatric Disorders among Persecution Victims," *Journal of Nervous and Mental Disease* 139 (1964): 458–474, 468, as quoted in Robert Jay Lifton, *Death in Life—Survivors of Hiroshima* (New York: Random House, 1968), 487.

86. Lawrence Langer, *Holocaust Testimonies: The Ruins of Memory* (New Haven, CT: Yale University Press, 1991), xii.

87. Arlene Stein, *Reluctant Witnesses: Survivors, Their Children, and the Rise of Holocaust Consciousness* (New York: Oxford University Press, 2014), 44–47.

88. Henry Greenspan, "Testimony and the Rise of Holocaust Consciousness," in *The Americanization of the Holocaust*, ed. Hilene Flanzbaum, (Baltimore: Johns Hopkins University Press, 1999), 64.

89. Eva Hoffman, *After Such Knowledge: Memory, History, and the Legacy of the Holocaust* (New York: Public Affairs, 2004), 46.

90. Greenspan, *On Listening*, 35.

91. William B. Helmreich, *Against All Odds: Holocaust Survivors and the Successful Lives They Made in America* (New Brunswick, NJ: Transaction Publishers, 1995), 38.

92. Greenspan, *On Listening*, 35.

93. Ruth Kluger, *Still Alive: A Holocaust Girlhood Remembered* (New York: Feminist Press at the City University of New York, 2001), 177.

94. Stein, *Reluctant Witnesses*, 40–44.

95. Greenspan, *On Listening*, 43–44.

96. Cohen, *Case Closed*, 156, 157.

97. Alexander Donat, *The Holocaust Kingdom: A Memoir* (New York: Holt Rinehart, 1965), 211; Primo Levi, *Survival in Auschwitz*, as quoted in Greenspan, *On Listening*, 38.

98. Primo Levi, *The Drowned and the Saved* (New York: Vintage/Random House, 1988), 12.

99. Ibid., 155–172.

100. Linenthal, *Preserving Memory*, 6.

101. Raul Hilberg, "I Was Not There," in *Writing and the Holocaust*, ed. Berel Lang (New York: Holmes & Meier, 1988), 18; Annette Wieviorka, who has done an extensive survey of survivor testimonies, describes the number in the 1950s as being "enormous." Wieviorka, *Era*, x–xi.

102. François Mauriac, introduction to *Night,* by Elie Wiesel (New York: Hill and Wang, 2006), xviii; Ruth Franklin, *A Thousand Darknesses: Lies and Truth in Holocaust Fiction* (New York: Oxford University Press, 2011), 70.

103. Diner, *We Remember.*

104. For an in-depth analysis of these novels and what they reflect about American society at the time see Leah Garrett, "Young Lions: Jewish American War Fiction of 1948," *Jewish Social Studies* 18, no. 2 (2012): 70–99.

105. For a detailed exposition on the trauma of antisemitism encountered by Jewish GIs, see Deborah Dash Moore, *GI Jews: How World War II Changed a Generation* (Cambridge, MA: Harvard University Press, 2006).

106. Irwin Shaw, "The Young Lions," as quoted in Garrett, *Young Lions,* 81.

107. Martha Gellhorn, *The Wine of Astonishment* (New York: Scribner's, 1948), 245; Merle Miller, *That Winter* (New York: Sloan Associates, 1948).

108. John Hersey, *The Wall* (New York: Borzoi, 1950); Alan Rosen, *Sounds of Defiance: The Holocaust, Multilingualism, and the Problem of English* (Lincoln: University of Nebraska Press, 2005), 200n.2; Nancy Sinkoff, "Fiction's Archive: Authenticity, Ethnography, and Philosemitism in John Hersey's *The Wall,*" *Jewish Social Studies* 17, no. 2 (2011): 49–50.

109. Daniel Schwarz, *Imagining the Holocaust* (New York: St. Martin's Press, 1999), 36. This was hardly the first book on the Holocaust to be published in the United States. It had been preceded by Mary Berg, *Warsaw Ghetto: A Diary* (New York: L. B. Fischer, 1945); Marek Edelman, *The Ghetto Fights* (New York: American Representation of the General Jewish Workers' Union of Poland, 1946); and Marie Syrkin, *Blessed Is the Match: The Story of Jewish Resistance* (Philadelphia: Jewish Publication Society of America, 1947), among others. None of these books, however, achieved the commercial success of Hersey's work.

110. John Hersey, "The Mechanics of a Novel," *Yale University Library Gazette* 27, no. 1 (1952): 1–11, as cited in Sinkoff, "Fiction's Archive," 54–55.

111. Hersey, *The Wall,* 628. For an analysis of how *The Wall* relates to Yiddish fiction see Anita Norich, *Discovering Exile: Yiddish and Jewish American Culture during the Holocaust* (Stanford, CA: Stanford University Press, 2007), 118–120.

112. Hersey, *The Wall,* 425, 550.

113. Sinkoff, "Fiction's Archive," 66, 68–70.

114. Robert D. McFadden, "Laura Z. Hobson, Author, Dies at 85," *New York Times,* March 2, 1986; Bosley Crowther, "Review: 'Gentleman's Agreement': A Study of Anti-Semitism," *New York Times,* November 12, 1947.

115. *Gentleman's Agreement,* directed by Elia Kazan (1947; Los Angeles: Twentieth Century–Fox, 2003), DVD, scene at 1:35–36.

116. Sara R. Horowitz, "The Cinematic Triangulation of Jewish American Identity," in *The Americanization of the Holocaust,* 148–151, 153.

117. Anne Frank Guide, 2005, accessed March 1, 2015, http://www.annefrankguide.net.

118. David Barnouw, "Anne Frank and Film," in *Anne Frank: Reflections on Her Life and Legacy*, ed. Hyman A. Enzer and Sandra Solotaroff-Enzer (Urbana: University of Illinois Press, 2000), 169 (hereafter *Anne Frank Reflections*).

119. Judith Doneson, "The American History of Anne Frank's Diary," in *Anne Frank Reflections*, 124.

120. Robert Alter, "The View from the Attic," *New Republic* 213 (December 4, 1995): 40.

121. Lawrence Langer, "The Americanization of the Holocaust on Stage and Screen," in *Anne Frank Reflections*, 200.

122. Hannah Arendt, letter to the editor, *Midstream*, September 1962, 85–87, as quoted in Lawrence Graver, *An Obsession with Anne Frank: Meyer Levin and the "Diary"* (Berkeley: University of California Press, 1995), 130.

123. Frances Goodrich and Albert Hackett, *The Diary of Anne Frank* (New York: Random House, 1956), 74.

124. Graver, *An Obsession with Anne Frank*, 95.

125. Bernard Kalb, "Diary Footnotes," *New York Times*, October 2, 1955; Walter K. Kerr, "Theater: Anne Frank and Family," *New York Herald Tribune* (Paris), October 23, 1955, as cited in Alvin H. Rosenfeld, "Popularization and Memory: The Case of Anne Frank," in *Lessons and Legacies*, ed. Peter Hayes (Evanston, IL: Northwestern University Press, 1991), 253, 258.

126. Judith Doneson, "The American History of Anne Frank's Diary," in *Anne Frank Reflections*, 128.

127. Kerr, "Theater: Anne Frank and Family"; *New York Post*, October 8, 1955.

128. Graver, *An Obsession with Anne Frank*, 94–95.

129. Brooks Atkinson, "Theatre: 'The Diary of Anne Frank,'" *New York Times*, October 6, 1955.

130. Tim Cole, *Selling the Holocaust: From Auschwitz to Schindler: How History Is Bought, Packaged, and Sold* (New York: Routledge, 1999), 42.

131. Cynthia Ozick, "Who Owns Anne Frank?" *New Yorker*, October 6, 1997, 81.

132. Rosenfeld, "Popularization and Memory," 252; Ozick, "Who Owns Anne Frank?," 7; Stephen J. Whitfield, "Value Added: Jews in Postwar World," *Studies in Contemporary Jewry* 8 (1992): 68–84.

133. Hannah Pick-Goslar, "Her Last Days," in *Anne Frank Reflections*, 50; Lienjte Rebling-Brillesijper, "Bergen-Belsen," in *Anne Frank Reflections*, 54.

134. On Anne's universalism see Alter, "The View from the Attic," 38–42.

135. Alter, "The View from the Attic," 42; Ozick, "Who Owns Anne Frank?," 78.

136. Barbara Kirshenblatt-Gimblett and Jeffrey Shandler, eds., *Anne Frank Unbound: Media, Imagination, Memory* (Bloomington: Indiana University Press, 2012).

137. Letter from John Stone to George Stevens, December 23, 1957, in Goodrich/Hackett File, Wisconsin Center for Film and Theater Research, as cited in Judith Doneson, "The American History of Anne Frank's Diary," *Holocaust and Genocide Studies* 2, no. 1 (1987): 153–154.

138. Lawrence Baron, "Film," in *The Oxford Handbook*, 446.

139. Alexander, *Social Construction of Moral Universals*, 5–86.

140. Cole, *Selling the Holocaust*, 42.

141. *This Is Your Life*, Season 1, Episode 6: Hanna Bloch Kohner, *This Is Your Life* video, 25:19, May 27, 1953, http://holocaustvisualarchive.wordpress.com/2012/05/10/this-is-your-life-hanna-kohner/, accessed March 5, 2015.

142. It is interesting to note that not once was Hannah described as a Jew. She was a "non-Aryan." It seems strange that the script avoided that aspect of her identity since her brother had been brought from Israel and the show ended with a call for viewers to aid the United Jewish Appeal in Hannah's honor in order to assist other survivors.

143. Leon Uris, *Exodus* (Garden City, NY: Doubleday, 1958); Rachel Weissbrod, "*Exodus* as a Zionist Melodrama," *Israel Studies* 4, no. 1 (1999): 129–152; Horowitz, "Cinematic Triangulation of Jewish American Identity," in *Americanization of the Holocaust*, 156.

144. Robert Cohen, "Review: *Our Exodus: Leon Uris and the Americanization of Israel's Founding Story*, M. M. Silver," Jewish Book Council, http://www.jewishbookcouncil.org/book/our-exodus-leon-uris-and-the-americanization-of-israels-founding-story.

145. Dalton Trumbo, *Exodus: Screenplay* (Los Angeles: Carlyle-Alpina, Otto Preminger, 1960); *Exodus*, directed by Otto Preminger (1960; Beverly Hills: MGM, 2002), scene at approximately 1:35 hours.

146. Horowitz, "The Cinematic Triangulation of Jewish American Identity," in *Americanization of the Holocaust*, 156.

147. Matt Wiener, writer, producer, and director of the television show *Mad Men*, which was set in the late 1950s and early 1960s, made a point of including in the show cultural artifacts from the era. In one episode the lead character, Don Draper, is reading *Exodus*. Discussing the book with his wife he learns that her first kiss was from a Jewish boy at a dance to raise money for "those skinny people on boats," that is, Holocaust survivors.

148. Amy Kaplan, "Zionism as Anticolonialism: The Case of *Exodus*," *American Literary History* 25, no. 4 (2013): 870–895; Rudolf Flesch, "Conversation Piece: A Book with Universal Appeal," *Los Angeles Times*, February 8, 1960.

149. Frank Cantor, "A Second Look at *Exodus*," *Jewish Currents* (1959): 20–21, as quoted in Deborah Dash Moore, *To the Golden Cities: Pursuing the American Jewish Dream in Miami and L.A.* (Cambridge, MA: Harvard University Press, 1994), 249.

150. Philip Roth, "Some New Jewish Stereotypes," in *Reading Myself and Others* (New York: Farrar, Straus, Giroux, 1975), 145–146, as quoted in Moore, *To the Golden Cities*, 250.

151. Lester Friedman, *Hollywood's Image of the Jew* (New York: Frederick Ungar, 1982), 192.

152. Gavriel D. Rosenfeld, "The Reception of William L. Shirer's *The Rise and Fall of the Third Reich* in the United States and West Germany, 1960–62," *Journal of Contemporary History* 29, no. 1 (1994): 95, 100.

153. William Shirer, *The Rise and Fall of the Third Reich: A History of Nazi Germany* (New York: Simon & Schuster, 1960), 90.

154. Peter Novick, *The Holocaust in American Life* (Boston: Houghton Mifflin, 1999), 101.

155. *New York Times*, February 22, 1963.

156. Geoffrey Barraclough, "Hitler in Cinerama," *The Nation* 191, no. 14 (1960): 330–331.

157. For example, Felix Morley, writing in *Modern Age*, took Shirer to task for the book's "pro-Communist suggestiveness," and observes that if Shirer's "pernicious thesis" were correct it would be "wise to stop immediately all re-arming of the Federal Republic and to hand West Berlin over to Communist control." Felix Morley, "Those Incorrigible Germans," *Modern Age* 5, no. 2 (1961): 192–193. For another highly critical review of Shirer's perspective on Germany see Klaus Epstein, "Shirer's History of Nazi Germany," *Review of Politics* 23, no. 2 (1961): 30–45.

CHAPTER 2 — STATE OF THE QUESTION

1. Adolf Eichmann, *The Trial of Adolf Eichmann: Record of Proceedings in the District Court of Jerusalem* (Jerusalem: Trust for the Publication of the Proceedings of the Eichmann Trial, in cooperation with the Israel State Archives and Yad Vashem, the Holocaust Martyrs' and Heroes' Remembrance Authority, 1992), 1680–1681 (hereafter *TAE*).

2. Robert H. Jackson, *Justice Jackson's Report to the President on Atrocities and War Crimes; June 7, 1945* (Washington, DC: United States Government Printing Office, 1945), http://avalon.law.yale.edu/imt/imt_jack01.asp, accessed March 4, 2015.

3. Raul Hilberg, "Opening Remarks," in *Lessons and Legacies*, ed. Peter Hayes, (Evanston, IL: Northwestern University Press, 1991), 12 (hereafter *Lessons and Legacies*).

4. Annette Wieviorka, *The Era of the Witness* (Ithaca, NY: Cornell University Press, 2006), 67.

5. Susan Sontag, "Reflections on the Deputy," *New York Herald Tribune* (Paris), March 1, 1964, reprinted in Eric Bentley, ed., *Storm over the Deputy* (New York: Grove Press, 1964), 118.

6. Dorothy Rabinowitz, *New Lives: Survivors of the Holocaust Living in America* (New York: Alfred A. Knopf, 1976), 193.

7. Geoffrey Hartman, "Closing Remarks," in *Lessons and Legacies*, 331.

8. Wieviorka, *Era of the Witness*, 83.

9. Haim Gouri, *Facing the Glass Booth: The Jerusalem Trial of Adolf Eichmann* (Detroit: Wayne State University Press, 2004), 37, 269.

10. *TAE*, 2082–2084; Wieviorka, *Era of the Witness*, 88.

11. Richard I. Cohen, "A Generation's Response to *Eichmann in Jerusalem*," in *Hannah Arendt in Jerusalem*, ed. Steven E. Aschheim (Berkeley: University of California Press, 2001), 256.

12. Tim Cole, *Selling the Holocaust: From Auschwitz to Schindler: How History Is Bought, Packaged, and Sold* (New York: Routledge, 1999), 8.

13. *Jewish Chronicle* (London), November 1, 1963; Konrad Kellen, "Reflections on Eichmann in Jerusalem," *Midstream* 9, no. 3 (1963): 25; John Gross, "Arendt on Eichmann," *Encounter* 21, no. 5 (1963): 66, 68; Hugh Trevor Roper, "How Innocent Was Eichmann?" *Sunday Times* (London), October 13, 1963; Louis Harap, "Notes and Communications: On Arendt's Eichmann and Jewish Identity," *Studies on the Left* 5, no. 4 (1965): 52–79 as quoted in Michael Ezra, "The Eichmann Polemics: Hannah Arendt and Her Critics," *Dissent*, Summer 2007, 155–156, http://www.dissentmagazine.org/democratiya_article/the-eichmann-polemics-hannah-arendt-and-her-critics, accessed March 6, 2015.

14. Stephen Spender, "Death in Jerusalem," *New York Review of Books* 1, no. 2 (1963); "Arguments: More on Eichmann: Comments by Marie Syrkin, Harold Weisberg, Irving Howe, Robert Lowell, Dwight Macdonald, Lionel Abel, Mary McCarthy, and William Phillips," *Partisan Review* 31, no. 2 (1964): 253–283; Mary McCarthy, "The Hue and Cry," *Partisan Review* 31, no. 1 (1964): 82; Richard Wolin, "The Banality of Evil: The Demise of a Legend," *Jewish Review of Books* 19 (2014): 28.

15. Gavriel D. Rosenfeld, "The Politics of Uniqueness: Reflections on the Recent Polemical Turn in Holocaust and Genocide Scholarship," *Holocaust and Genocide Studies* 13, no. 1 (1999): 31, 50n.8; Hannah Arendt, *The Origins of Totalitarianism* (New York: Harcourt, Brace & World, 1979), 437–440.

16. Michael Marrus, *Lessons of the Holocaust* (Toronto: University of Toronto Press, 2016), 18.

17. Hannah Arendt, *Eichmann in Jerusalem: A Report on the Banality of Evil,* revised and enlarged ed. (New York: Penguin, 1994), 27 (hereafter *EIJ*); Hannah Arendt to Karl Jaspers, December 23, 1960, in *Correspondence, 1926–1969,* ed. Lotte Kohler and Hans Saner (New York: Harcourt, 1992), 414–415.

18. Salo W. Baron, "Opening Remarks," *Jewish Social Studies* 12, no. 1 (1950): 13–15; Hannah Arendt, "Social Science Techniques and the Study of Concentration Camps," *Jewish Social Studies* 12, no. 1 (1950): 50–51.

19. Arendt, *EIJ*, 54; Arendt to Jaspers, December 2, 1960, in *Correspondence*, 409–410.

20. Christopher Browning, *Collected Memoirs: Holocaust History and Postwar Testimony* (Madison: University of Wisconsin Press, 2003), 3–4.

21. Bettina Stangneth, *Eichmann before Jerusalem: The Unexamined Life of a Mass Murderer* (New York: Alfred A. Knopf, 2014), 302.

22. Arendt, *EIJ*, 117–118, 125–126.

23. Arieh Leon Kubovy, "Medinah posha'at," *Yediot Yad Vashem* 31 (1964): 1–7; M. Muszkat, "Eichmann b'New York," *Yediot Yad Vashem* 31 (1964): 8–15, both as cited in David Engel, *Historians of the Jews and the Holocaust* (Stanford, CA: Stanford University Press, 2010), 151.

24. Alexander Donat, "An Empiric Examination," *Judaism* 12, no. 4 (1963): 416–417.

25. Philip Friedman, "Aspects of Research on the Judenrat," in *Roads to Extinction: Essays on the Holocaust,* ed. Ada June Friedman (New York: Jewish Publication Society of America, 1980), 547, 551 (hereafter *Roads to Extinction*).

26. Arendt, *EIJ*, 11, 12.

27. Yehuda Bauer, "Jewish Leadership Reactions to Nazi Policies," in *Holocaust as a Historical Experience: Essays and a Discussion,* ed. Yehuda Bauer and Nathan Rotenstreich (New York: Holmes & Meier, 1981), 173–192; Michael Marrus, *The Holocaust in History* (New York: Meridian, 1987), 118.

28. At this point, of course, the Reich was already murdering "those unworthy of life," that is, handicapped, mentally deficient, bearers of hereditary diseases, and others. While this would be a prototype for the Judeocide that would follow, there was no mass annihilation of Jews at the time.

29. Hannah Arendt, "Comment," *Midstream* 8, no. 6 (1962): 86–88, as quoted in Engel, *Historians,* 147.

30. Elisabeth Young-Bruehl, *Hannah Arendt: For the Love of the World* (New Haven, CT: Yale University Press, 1982), 338; Richard J. Bernstein, *Hannah Arendt and the Jewish Question* (Cambridge, MA: MIT Press, 1996), 159. For additional examples of the anger provoked by her cynicism see Deborah Lipstadt, *The Eichmann Trial* (New York: Schocken/Nextbook, 2011), 148–175.

31. "Eichmann in Jerusalem: An Exchange of Letters between Gershom Scholem and Hannah Arendt," *Encounter* 22, no. 1 (1964): 51.

32. Nathan Abrams, *Norman Podhoretz and Commentary Magazine: The Rise and Fall of the Neocons* (New York: Bloomsbury Academic, 2010), 38.

33. Arendt, *EIJ*, 259–260, 271.

34. Ibid., 15–18.

35. Engel, *Historians,* 154–158.

36. Hannah Arendt, *The Origins of Totalitarianism* (New York: Meridian Books, 1958), 9–10.

37. Wolin, *Banality of Evil,* 28.

38. Robert H. Glauber, "The Eichmann Case," *The Christian Century* 80, no. 21 (1963): 682.

39. Paul Jacobs, "Eichmann and Jewish Identity," *Midstream* (1961): 65.

40. Pinchas Lapide, *The Last Three Popes and the Jews* (New York: Hawthorn Books, 1967), 268, as quoted in Tom Lawson, *Debates on the Holocaust* (New York: Palgrave Macmillan, 2010), 94; Eric Bentley, "Foreword," *Storm over The Deputy* (New York: Grove Press, 1964), 10.

41. Hannah Arendt, "*The Deputy:* Guilt by Silence?," in *Amor Mundi: Explorations in the Faith and Thought of Hannah Arendt,* ed. J. W. Bernauer (Boston: Martinus Nijhoff, 1987), 51–52.

42. Lawson, *Debates,* 94.

43. The same editorial also used the term "the holocaust," albeit in lowercase. It noted that the reaction to the play proved that "ripples of the holocaust still reach the far corners of the earth." "Silence," *New York Times,* February 28, 1964.

44. Kirsten Fermaglich, *American Dreams and Nazi Nightmares: Early Holocaust Consciousness and Liberal America, 1957–1965* (Waltham, MA: Brandeis University Press, 2006), 4–5, 13, 19–20, 59.

45. Though his thesis would eventually fall out of favor, it apparently influenced then Assistant Secretary of Labor Daniel Patrick Moynihan, who argued that the problems African Americans faced were not just rooted in racial discrimination but in the environmental conditions in which they lived. Ending discrimination simply was not enough. Fermaglich, *American Dreams,* 47–48, 50.

46. Sylvia Plath, "Daddy," in *Collected Poems* (New York: HarperCollins, 1992), http://www.poetryfoundation.org/poem/178960, accessed August 5, 2014. In "Mary's Song," Plath lamented about "This holocaust I walk in, O golden child the world will kill and eat." In *Collected Poems,* http://www.americanpoems.com/poets/sylviaplath/7853, accessed August 5, 2014. In "Lady Lazarus," she wrote of "my skin Bright as a Nazi lampshade." In *Collected Poems,* http://www.americanpoems.com/poets/sylvia-plath/1404, accessed August 5, 2014.

47. Kurt Vonnegut, *Mother Night* (New York: Dell, 1961), 22; Fermaglich, *American Dreams,* 14.

48. Betty Friedan, *The Feminine Mystique* (New York: Dell, 1964), 294, as quoted in Fermaglich, *American Dreams,* 58. Friedan later acknowledged that the analogy was inappropriate and that she was "ashamed" of having used it. Betty Friedan, *Life So Far* (New York: Simon and Schuster, 2000), 132 as quoted in Fermaglich, *American Dreams,* 58.

49. Stanley Milgram, *Obedience to Authority: An Experimental View* (New York: Harper Perennial, 2009), xii, 5–6.

50. Fermaglich, *American Dreams,* 88–90, 111; Omer Bartov, "Reception and Perception: Goldhagen's Holocaust and the World," in *The 'Goldhagen Effect': History, Memory, Nazism—Facing the German Past,* ed. Geoff Eley (Ann Arbor: University of Michigan Press, 2000), 78–87.

51. Bernd Greiner, *War without Fronts: The USA in Vietnam* (New Haven, CT: Yale University Press, 2009).

52. Dana Villa, *Politics, Philosophy, Terror: Essays on the Thought of Hannah Arendt* (Princeton, NJ: Princeton University Press, 1999), 54.

53. Among these scientists were many war criminals who used concentration camp inmates at Dachau and Ravensbrück in research on biological and chemical weapons and subjected inmates in slave labor camps to inhuman conditions. They had been responsible for the death of thousands. Nonetheless, after the war they lived privileged lives in this country. Annie Jacobsen, *Operation Paperclip: The Secret Intelligence Program That Brought Nazi Scientists to America* (Boston: Little, Brown, 2014).

54. There were, of course, other works being produced at this time that explored questions of evil and obedience and that did not make any direct reference to the Final Solution. Joseph Heller's *Catch-22* (New York: Simon & Schuster, 1961) depicted World War II as a brutal, if not senseless, war. Both Richard Condon's *The Manchurian Candidate* (New York: The New American Library, 1962) and Ken Kesey's *One Flew Over the Cuckoo's Nest* (New York: Viking Press, 1962) provoked Americans to reflect upon the mindlessness of those in positions of authority in America.

55. Arthur Miller, *After the Fall* (New York: Viking Press, 1964), 1, 58–59, 100–101; Howard Taubman, "Theater: 'After the Fall,'" *New York Times*, January 24, 1964; Howard Taubman, "A Cheer for Controversy," *New York Times*, February 2, 1964.

56. Christopher Bigsby, "Arthur Miller, The Art of Theater No. 2, Part 2," *Paris Review* 41, no. 152 (1999), http://www.theparisreview.org/interviews/895/the-art-of-theater-no-2-part-2-arthur-miller, accessed March 5, 2014.

57. Arthur Miller, *Focus* (Harmondsworth: Penguin Books, 1984), v–vi.

58. See Fermaglich for a comparative analysis of how these various author's Jewish or non-Jewish identities might have influenced their work. Fermaglich, *American Dreams*.

59. James E. Young, "America's Holocaust: Memory and the Politics of Identity," in *The Americanization of the Holocaust*, ed. Hilene Flanzbaum (Baltimore: Johns Hopkins University Press, 1999), 70 (hereafter *Americanization of the Holocaust*).

60. Rogers Brubaker and Frederick Cooper, "Beyond 'Identity,'" *Theory and Society* 29 (2000): 1–47. I thank Doris Bergen for bringing this article to my attention.

61. Will Herberg, *Protestant, Catholic, Jew* (Garden City, NY: Anchor Books, 1960), 20, as quoted in Matthew Frye Jacobson, *Roots Too: White Ethnic Revival in Post–Civil Rights America* (Cambridge, MA: Harvard University Press, 2006), 14, 16.

62. Fred Ferretti, "Levy's Jewish Rye Will Soon Be Arnold's," *New York Times*, June 6, 1979; Margalit Fox, "Judy Protas, Writer of Slogan for Levy's Read Jewish Rye, Dies at 91," *New York Times*, January 11, 2014. For an assessment of how revolutionary this ad was see Dave Trott, *44 Club: Ads That Changed the World*, video, 7:25, May 29, 2013, https://www.youtube.com/watch?v=iAVqVfaNtoo, accessed March 25, 2014.

63. David B. McDonald, *Identity Politics in the Age of Genocide: The Holocaust and Historical Representation* (New York: Routledge, 2008), 10.

64. Beth Bailey, *America's Army: Making the All-Volunteer Force* (Cambridge, MA: Belknap Press of Harvard University Press, 2009), 18–21.

65. "Police Again Rout 'Village' Youths: Outbreak by 400 Follows a Near-Riot Over Raid," *New York Times,* June 30, 1969; "Stonewall Riots: The Beginning of the LGBT Movement," *The Leadership Conference,* June 22, 2009, http://www.civilrights.org/archives/2009/06/449-stonewall.html, accessed March 3, 2014; David Carter, Andrew Scott Dolkart, Gale Harris, and Jay Shockley, "National Historic Landmark Nomination: Stonewall," ed. Kathleen La Frank, January 1999, http://www.columbia.edu/cu/lweb/eresources/exhibitions/sw25/gifs/stonewall_national_historic_landmark_nomination.pdf; Columbia University, "The Stonewall Riot and Its Aftermath," *Stonewall and Beyond: Lesbian and Gay Culture,* http://www.columbia.edu/cu/lweb/eresources/exhibitions/sw25/case1.html, last modified August 24, 2011, accessed March 5, 2015; David Carter, "What Made Stonewall Different," *The Free Library,* http://www.thefreelibrary.com/What made Stonewall different.-a0203192731, July, 1, 2009, accessed March 3, 2014; Elizabeth A. Armstrong and Suzanna M. Crage, "Movements and Memory: The Making of the Stonewall Myth," *American Sociological Review* 71, no. 5 (2006): 724–775, http://www-personal.umich.edu/~elarmstr/publications/Movements%20and%20Memory%20Armstrong%20and%20Crage.pdf, accessed March 3, 2014.

66. Stephen S. Hall, "Italian-Americans Coming into Their Own," *New York Times Magazine,* May 15, 1983; Ken Auletta, "I-Governors," *New Yorker,* April 9, 1984, 57–58; Lee Iacocca and William Novak, *Iacocca: An Autobiography* (New York: Bantam Books, 1984), chapters 10–12; Charles E. Silberman, *A Certain People: American Jews and Their Lives Today* (New York: Summit Books, 1985), 110–112.

67. Arthur Hertzberg, "Israel and American Jewry," *Commentary,* August 1, 1967.

68. Abraham Joshua Heschel, *Israel: An Echo of Eternity* (New York: Farrar, Straus and Giroux, 1969), 112; Morris M. Faierstein, "Abraham Joshua Heschel and the Holocaust," *Modern Judaism* 19, no. 3 (1999): 255–275.

69. Abraham Joshua Heschel, "To Save a Soul," in *Moral Grandeur and Spiritual Audacity: Essays,* ed. Susannah Heschel (New York: Farrar, Straus and Giroux, 1997), 64.

70. Riv-Ellen Prell, "Complicating a Jewish Modernity: The Jewish Theological Seminar, Columbia University, and the Rise of a Jewish Counterculture in 1968," in *Between Jewish Tradition and Modernity: Rethinking An Old Opposition: Essays in Honor of David Ellenson,* ed. Michael A. Meyer and David N. Myers (Detroit: Wayne State University Press, 2014), 271.

71. A. Roy Eckardt, "A Theology for the Jewish Question," *Christianity and Society* 11 (Spring 1946): 24–27.

72. Conversation with Hubert Locke, July 26, 2015.

73. Elwyn A. Smith, "Christian Meaning of the Holocaust," *Journal of Ecumenical Studies* 6 (Summer 1969): 419–442; Eva Fleischner, "The Christian and the Holocaust," *Journal of Ecumenical Studies* 7 (Spring 1970): 331–333.

74. A. Roy Eckardt, "Once and Not Future Partisan: A Plea for History," in *From the Unthinkable to the Unavoidable: American Christian and Jewish Scholars Encounter the Holocaust,* ed. Carol Ritttner and John K. Roth (Westport, CT: Praeger Publishers, 1997), 113.

75. Conversation with John Roth, July 24, 2014.

76. Harry James Cargas, "In the Name of the Father," in *From the Unthinkable to the Unavoidable,* 34–35.

77. Eugene J. Fisher, "Being Catholic, Learning Jewish: Personal Reflections on the Shoah," in *From the Unthinkable to the Unavoidable,* 44.

78. Rosemary Radford Ruether, *Faith and Fratricide* (New York: Seabury Press, 1974); A. Roy Eckardt, *Your People, My People* (New York: Quadrangle, 1974); Franklin H. Littell, *The Crucifixion of the Jews* (New York: Harper & Row, 1974); Frank Talmadge, "Christian Theology and the Holocaust," *Commentary,* October 1, 1975, https://www.commentary magazine.com/article/christian-theology-and-the-holocaust/, accessed July 15, 2015.

79. Rosemary Radford Ruether, "Christology and Jewish-Christian Relations," in *Jews and Christians after the Holocaust,* ed. Abraham J. Peck (Minneapolis: Fortress Press, 1982), 27; Alice Eckardt, "The Holocaust: Christian and Jewish Responses," *Journal of the American Academy of Religion* 42, no. 3 (September 1974): 453–459.

80. Conversation with Mary Boys, August 12, 2015.

81. Talmadge, "Christian Theology and the Holocaust."

82. Jules Isaac, "Notes about a Crucial Meeting with John XXIII," Jewish Documents & Statements, Created: June 13, 1960, http://www.ccjr.us/dialogika-resources/documents-and-statements/jewish/1123-isaac1960, accessed August 12, 2015.

83. Conversation with Carol Rittner, August 12, 2015.

84. Conversation with Alice Eckardt, August 13, 2015.

85. Conversation with Peggy Obrecht, August 11, 2015.

86. Carol Rittner, "From Ignorance to Insight," in *From the Unthinkable to the Unavoidable,* 127.

87. Conversation with John Pawlikowskis e, August 11, 2015.

88. Conversation with Victoria Barnett, August 12, 2015.

89. Eva Fleischner, "Encounter Anew the Living God—In a Living People," in *Faith Transformed: Christian Encounters with Jews and Judaism,* ed. John Merkle (Collegeville, MN: Liturgical Press, 2003), 41.

90. I am struck by the number of women who were actively involved as this theological conversation evolved. While I am not sure any hard conclusions can be drawn from that fact, it certainly bears noting.

91. Eva Fleischner, "Response to Emil Fackenheim," in *Auschwitz: Beginning of a New Era: Reflections on the Holocaust,* ed. Eva Fleischner (New York: Ktav, 1974), 225.

92. Emil Fackenheim, *To Mend the World: Foundations of Future Jewish Thought* (New York: Schocken Books, 1982), 213.

93. Irving Greenberg, "Part III: The Third Era—Power and Politics," *Perspectives* (New York: National Jewish Center for Learning and Leadership [CLAL], 1987), http://rabbiirvinggreenberg.com/writing/monographs/, accessed June 20, 2015.

94. Conversation with John Pawlikowski.

95. Enid Nemy, "Young Women Challenge Their '2d-Class Status' in Judaism," *New York Times,* June 12, 1972, 43; Irving Spiegel, "Conservative Jews Vote for Women in Minyan," *New York Times,* September 11, 1973, 1.

96. Arthur D. Morse, *While Six Million Died: A Chronicle of American Apathy* (Woodstock, NY: Overlook Press, 1968); Lawson, *Debates,* 103; J. J. Goldberg, *Jewish Power: Inside the American Jewish Establishment* (New York: Basic Books, 1997), 145.

97. Tony Kushner, "Britain, the United States and the Holocaust: In Search of a Historiography," in *The Historiography of the Holocaust,* ed. Dan Stone (New York: Palgrave Macmillan, 2004), 259.

98. David Wyman, *Paper Walls: America and the Refugee Crisis, 1938–1941* (Amherst: University of Massachusetts Press, 1968); Henry Feingold, *The Politics of Rescue: The Roosevelt Administration and the Holocaust, 1938–1945* (New Brunswick, NJ: Rutgers University Press, 1970).

99. Monty Noam Penkower, *The Jews Were Expendable: Free World Diplomacy and the Holocaust* (Urbana: University of Illinois Press, 1983); Saul Friedman, *No Haven for the Oppressed* (Detroit: Wayne State University Press, 1973); Herbert Druks, *The Failure to Rescue* (New York: Robert Speller & Sons, 1977); Peter Novick, *The Holocaust in American Life* (Boston: Houghton Mifflin, 1999), 47.

100. Lawson, *Debates,* 106.

101. They ran ads addressed to President Roosevelt asking him "how well he was sleeping" while Jews were being murdered.

102. Peter Hayes, email to author, July 5, 2015; conversation with Peter Hayes, July 23, 2015; Peter Hayes, "From Aryanization to Auschwitz: German Corporate Complicity in the Holocaust," Oregon State University, May 2013, www.youtube.com/watch?v=pQwDm5iQaCw, accessed August 11, 2015.

103. Conversation with John Roth.

104. Conversation with Karl Schleunes, July 26, 2015.

105. Christopher Browning, "The Personal Contexts of a Holocaust Historian: War, Politics, Trials, and Professional Rivalry," in *Holocaust Scholarship: Personal Trajectories and Professional Interpretations,* ed. Christopher R. Browning, Susannah Heschel,

Michael R. Marrus, and Milton Shain (New York: Palgrave Macmillan, 2015), 48–66; conversation with Christopher Browning, July 21, 2015.

106. Conversation with Robert Ericksen, July 24, 2015.

107. Browning, "Personal Contexts"; conversation with Christopher Browning, July 21, 2015.

108. "Nasser Pledges to Destroy Israel If There Is War," *New York Times,* May 27, 1967.

109. Bassil Mardelli, *Middle-East Perspective: From Lebanon (1968–1988)* (Bloomington, IN: iUniverse, 2012), 11.

110. Silberman, *A Certain People,* 183; Lucy Dawidowicz, "American Public Opinion," *American Jewish Year Book* 69 (1968): 204–205, 209.

111. Robert Alter, "Deformations of the Holocaust," *Commentary,* February 1, 1981, https://www.commentarymagazine.com/articles/deformations-of-the-holocaust/, accessed March 4, 2015.

112. Melvin I. Urofsky, *We Are One! American Jewry and Israel* (Garden City, NY: Anchor Press, 1978), 350; Silberman, *A Certain People,* 182–183.

113. Dawidowicz, "American Public Opinion," 209.

114. Ibid., 206, 209ff.

115. Milton Himmelfarb, "In the Light of Israel's Victory," *Commentary,* October 1, 1967.

116. Hillel Levine, "The Decline of the Incredible," *New Leader* 82, no. 7 (1999): 23ff.

117. Abraham Joshua Heschel, *Israel: An Echo of Eternity,* as quoted in Jonathan Kaufman, *Broken Alliance: The Turbulent Times between Blacks and Jews in America* (New York: New American Library, 1988), 192.

118. Marshall Sklare, "Lakeville and Israel: The Six-Day War and Its Aftermath," *Midstream* 14, no. 8 (1968): 10–11.

119. Robert Alter, "Israel and the Intellectuals," *Commentary,* October 1, 1967, http://www.commentarymagazine.com/articles/israel-the-intellectuals, accessed February 27, 2014.

120. Eli N. Evans, *The Provincials: A Personal History of Jews in the South* (New York: Atheneum, 1973), 108.

121. Sklare, "Lakeville and Israel," 18, 19.

122. Deborah Lipstadt, "The Holocaust: Symbol and 'Myth' in American Jewish Life," *Forum on the Jewish People, Zionism, and Israel* 40 (1980/1981): 78; Cole, *Selling the Holocaust,* 10–11.

123. Gal Beckerman, *When They Come For Us, We'll Be Gone: The Epic Struggle to Save Soviet Jewry* (Boston: Houghton Mifflin Harcourt, 2010), 79, 164; conversation with Gal Beckerman, March 26, 2014.

124. Beckerman, *When They Come For Us*, 64, 83, 142; Elie Wiesel, *All Rivers Run to the Sea: Memoirs* (New York: Alfred A, Knopf, 1995), 377.

125. Elie Wiesel, *The Jews of Silence: A Personal Report on Soviet Jewry* (New York: Holt, Rinehart and Winston, 1966), 13–14, 19–20, 23–24, as cited in Beckerman, *When They Come For Us*, 144–145.

126. Benjamin Nathans, "The Wild Desire to Leave: On Soviet Jewry," *The Nation*, November 29, 2010, http://www.thenation.com/article/156375/wild-desire-leave-soviet-jewry?page=full, accessed March 14, 2014.

127. Ismar Schorsch, "The Holocaust and Jewish Survival," *Midstream* 27, no. 1 (1981): 38.

128. Wiesel, *Jews of Silence*, 58–59.

129. Irving Spiegel, "Inaction Charged to Western Jews on Soviet Issue," *New York Times*, May 17, 1966.

130. In 1972 I delivered a talk at Boston's Faneuil Hall at a rally on behalf of Soviet Jewry in which I made this very point.

131. Lenore Bell, director of the library, United States Holocaust Memorial Museum, email to author, July 11, 2013; Lenore Bell, interview with author, March 7, 2014; Janis L. Young, Senior Cataloging Policy Specialist Policy and Standards Division, Library of Congress, email to author, April 11, 2014.

132. Lenore Bell email to author, March 6, 2014; Lenore Bell, "LC Holocaust Headings Survey: Analysis of Results," June 12, 1996, from the files of the Cataloging Policy and Support Office of the LOC (Washington, DC: Library of Congress, 1996), copy provided to author by Lenore Bell, July 11, 2013.

133. Hilberg, "Opening Remarks," in *Lessons and Legacies*, 13.

134. Rabinowitz, *New Lives*, 195, 196.

135. Henry Greenspan, *On Listening to Holocaust Survivors: Recounting and Life History* (Westport, CT: Praeger, 1998), 40–42.

136. Conversation with Robert Jay Lifton, November 6, 2013.

137. Robert Jay Lifton, *Death in Life—Survivors of Hiroshima* (New York: Random House, 1968), 480.

138. Robert Jay Lifton, *Witness to an Extreme Century: A Memoir* (New York: Free Press, 2011), 110.

139. Terrence Des Pres, *The Survivor: An Anatomy of Life in the Death Camps* (New York: Oxford University Press, 1976), 49, 52, 185–186, 190.

140. See Marion Kaplan, *Between Dignity and Despair: Jewish Life in Nazi Germany* (New York: Oxford University Press, 1999); Saul Friedlander, *Nazi Germany and the Jews: Vol. 1, The Years of Persecution, 1933–1939* (New York: HarperCollins, 1997).

141. Lucy Dawidowicz, *The War against the Jews, 1933–1945* (New York: Holt, Rinehart and Winston, 1975); Lucy Dawidowicz, *A Holocaust Reader* (New York: Berman House, 1976). Neither work utilized interviews with survivors.

142. It is worth noting that in Germany historians have tended to "canonize" written documents particularly from German sources but give rather short shrift to testimonies, particularly by Jewish victims, because they suffer from a putative "lack of objectivity." Dan Mikhman, "Introduction," in *Holocaust Historiography in Context: Emergence, Challenges, Polemic and Achievements*, ed. David Bankier and Dan Mikhman (Jerusalem: Yad Vashem, 2008), 58.

143. Hartman, "Closing Remarks," in *Lessons and Legacies*, 331.

144. Arlene Stein, *Reluctant Witnesses: Survivors, Their Children, and the Rise of Holocaust Consciousness* (New York: Oxford University Press, 2014), 105.

145. Rabinowitz, *New Lives*, 174.

146. *New Yorker*, January 8, 1979, 40; Hank Greenspan, "On Being a Real Survivor," *Sh'ma: A Journal of Jewish Ideas* 26, no. 511 (1996): 1–3, http://www.bjpa.org/Publications/details.cfm?PublicationID=8384, accessed March 25, 2015; Efraim Sicher, "The Future of the Past: Contemporary and Postmemory in Contemporary American Post-Holocaust Narratives," *History and Memory: Studies in Representation of the Past* 12, no. 2 (2000): 63.

147. Arlene Stein, *Reluctant Witnesses*, 164; Henry Greenspan, "Survivors' Accounts," in *Oxford Handbook of Holocaust Studies*, ed. Peter Hayes and John Roth (New York: Oxford University Press, 2010), 418 (hereafter *Oxford Handbook*); Jeffrey Shandler, "Jewish Culture," in *Oxford Handbook*, 598.

148. Judith Kestenberg, "Psychoanalytic Contributions to the Problem of Children of Survivors from Nazi Persecution," *Israeli Annals of Psychiatry and Related Sciences* 10 (1972): 311–325; Aaron Hass, *In the Shadow of the Holocaust: The Second Generation* (Cambridge: Cambridge University Press, 1990).

149. For a survey of this development see Stein, *Reluctant Witnesses*, chapter 3.

150. Helen Epstein, *Children of the Holocaust: Conversations with Sons and Daughters of Survivors* (New York: Putnam, 1979), 88.

151. Silberman, *A Certain People*, 203.

152. Irving Spiegel, "Rabbis Score Christians for Silence on Mideast," *New York Times*, June 23, 1967, 10; "Rabbinical Leaders Criticize Christians," *New York Times*, June 27, 1967, 15; Manfred Vogel, "Some Reflections on the Jewish-Christian Dialogue in Light of the Six-Day War," *Annals of American Academy of Political and Social Science* 387 (January 1970): 96–108.

153. Dawidowicz, "American Public Opinion," 219; Henry P. Van Dusen, "Letters to the Editor of the Times," *New York Times*, July 7, 1967, 32. For a response by a Christian theologian to Van Dusen's charges see Roy Eckardt, "Letters to the Editor of the

Times," *New York Times,* July 13, 1967, 36; Edward B. Fiske, "Religion: The June War—A Christian-Jewish Issue Politics or Morals Return Fire American Reaction," *New York Times,* December 31, 1967; Alice L. Eckardt and A. Roy Eckardt, "Again, Silence in the Churches," *Christian Century,* July 26, 1967, 97–72, and August 2, 1967, 922–925.

154. Renata Adler, "Letter from the Palmer House," *New Yorker,* September 23, 1967, 56ff.

155. Himmelfarb, "In the Light of Israel's Victory."

156. Kaufman, *Broken Alliance,* 44.

157. James Baldwin, "Negroes Are Anti-Semitic Because They're Anti-White," *New York Times Magazine,* April 9, 1967, 26ff.

158. Robert Gordis, "Negroes Are Anti-Semitic Because They Want a Scapegoat: A Reply to James Baldwin," *New York Times Magazine,* April 23, 1967, 28ff.

159. Robert G. Weisbord and Arthur Benjamin Stein, *Bittersweet Encounter: The Afro-American and the American Jew* (Westport, CT: Negro Universities Press, 1970), 168ff.; Goldberg, *Jewish Power,* 141.

160. Julius Lester, *All Is Well* (New York: Morrow, 1976), 153, as quoted in Clayborne Carson, "Blacks and Jews in the Civil Rights Movement," in *Strangers and Neighbors: Relations between Blacks and Jews in the United States,* ed. Maurianne Adams and John Bracey (Amherst: University of Massachusetts Press, 1999), 587; Julius Lester, *Lovesong: Becoming a Jew* (New York: Henry Holt, 1988).

161. James Baldwin and Shlomo Katz, "Of Angela Davis and 'the Jewish Housewife Headed for Dachau': An Exchange," *Midstream* 17, no. 6 (1971): 6.

162. Andrew Geddings Childs, "Ocean Hill–Brownsville and the Change in American Liberalism" (PhD diss., Florida State University, 2008), http://diginole.lib.fsu.edu/etd/3815/, accessed February 5, 2014.

163. "Third World Round Up; The Palestine Problem: Test Your Knowledge," *SNCC Newsletter,* June–July 1967, 4–5, as cited in Carson, "Blacks and Jews in the Civil Rights Movement," 583.

164. Kaufman, *Broken Alliance,* 251.

165. Baldwin, "Negroes Are Anti-Semitic Because They're Anti-White."

166. Combahee River Collective, "The Combahee River Collective Statement," in *Home Girls: A Black Feminist Anthology,* ed. Barbara Smith (New Brunswick, NJ: Rutgers University Press, 2000), 273, 275; Stein, *Reluctant Witnesses,* 150.

167. Carson, "Blacks and Jews in the Civil Rights Movement," 575.

168. Alexander, *Social Construction of Moral Universals,* 47.

169. Cynthia Ozick, "All the World Wants the Jews Dead," *Esquire,* November 1974, 103–107.

170. William Safire, "Marching through Skokie," *New York Times,* March 27, 1978.

171. Lee C. *Bollinger,* "The *Skokie* Legacy: Reflections on an 'Easy Case' and Free Speech Theory (Review of *Defending My Enemy: American Nazis, the Skokie Case, and the Risks of Freedom* by Aryeh Neier)," *Michigan Law Review* 80, no. 4 (1982): 617.

172. Philippa Strum, *When the Nazis Came to Skokie: Freedom for Speech We Hate* (Lawrence: University Press of Kansas, 1999), 4.

173. Bollinger, "The Skokie Legacy," 625–626.

174. Strum, *When the Nazis Came to Skokie,* 82–96, 147; Safire, "Marching through Skokie."

175. Historian Marion Kaplan was prompted in great measure to write her book on German Jewry during the Third Reich in order to counter this perception. Marion Kaplan, *Between Dignity and Despair* (New York: Oxford University Press, 1998).

176. Strum, *When the Nazis Came to Skokie,* 147.

177. Ibid., 10; David G. Barnum, "Decision Making in a Constitutional Democracy: Policy Formation in the Skokie Free Speech Controversy," *Journal of Politics* 44, no. 2 (1982): 492–493, http://www.jstor.org/stable/2130597, accessed March 4, 2015.

178. Strum, *When the Nazis Came to Skokie,* 147.

179. Ibid., 20, 149.

180. Daniel Dayan and Elihu Katz, *Media Events: The Live Broadcasting of History* (Cambridge, MA: Harvard University Press, 1992).

181. Gerald Green, "TV View: In Defense of *Holocaust,*" *New York Times,* April 23, 1978; Frank Rich, "Television: Reliving the Nazi Nightmare," *Time,* April 17, 1978; Ilan Avisar, *Screening the Holocaust: Cinema's Images of the Unimaginable* (Bloomington: Indiana University Press, 1988), 129; Pierre Vidal-Naquet, *Assassins of Memory: Essays on the Denial of the Holocaust* (New York: Columbia University Press, 1993), xii, xviii; Cole, *Selling the Holocaust,* 13; Ismar Schorsch, "The Holocaust and Jewish Survival," *Midstream* 27, no. 1 (1981): 38; Lance Morrow, "Television and the Holocaust," *Time,* May 1, 1978, 53.

182. Elie Wiesel, "Trivializing the Holocaust: Semi-Fact and Semi-Fiction," *New York Times,* April 16, 1978; Lawrence Langer, "The Americanization of the Holocaust on Stage and Screen," in *From Hester Street to Hollywood: The Jewish-American Stage and Screen,* ed. Sarah Blacher Cohen (Bloomington: Indiana University Press, 1983), 213–230; Alvin Rosenfeld, "The Holocaust in American Popular Culture," *Midstream* 29, no. 6 (1983): 53–59.

183. Daniel Levy and Natan Sznaider, "Memory Unbound: The Holocaust and the Formation of Cosmopolitan Memory," *European Journal of Social Theory* 5, no. 1 (2002): 7, 91, 96.

184. Jeffrey Shandler, *While America Watches: Televising the Holocaust* (New York: Oxford University Press, 1999), 164–175.

185. Hartman, "Closing Remarks," in *Lessons and Legacies,* 331. My own experience mirrored Hartman's. In the months following the broadcast many survivors related to

me that they were going to speak at schools and community venues and tell their stories for the first time.

186. Judith E. Doneson, "Holocaust Revisited: A Catalyst for Memory or Trivialization?," *Annals of the American Academy of Political and Social Science* 548 (1996): 70–77.

187. Lawrence Baron, "Film," in *The Oxford Handbook,* 450.

188. Ian Kershaw, *Hitler, the Germans, and the Final Solution* (New Haven, CT: Yale University Press, 2008), 317.

189. As quoted in Ian Buruma, "From Hirohito to Heimat," *New York Review of Books,* October 26, 1989, http://www.nybooks.com.proxy.library.emory.edu/articles/archives/1989/oct/26/from-hirohito-to-heimat/?page=2, accessed March 25, 2015.

190. David Wyman, *The Abandonment of the Jews* (New York: Pantheon Books, 1984); http://www.wymaninstitute.org/about/bio-wyman.php, accessed July 16, 2015.

191. Samuel Merlin, "American Jews and the Holocaust," *Commentary,* September 1, 1983.

192. Goldberg, *Jewish Power,* 114.

193. Refused entry into the United States, they were allowed entry by Western European nations. Many of them were later murdered when the Germans took control of those lands. Rafael Medoff, "Reply to Noah Feldman: Could FDR Have Done More to Save the Jews?," *New York Review of Books,* June 5, 2014.

194. Henry Feingold, *Bearing Witness: How America and Its Jews Responded to the Holocaust* (Syracuse, NY: Syracuse University Press, 1995), 184; Michael Marrus, "Bystanders to the Holocaust" (review of Monty Penkower's *The Jews Were Expendable: Free World Diplomacy and the Holocaust* and David Wyman's *The Abandonment of the Jews: America and the Holocaust, 1941–1945*), in *FDR and the Holocaust,* ed. Verne W. Newton (New York: St. Martin's Press, 1996).

195. Noah Feldman, "Could FDR Have Done More to Save the Jews?," *New York Review of Books,* May 8, 2014.

196. John P. Fox, "Review of *Britain and the Jews of Europe, 1939–1945* by Bernard Wasserstein," *International Affairs* 56, no. 1 (1980): 143; Lawson, *Debates on the* Holocaust, 110–111.

197. Yehuda Bauer, *The Holocaust in Historical Perspective* (Seattle: University of Washington Press, 1978), 39; Yehuda Bauer, "Whose Holocaust?" *Midstream* 26, no. 9 (1980): 43.

198. Edward T. Linenthal, *Preserving Memory: The Struggle to Create America's Holocaust Museum* (New York: Viking, 1995), 18.

199. Ibid.

200. Safire, "Marching through Skokie."

201. Stuart Eizenstat, "Interview," in *Bitburg and Beyond: Encounters in American, German, and Jewish History,* ed. Ilya Levkov (New York: Shapolsky Publishers, 1987), 339.

202. Elie Wiesel, "An Interview Unlike Any Other," in *A Jew Today*, trans. Marion Wiesel (New York: Random House, 1979), 15.

203. Rochelle G. Saidel, *Never Too Late to Remember: The Politics behind New York City's Holocaust Museum* (New York: Holmes & Meier, 1996), 34.

204. Harold Flender, "Conversation with Elie Wiesel," in *Conversations with Elie Wiesel*, ed. Robert Franciosi (Jackson: University Press of Mississippi, 2002), 25.

205. Robert Alter, *After the Tradition: Essays on Modern Jewish Writing* (New York: E. P. Dutton, 1969), 151.

206. Michael Berenbaum, "Is the Memory of Holocaust Being Exploited?," *Midstream* 50, no. 3 (2004): 2–8, http://www.midstreamthf.com/200404/feature.html, accessed February 20, 2015.

207. Steven Schwarzschild, "Toward Jewish Unity," *Judaism*, 15, no 2 (Spring 1966): 157. For a comprehensive analysis of Wiesel's work see Michael Berenbaum, *Elie Wiesel: God, the Holocaust, and the Children of Israel* (New York: Berman House, 1994).

208. Lifton, *Death in Life*, 484, 491, 496, 502, 521, 527, 538, 553.

209. I. B. Singer, "A State of Fear," *New York Times*, January 8, 1967.

210. Herbert Lottman, "Paris Literary Letter," *New York Times Book Review*, February 16, 1969.

211. Israel Shenker, "The Concerns of Elie Wiesel: Today and Yesterday," *New York Times*, February 10, 1970.

212. Saidel, *Never Too Late*, 47.

213. Carter mandated and the commission agreed that it would be a federal museum but would be built primarily with private funds. Elie Wiesel, chairman, *Report to the President: President's Commission on the Holocaust*, September 27, 1979, 17 (Washington, DC: Reprinted by the United States Holocaust Memorial Museum, 2005), http://www.ushmm.org/m/pdfs/20050707-presidents-commission-holocaust.pdf, accessed March 25, 2015 (hereafter *President's Commission Report*).

214. Jimmy Carter, "30th Anniversary of the State of Israel Remarks of the President and Prime Minister Menachem Begin at a White House Reception," in *The American Presidency Project*, ed. Gerhard Peters and John T. Woolley, May 1, 1978, http://www.presidency.ucsb.edu/ws/?pid=30730, accessed February 24, 2014. For additional comments made by President Carter see Young, "America's Holocaust," 73.

215. Emil Fackenheim, *The Jewish Return into History: Reflections in the Age of Auschwitz and a New Jerusalem* (New York: Schocken Books, 1978), iii, 279.

216. Timothy Snyder, *Black Earth: The Holocaust as History and Warning* (New York: Tim Duggan Books, 2015), 140.

217. Eichmann had come to Hungary in March 1944 with approximately 200 SS men. Yet he managed to murder over 400,000 Jews in approximately ten weeks. The

secret to his "success" was that he had the enthusiastic aid of scores of Hungarian police, gendarmes, and ordinary citizens.

218. Eric Lichtblau, *The Nazis Next Door: How America Became a Safe Haven for Hitler's Men* (New York: Houghton Mifflin Harcourt, 2014).

219. Linenthal, *Preserving Memory*, 39, 41, 42, 45.

220. *President's Commission Report*, 3.

221. In 1941 Reichskommissar Lohse asked Alfred Rosenberg, the Reich's specialist on the Jews, if Jews in the East should be exterminated "without taking economic interest into consideration, Wehrmacht needs for skilled workers in the arms industry, for example." He was told quite explicitly: "No economic consideration whatever will be taken into account in the solution of this problem." "Nuremberg Documents PS-3666," as cited in Saul Friedlander, *Reflections of Nazism: An Essay on Kitsch and Death* (New York: Harper & Row, 1982), 124.

222. *President's Commission Report*, 3–4.

223. Henryk Grynberg, "Appropriating the Holocaust," *Commentary*, November 1, 1982.

224. Elie Wiesel, "Pilgrimage to the Country of Night," *New York Times Magazine*, November 4, 1979.

225. Mordechai Altshuler, "Jewish Holocaust Commemoration Activity in the USSR under Stalin," *Shoah Resource Center*, http://www.yadvashem.org/odot_pdf/Microsoft%20Word%20-%205422.pdf , accessed March 25, 2015.

226. Andrew Charlesworth, "Contesting Places of Memory: The Case of Auschwitz," *Environmental and Planning D* 12, no. 5 (1994): 582ff.

227. Paula Hyman, "New Debate on the Holocaust," *New York Times Magazine*, September 14, 1980, 78.

228. Manfred Gerstenfeld, *The Abuse of Holocaust Memory: Distortions and Responses* (Jerusalem: Jerusalem Center for Public Affairs, 2009), 87.

229. Conversation with John Pawlikowski.

230. During the war itself Jews were not the only ones who thought that what was being done to them was fundamentally different from the oppression faced by other groups. Other European victims of Nazi oppression had the same perspective. Many Poles, for example, feared that, if the Germans won, eventually they might be subjected to the same fate as the Jews. The commander of the Polish underground Home Army issued an order in late 1942 that referred to the "extermination of the Jews" and that articulated his fear that, should the Germans prevail, they would "commence to liquidate the Poles in the same manner." When the Polish uprising against the Nazis in August 1944 collapsed and the Germans deported the inhabitants of Warsaw, many among them anticipated that they would share the same fate as the Jews. Bauer, *The Holocaust in Historical Perspective*, 35–36.

231. Karl Jaspers, "The Criminal State and German Responsibility: A Dialogue," *Commentary*, February 1, 1966, 35; George M. Kren and Leon Rappoport, *The Holocaust and the Crisis of Human Behavior* (New York: Holmes & Meier, 1980), 3; Isaac Deutscher, *The Non-Jewish Jew and Other Essays*, ed. Tamara Deutscher (New York: Hill and Wang, 1968), as cited in Marrus, *The Holocaust in History*, 8.

232. Arendt, *EIJ*, 267–268.

CHAPTER 3 — IN A NEW KEY

1. Jimmy Carter, "Address by President Jimmy Carter, April 1979, Capitol Rotunda, April 24, 1979," in *Report to the President: President's Commission on the Holocaust*, Appendix C, September 27, 1979, 26 (Washington, DC: Reprinted by the United States Holocaust Memorial Museum, 2005), http://www.ushmm.org/m/pdfs/20050707-presidents-commission-holocaust.pdf, accessed March 25, 2015 (hereafter *President's Commission Report*).

2. Walter F. Mondale, "Remarks by Vice President Walter F. Mondale, April 24, 1979, Capitol Rotunda," in *President's*, Appendix D, *Commission Report* 28.

3. Peter Novick, *The Holocaust in American Life* (Boston: Houghton Mifflin, 1999), 214. There were, of course, other death tolls that were used. At Nuremberg, Justice Robert Jackson, the American prosecutor, used the figure of 5.7 million. Hilberg calculated the toll as 5.2 million. But no serious historian had even contemplated such a numerical construct as eleven million. Before the Carter White House's use of this figure, other politicians and public officials cited it. In April 1978, shortly before the White House announcement of the Holocaust council, Senator Wendell Anderson, a Democrat from Minnesota, introduced legislation calling for a "President's Commission on the Victims of the Holocaust," which would oversee a national design competition for a memorial to honor the "eleven million innocent victims." Edward T. Linenthal, *Preserving Memory: The Struggle to Create America's Holocaust Museum* (New York: Viking, 1995), 20.

4. Despite the fact that the number makes no historical sense, it has gained significant popular currency. See, for example, Terese Pencak Schwartz, *Holocaust—Non-Jewish Holocaust Victims*, http://www.holocaustforgotten.com/, accessed February 18, 2014, and Terese Pencak Schwartz, "Holocaust Forgotten—Five Million Non-Jewish Victims (Volume 1)," *Polonia Music*, http://www.poloniamusic.com/Books_Holocaust_Forgotten-Five_Million_Non-Jewish_Victims_Volume_1.html, accessed February 18, 2014.

5. Michael Berenbaum insists that Wiesel knew that the White House intended to use this number. Michael Berenbaum, "Is the Holocaust Being Exploited?," *Midstream* 50, no. 3 (2004): 28, http://www.midstreamthf.com/200404/feature.html, accessed June 9, 2015.

6. Linenthal, *Preserving Memory*, 43.

7. Bettina Stangneth, *Eichmann before Jerusalem: The Unexamined Life of a Mass Murderer* (New York: Alfred A. Knopf, 2014).

8. Tom Segev, *Simon Wiesenthal: The Life and Legends* (New York: Doubleday, 2010), 344.

9. Wiesenthal figured as a character in the film version of Frederick Forsyth's *The Odessa File* (1974). In the film adaptation of Ira Levin's novel *The Boys from Brazil*, the main character was based on a Wiesenthal-like character and was played by Olivier. Frederick Forsyth, *The Odessa File* (New York: Viking Press, 1972); *The Odessa File*, directed by Ronald Neame (1974; Culver City, CA: Columbia TriStar Home Video, 1999), DVD; Ira Levin, *The Boys from Brazil* (New York: Random House, 1976); *The Boys from Brazil* (Los Angeles: Twentieth Century–Fox, 1978).

10. Norbert Frei, *Adenauer's Germany and the Nazi Past: The Politics of Amnesty and Integration* (New York: Columbia University Press, 2002), 55.

11. Daniel Finkelstein, "Is It Right to Expose Wiesenthal?," *Jewish Chronicle* (London), August 20, 2009, http://www.thejc.com/comment/columnists/it-right-expose-wiesenthal, accessed June 25, 2014.

12. Segev, *Wiesenthal*, 345, 400ff.

13. Michael Getler, "The Hunter's Remembrance," *Washington Post*, April 1, 1979.

14. Segev, *Wiesenthal*, 322.

15. Elie Wiesel, *And the Sea Is Never Full: Memoirs, 1969–*, trans. Marion Wiesel (New York: Alfred A. Knopf, 1999), 129. For the Wiesel/Wiesenthal relationship see Tom Segev's in-depth and sympathetic *Wiesenthal*, 319–327.

16. Yehuda Bauer, "Don't Resist," *Tikkun* 4, no. 3 (1989): 67ff.; Yehuda Bauer, "Po tamun hahevdel," *Ha'aretz*, November 23, 2005, as quoted in Tom Segev, *Wiesenthal*, 322; Novick, *The Holocaust in American Life*, 215. At a meeting I had with Bauer and Guttman in Jerusalem in 1999 they both recalled how appalled they had been by Wiesenthal's manipulation of history.

17. Timothy Snyder, *Bloodlands* (New York: Basic Books, 2010), 355–357; Timothy Snyder, *Black Earth: The Holocaust as History and Warning* (New York: Crown, 2015), 166ff.

18. Over the years I have received frequent complaints from people, many of whom make a point of identifying themselves as non-Jews, about my references to "the Six Million." They contend that I am ignoring five million non-Jewish victims and privileging Jewish ones. When I try to explain the source of the eleven million figure they generally become even more convinced of my narrow chauvinism.

19. Robert Alter, "Deformations of the Holocaust," *Commentary*, February 1, 1981, https://www.commentarymagazine.com/articles/deformations-of-the-holocaust/, accessed March 4, 2015.

20. Jacob Neusner, *Stranger at Home: 'The Holocaust,' Zionism, and American Judaism* (Chicago: University of Chicago Press, 1981), 83–86.

21. Paula Hyman, "New Debate on the Holocaust," *New York Times Magazine*, September 14, 1980, 78.

22. Ismar Schorsch, "The Holocaust and Jewish Survival," *Midstream* 27, no. 1 (1981): 38, 40.

23. Conversation with John Roth, July 25, 2015.

24. David Engel, *Historians of the Jews and the Holocaust* (Stanford, CA: Stanford University Press, 2010), 68–69, 245n.60, 251n.188.

25. Yaffa Eliach, "President's Commission on the Holocaust: Reflections," n.d., Yaffa Eliach Papers, as quoted in Linenthal, *Preserving Memory*, 13.

26. Deborah E. Lipstadt, "Invoking the Holocaust," *Judaism* 30, no. 3 (1981): 336–337.

27. I saw this advertisement on the wall of a campus Hillel in the late 1970s and was discomfited by it. Ibid., 337.

28. Hyman, "New Debate," 78.

29. Arthur M. Schlesinger Jr., "The Rush to Reconcile," in *Bitburg in Moral and Political Perspective*, ed. Geoffrey Hartman (Bloomington: Indiana University Press, 1986), 182 (hereafter *Bitburg in Moral and Political Perspective*); Peter Baldwin, "The *Historikerstreit* in Context," in *Reworking the Past: Hitler, the Holocaust, and the Historians' Debate*, ed. Peter Baldwin (Boston: Beacon Press, 1990), 28 (hereafter *Reworking the Past*).

30. Charles Maier, *The Unmasterable Past: History, Holocaust, and German National Identity* (Cambridge, MA: Harvard University Press, 1988), 9–10; Baldwin, "The *Historikerstreit*," 28.

31. James F. Clarity and Warren Weaver Jr., "Briefing: Dachau Visit Unlikely," *New York Times*, January 24, 1985.

32. Ronald Reagan, "The President's News Conference," in *The American Presidency Project*, ed. Gerhard Peters and John T. Woolley, March 21, 1985, http://www.presidency.ucsb.edu/ws/index.php?pid=38372, accessed July 10, 2014.

33. Geoffrey Hartman, "Introduction: 1985," in *Bitburg in Moral and Political Perspective*, 9.

34. Raul Hilberg, "Bitburg as Symbol," in ibid., 18.

35. William Bole, "Bitburg: The American Scene," in ibid., 68.

36. "SS War Veterans Hold Reunion, Support Reagan's Graves Visit," *Los Angeles Times*, May 4, 1985.

37. Ronald Reagan, "Remarks and a Question-and-Answer Session with Regional Editors and Broadcasters," in *The American Presidency Project*, ed. Gerhard Peters and John T. Woolley, April 18, 1985, http://www.presidency.ucsb.edu/ws/index.php?pid=38498&st=reagan&st1., accessed July 10, 2014; Hilberg, "Bitburg as Symbol," in *Bitburg in Moral and Political Perspective*, 19.

38. Alvin H. Rosenfeld, "Another Revisionism: Popular Culture and the Changing Image of the Holocaust," in *Bitburg in Moral and Political Perspective*, 94.

39. Bole, "Bitburg: The American Scene," 68.

40. John Tagliabue, "Summit in Europe: Bitburg Graves Cast a Pall; SS Veterans Feel 'Rehabilitated' by Reagan Visit," *New York Times*, May 3, 1985.

41. Charles Silberman, "Speaking Truth to Power," in *Bitburg and Beyond: Encounters in American, German, and Jewish History*, ed. Ilya Levkov (New York: Shapolsky Publishers, 1987), 346 (hereafter *Bitburg and Beyond*).

42. Elie Wiesel, "Remarks, White House, April 19, 1985," in *Bitburg and Beyond*, 42.

43. The *Washington Post* published two side-by-side stories about the incident on the front page. Under a banner headline, "Honoring Wiesel, Reagan Confronts the Holocaust," there was a story by David Hoffman, "Bergen-Belsen Put on Trip Itinerary: Honoring a Survivor, Reagan Faces Holocaust," and one by Lou Cannon, "Reagan Team Falters on Damage Control," *Washington Post*, April 20, 1985; Jeffrey Shandler, *While America Watches: Televising the Holocaust* (New York: Oxford University Press, 1999), 207.

44. A. Roy Eckardt, "The Christian World Goes to Bitburg," in *Bitburg in Moral and Political Perspective*, 80–89; Bole, "Bitburg: The American Scene," 71–72; Simone Veil, "Reconciliation Does Not Mean Forgetting," in *Bitburg and Beyond*, 630; Charles Maier, "Immoral Equivalence: Revising the Past for the Kohl Era," in *Reworking the Past*, 39.

45. "82 Senators Urge Reagan to Cancel His Cemetery Visit: Anger over German Trip; Lawmakers Also Call on Kohl to Withdraw Invitation to See Graves in Bitburg," *New York Times*, April 27, 1985.

46. Hedrick Smith, "Delicate Reagan Path: He Tries to End Damage from Bitburg by Carefully Balancing His Comments," *New York Times*, May 6, 1985. For a sampling of media reactions see Hartman, *Bitburg*, 173–178; and Levkov, *Bitburg and Beyond*, 440–482.

47. Boyle, "Bitburg: The American Scene," 71, 77.

48. Lance Morrow, "Essay: Forgiveness to the Injured Doth Belong," *Time*, May 20, 1985, 90.

49. Maier, *The Unmasterable Past*, 14.

50. Helmut Kohl, "Address by Helmut Kohl, Chancellor of the Federation Republic of Germany, during the Ceremony Marking the 40th Anniversary of the Liberation of the Concentration Camps, April 21, 1945," in *Bitburg in Moral and Political Perspective*, 244; James M. Markham, "Kohl Says Shame of Nazis Persists: At Belsen Rites, He Accepts Responsibility for Crimes," *New York Times*, April 22, 1985.

51. Markham, "Kohl Says Shame of Nazis Persists."

52. Richard von Weizsäcker, "President Richard von Weizsäcker, May 8, 1985," in *Verhandlungen des Bundestages*, trans. in *Bitburg in Moral and Political Perspective*, 262–271.

53. Leslie Maitland Werner, "Waldheim Barred from Entering U.S. over Role in War: Tied to Nazi Oppression in U.S. Action Is First Such Move against a Head of State," *New York Times*, April 28, 1987. See also Segev, *Wiesenthal*, 362–375; Eli M. Rosenbaum, *Betrayal: The Untold Story of the Kurt Waldheim Investigation and Cover-Up* (New York: St. Martin's Press, 1993).

54. Gregor Thum, "Ethnic Cleansing in Eastern Europe after 1945," *Contemporary European History* 19, no. 1 (2010): 75–81.

55. Roy Gutman, "American Public Opinion, the Media, and Genocide Prevention Transcript," *United States Holocaust Memorial Museum.org*, May 2002, transcription of event, http://www.ushmm.org/confront-genocide/speakers-and-events/all-speakers-and-events/genocide-prevention-morality-and-the-national-interest/american-public-opinion-the-media-and-genocide-prevention-transcript, accessed May 24, 2015.

56. I conducted the research on and helped design a portion of the exhibit that dealt with the American response to the Holocaust. The notion of America's failure to respond is a central motif of this portion of the exhibit. After the museum opened President Bill Clinton appointed me to two consecutive terms on the Holocaust Council. President Barack Obama reappointed me to one term. I also received the Resnick fellowship and was in residence at the museum while writing my book *The Eichmann Trial*.

57. This comment was made to me at the dedication of the museum.

58. Pierre Nora and Lawrence D. Kritzman, *Realms of Memory: Rethinking the French Past*, vol. 1, trans. Arthur Goldhammer (New York: Columbia University Press, 1996); Pierre Nora, *The State*, vol. 1 of *Rethinking France: Les Lieux de Mémoire* (Chicago: University of Chicago Press, 1999). It is hard to speak of the intellectual focus on memory without mentioning Yosef Hayim Yerushalmi's *Zakhor: Jewish History and Jewish Memory* (Seattle: University of Washington Press, 1982). It appeared shortly before both Nora's work and that of E. J. Hobsbawn and T. O. Ranger, eds., *The Invention of Tradition* (New York: Cambridge University Press, 1983).

59. Gavriel D. Rosenfeld, *Hi Hitler: How the Nazi Past Is Being Normalized in Contemporary Culture* (Cambridge: Cambridge University Press, 2014), 15–16.

60. Peter Hayes, *Industry and Ideology: I.G. Farben in the Nazi Era* (New York: Cambridge, 2000); Peter Hayes, "Industry under the Swastika," in *Enterprise in the Period of Fascism in Europe*, ed. Harold James and Jakob Tanner (Aldershot: Ashgate, 2002), 26–37; Wolf Gruner, *Jewish Forced Labor under The Nazis: Economic Needs and Racial Aims, 1938–1944* (New York: Cambridge University Press, 2006); Christopher R. Browning, *Remembering Survival: Inside a Nazi Slave-Labor Camp* (New York: W. W. Norton, 2010).

61. Lynn H. Nicholas, *The Rape of Europa: The Fate of Europe's Treasures in the Third Reich and the Second World War* (New York: Alfred A. Knopf, 1995).

62. Avi Beker, "Restitution Issues Destroy National Myths," in *Europe's Crumbling Myths: The Post-Holocaust Origins of Today's Anti-Semitism*, ed. Manfred Gerstenfeld (Jerusalem: Jerusalem Center for Public Affairs, 2003).

63. Peter Hayes, "Plunder and Restitution," in *Oxford Handbook of Holocaust Studies*, ed. Peter Hayes and John Roth (New York: Oxford University Press, 2010), 551–553 (hereafter *Oxford Handbook*); Michael Marrus, "Restitution and Its Discontents," in *How Was It Possible? A Holocaust Reader*, ed. Peter Hayes (Lincoln: University of Nebraska Press,

2015), 852; Gerald Feldman, "The Historian and Holocaust Restitution: Personal Experiences and Reflections," *Berkeley Journal of International Law* 23, no. 3, article 6 (2005), http://dx.doi.org/doi:10.15779/Z38DH18, accessed December 21, 2015.

64. These cases instigated significant work on the topic. Martin Dean, *Robbing the Jews: The Confiscation of Jewish Property in the Holocaust, 1933–1945* (New York: Cambridge University Press, 2008); Gerald Feldman, *Allianz and the German Insurance Business 1933–1945* (New York: Cambridge University Press, 2001); Peter Hayes, *From Cooperation to Complicity: Degussa in the Third Reich* (New York: Cambridge University Press, 2004); Michael Marrus, *Some Measure of Justice: The Holocaust Era Restitution Campaign of the 1990s* (Madison: University of Wisconsin Press, 2009).

65. "The ICRC in WW II: The Holocaust," *International Committee of the Red Cross.org*, January 24, 2014, https://www.icrc.org/eng/resources/documents/misc/history-holocauste-020205.htm, accessed November 11, 2015.

66. Irvin Molotsky, "Red Cross Admits Knowing of the Holocaust during the War," *New York Times*, December 19, 1996; Jean-Claude Favez, *The Red Cross and the Holocaust*, trans. John and Beryl Fletcher (Cambridge: Cambridge University Press, 1999).

67. Cardinal Edward Idris Cassidy, "We Remember: A Reflection on the Vatican and the Shoah" (presentation, Press Conference for Commission for Religious Relations with the Jews, the Vatican, March 16, 1998), http://www.vatican.va/roman_curia/pontifical_councils/chrstuni/documents/rc_pc_chrstuni_doc_16031998_shoah_en.html, accessed March 1, 2015.

68. Undersecretary Stuart Eizenstat, "Closing Plenary Statement at the London Conference on Nazi Gold," December 4, 1997, http://www.state.gov/1997–2001-NOPDFS/////policy_remarks/971204_eizen_nazigold.html, accessed March 2015.

69. Michael Dobbs, "Albright's Family Tragedy Comes to Light: Secretary Says She Didn't Know That 3 Grandparents Were Jewish Victims of Holocaust," *Washington Post*, February 4, 1997.

70. Frank Rich, "The Albright Question," *New York Times*, February 19, 1997.

71. Lisa Hostein, "Coming to Terms with Madeleine Albright Revelations," *J-weekly.com*, February 14, 1997, http://www.jweekly.com/article/full/5071/coming-to-terms-with-madeleine-albright-revelations/, accessed March 3, 2015.

72. Maier, *The Unmasterable Past*, 30.

73. Ernst Nolte, "Between Myth and Revisionism? The Third Reich in the Perspective of the 1980s," in *Aspects of the Third Reich*, ed. H. W. Koch (New York: St. Martin's Press, 1985), as cited in Anson Rabinbach, "The Jewish Question in the German Question," in *Reworking the Past*, 62–63.

74. Maier, *The Unmasterable Past*, 15.

75. William John Niven, *Facing the Nazi Past: United Germany and the Legacy of the Third Reich* (London: Routledge, 2002).

76. Peter Baldwin, *Reworking the Past: Hitler, the Holocaust, and the Historians' Debate*, ed. Peter Baldwin (Boston: Beacon Press, 1990), 28–29.

77. Warwick Hester, "On the Streets of Truth," *Der Weg* 8 (1954): 574, as quoted in Stangneth, *Eichmann before Jerusalem*, 152; see also 152–153.

78. Deborah Lipstadt, *History on Trial: My Day in Court with a Holocaust Denier* (New York: Ecco, 2006).

79. Samantha Power, *A Problem from Hell: America and the Age of Genocide* (New York: Harper Perennial, 2003); Samantha Power, "To Suffer by Comparison," *Daedalus* 128, no. 2 (1999): 52–53.

80. John Torpey, "Making Whole What Has Been Smashed: Reflections on Reparations," *Journal of Modern History* 73, no. 2 (2001): 341.

81. Samuel Freedman, "Laying Claim to Sorrow Beyond Words," *New York Times*, December 13, 1997.

82. Novick, *The Holocaust in American Life*, 194, 330n.100.

83. Power, "To Suffer," 52–53; Novick, *The Holocaust in American Life*, 241.

84. James M. Jasper and Dorothy Nelkin, *The Animal Rights Crusade: The Growth of a Moral Protest* (New York: Free Press, 1992), 47, as cited in Manfred Gerstenfeld, *The Abuse of Holocaust Memory: Distortions and Responses* (Jerusalem: Jerusalem Center for Public Affairs, 2009), 120–121.

85. Al Gore, "An Ecological Kristallnacht," *New York Times*, March 19, 1989.

86. Yitzchak Mais, "Institutionalizing the Holocaust: Issues Related to the Establishment of Holocaust Memorial Centers," *Midstream* 34, no. 9 (1988): 16–20.

87. Jeffrey Alexander, *Remembering the Holocaust: A Debate* (New York: Oxford University Press, 2009), 52–53.

88. Lucy Dawidowicz, *The Holocaust and the Historians* (Cambridge, MA: Harvard University Press, 1981), 15.

89. Yehuda Bauer, *The Holocaust in Historical Perspective* (Seattle: University of Washington Press, 1978), 35–36; Dawidowicz, *The Holocaust and the Historians*, 11–15.

90. Michael Marrus, *The Holocaust in History* (New York: Meridian, 1987), 24; Linenthal, *Preserving Memory*, 11.

91. Elie Wiesel, "Trivializing the Holocaust: Semi-Fact and Semi-Fiction," *New York Times*, April 16, 1978; A. Roy Eckardt with Alice L. Eckardt, *Long Night's Journey into Day: Life and Faith after the Holocaust* (Detroit: Wayne State University Press, 1982), 43–50.

92. Bauer, *The Holocaust in Historical Perspective*, 30–31, 37.

93. Yehuda Bauer, as quoted in Alan Rosenberg and Evelyn Silverman, "The Issue of the Holocaust as a Unique Event," in *Genocide in Our Time: An Annotated Bibliography with Analytical Introductions*, ed. Michael N. Dobkowski and Isidor Wallimann (Ann Arbor, MI: Pierian Press, 1992), 48.

94. Yehuda Bauer, "Holocaust and Genocide: Some Comparisons," in *Lessons and Legacies*, ed. Peter Hayes (Evanston, IL: Northwestern University Press, 1991), 37.

95. Alan Rosenberg, "The Crisis in Knowing," in *Echoes from the Holocaust: Philosophical Reflections on a Dark Time*, ed. Alan Rosenberg and Gerald E. Myers (Philadelphia: Temple University Press, 1988), 381–382.

96. Schorsch, "The Holocaust and Jewish Survival," 39.

97. Gavriel D. Rosenfeld, "The Politics of Uniqueness: Reflections on the Recent Polemical Turn in Holocaust and Genocide Scholarship," *Holocaust and Genocide Studies* 13, no. 1 (1999): 28–61; Steven Katz, *The Holocaust in Historical Context* (New York: Oxford University Press, 1994).

98. Hubert Locke, "The Goldhagen Fallacy," in *Hyping the Holocaust: Scholars Answer Goldhagen*, ed. Franklin H. Littell (East Rockaway, NY: Cummings & Hathaway, 1997), 21 (hereafter *Hyping the Holocaust*); Roger W. Smith, "'Ordinary Germans,' the Holocaust, and Responsibility: *Hitler's Willing Executioners* in Moral Perspective," in *Hyping the Holocaust*, 56, 57; Yehuda Bauer, "Daniel J. Goldhagen's View of the Holocaust," in *Hyping the Holocaust*, 62; Raul Hilberg, "Is There a New Anti-Semitism? A Conversation with Raul Hilberg," *Logos: A Journal of Modern Society and Culture* 6, no. 1–2 (2007), http://www.logosjournal.com/issue_6.1–2/hilberg.htm, accessed November 6, 2015.

99. Adi Gordon, Amos Morris Reich, and Amos Goldberg, "An Interview with Professor Hans Mommsen," *Yad Vashem*, December 12, 1997, 36, 38–39, http://goo.gl/MlCQUU, accessed November 11, 2015.

100. Bauer, "Goldhagen's View," 71; Erich Geldbach, "Goldhagen—Another Kind of Revisionism," in *Hyping the Holocaust*, 93.

101. Dalia Ofer and Lenore Weitzman, eds., *Women and the Holocaust* (New Haven, CT: Yale University Press, 1998).

102. Gabriel Schoenfeld, "Auschwitz and the Professors," *Commentary*, June 1, 1998, 45.

103. David Stannard, "Uniqueness as Denial: The Politics of Genocide Scholarship," in *Is the Holocaust Unique? Perspectives on Comparative Genocide*, ed. Alan S. Rosenbaum (Boulder, CO: Westview Press, 1996), 198; Rosenfeld, *Hi Hitler*, 82–84. Churchill challenged the university decision; though a jury upheld his challenge, the higher courts did not.

104. Novick, *The Holocaust in American Life*, 154–159, 202.

105. Ibid., 1; Berel Lang, "On Peter Novick's 'The Holocaust in American Life,'" *Jewish Social Studies* 7, no. 3 (2001): 149–158; Novick, *The Holocaust in American Life*, 98, 171.

106. David Roskies and Naomi Diamant, *Holocaust Literature (A History and Guide)* (Waltham, MA: Brandeis University Press, 2013), 9.

107. Lang, "On Peter Novick," 150.

108. Lipstadt, "Invoking," 337ff.

109. Novick, *The Holocaust in American Life*, 103, 195, 198, 202; Lang, "On Peter Novick," 150.

110. Goldberg, *Jewish Power*, 9.

111. Conversation with Christopher Browning, July 17, 2015.

112. Doris L. Bergen, "Protestants, Catholics, Mennonites, and Jews: Identities and Institutions in Holocaust Studies," in *Holocaust Scholarship: Personal Trajectories and Professional Interpretations*, ed. Christopher R. Browning, Susannah Heschel, Michael R. Marrus, and Milton Shain (Houndmills, Basingstoke: Palgrave Macmillan, 2015), 144–156.

113. Saul Friedlander, "Prologue," in *Lessons and Legacies IX*, ed. Jonathan Petropoulos, Lynn Rapaport, and John K. Roth (Evanston, IL: Northwestern University Press, 2010), 3, emphasis in original. My thanks to Doris Bergen for bringing Friedlander's observation to my attention.

114. Bergen, "Protestants, Catholics, Mennonites, and Jews."

115. Novick, *The Holocaust in American Life*, 219.

116. A. J. Wolf, "The Centrality of the Holocaust as a Mistake," in *After Tragedy and Triumph: Essays in Modern Jewish Thought and the American Experience*, ed. Michael Berenbaum (New York: Cambridge University Press, 1990), 44–45, as quoted in Tim Cole, *Selling the Holocaust: From Auschwitz to Schindler: How History Is Bought, Packaged, and Sold* (New York: Routledge, 1999), 1.

117. He bases his comments about the cookbook on a quote from Norman Finkelstein's *The Holocaust Industry: Reflections on the Exploitation of Jewish Suffering* (New York: Verso, 2003), a highly polemical book that I have chosen not to analyze because it is so riddled with errors and misstatements of fact, such as this one about the cookbook.

118. Conversation with Michael Berenbaum, June 20, 2015.

119. Berenbaum, "Is the Holocaust Being Exploited?" One of the major donors to the museum wanted the exhibit to end with a display of the flags of the various American military units that participated in the liberation of the camps. (I was privy to this exchange between the donor and the director at the time.) Having visited the museum countless times I can personally attest to the fact that for most visitors the flags are something they pass by with some interest while the filmed interviews with the survivors mesmerize them. Visitors tend to watch the films far longer than museum designers had anticipated.

120. Brad Prager, "Mediated Memories: The Influence of Spielberg's Hollywood Hit on *Inheritance* and *Spielberg's List*," in *After the Fact: The Holocaust in Twenty-First Century Documentary Film* (New York: Bloomsbury, 2015), 69–70.

121. Novick, *The Holocaust in American Life*, 214.

122. Cole, *Selling the Holocaust*, 116, 118–120.

123. Ibid., 81.

124. For the background on the two versions of this text see Gilbert Rosenthal, "The Strange Tale of a Familiar Text," *G'vanim: The Journal of the Academy for Jewish Religion* 3, no. 1 (2007): 57ff.

125. Cole, *Selling the Holocaust*, 19. Philip Gourevitch originally applied the term "peepshow" to this portion of the museum exhibit. Cole's repeated use of it suggests that he wholeheartedly embraces it as appropriate. Philip Gourevitch, "Behold Now Behemoth: The Holocaust Museum," *Harper's Magazine*, July 1993, 61.

126. Yehuda Bauer wondered in 1988 whether the fact that the Holocaust had become "a ruling symbol in our culture . . . is good or bad." Cole picked up on that rumination. Cole, *Selling the Holocaust*, 18.

127. Ibid., 188.

128. In recent years members of the ultra-Orthodox community have come to recognize that the story as told, however affirming, cannot be true. As one teacher in a *Bais Yaakov* seminary, a school that is part of the same system that the ninety-three girls attended, observed, there are "enough stories of true bravery by Jewish girls in the Holocaust" that using this one is unnecessary. Here, too, as in the case with Simon Wiesenthal, good intentions led to a false result. Ezra Reichman, "The Myth of the 93 Cracow Girls Who Took Their Lives in the Holocaust Exposed," *What's News? The Voice of the Orthodox Jewish Community*, April 27, 2009, http://www.vosizneias .com/30766/2009/04/27/israel-the-myth-of-the-93-cracow-girls-who-took-their-lives-in-the-holocaust-exposed/, accessed June 9, 2014.

129. Cole, *Selling the Holocaust*, 188.

130. In 1964 in *New York Times Co. v. Sullivan* the Supreme Court ruled that a "public figure" (politician, celebrity, business leader, or someone who willingly puts themselves in the public eye) cannot sue for defamation unless they can prove the writer acted with actual malice, that is, either with reckless disregard for the truth or with knowledge that what they were writing was false.

131. Lipstadt, *History on Trial*. Much of the documentation on that trial can be found at the website Holocaust Denial on Trial, http://www.hdot.org. The closest parallel to my trial was the suit against *Exodus* author Leon Uris in England in 1964 by a Polish doctor who, as a prisoner in Auschwitz, conducted cruel medical experiments. Because Uris exaggerated the number of deaths for which the doctor was responsible, he was found guilty. However, in a symbolic commentary, the court awarded the doctor a half-penny, "the smallest coin in the realm," in damages.

132. Torpey, "Making Whole," 338; Rosenfeld, *Hi Hitler*, 91–92.

133. A. Dirk Moses, "Revisiting a Founding Assumption of Genocide Studies," *Genocide Studies and Prevention* 6, no. 3 (2011): 287–300, https://muse.jhu.edu/journals/ genocide_studies_and_prevention/summary/v006/6.3.moses.html, accessed June 9, 2015.

134. Novick, *The Holocaust in American Life*, 14; Lang, "On Peter Novick," 157–158n.3.

135. Marla Stone, "When Memory Makes Policy: Bosnia, Kosovo, and the Holocaust," *New England Journal of History* 5, no. 1 (2003): 20.

136. Roy Gutman, *A Witness to Genocide: The 1993 Pulitzer Prize–Winning Dispatches on the "Ethnic Cleansing" of Bosnia* (New York: Macmillan, 1993), xiii; Power, "To Suffer," 65n.44.

137. Power, "To Suffer," 53; Stone, "When Memory Makes Policy," 27–28.

138. Elaine Sciolino, "U.S. Goals on Bosnia," *New York Times*, May 19, 1993.

139. Samantha Power, *A Problem from Hell*, 298.

140. Alan Steinweis, "The Auschwitz Analogy: Holocaust Memory and American Debates over Intervention in Bosnia and Kosovo in the 1990s," *Holocaust and Genocide Studies* 19, no. 2 (2005): 282–283; Rosenfeld, *Hi Hitler*, 89–92.

141. Madeleine K. Albright, *Voices on Anti-Semitism Podcast: Madeleine K. Albright*, podcast audio, United States Holocaust Memorial Museum, MP3, 7:11, http://www.ushmm.org/confront-antisemitism/antisemitism-podcast/madeleine-k-albright, accessed March 21, 2015; Steinweis, "The Auschwitz Analogy," 276–289; Power, *A Problem from Hell*, 326.

142. Torpey, "Making Whole," 335–358; Rosenfeld, *Hi Hitler*, 91–92.

143. Wole Soyinka, *The Burden of Memory, the Muse of Forgiveness* (New York: Oxford University Press, 1999), 83.

144. Ali A. Mazrui, "Who Should Pay for Slavery?," *World Press Review* 40, no. 8 (1993): 22, as cited in Torpey, "Making Whole," 341.

145. Power, "To Suffer by Comparison," 52–66; Power, *A Problem from Hell*, xxi.

146. Conversation with John Pawlikowski.

147. Jeffrey Alexander, *Remembering the Holocaust*, 58–59; Torpey, "Making Whole," 341; Rosenfeld, *Hi Hitler*, 91–92.

148. David Cesarani, "Two Books on Genocide Today," *History Today*, http://www.historytoday.com/reviews/two-books-genocide, accessed December 21, 2015; Doris Bergen, "Challenging Uniqueness: Decentering and Recentering the Holocaust," *Journal of Genocide Research* 13, no. 1–2 (2011): 130–131; and Jürgen Matthäus, "The Precision of the Indefinite," *Journal of Genocide Research* 13, no. 1–2 (2011): 107. Bergen and Matthäus were responding to Donald Bloxham's *The Final Solution: A Genocide* (Oxford: Oxford University Press, 2009).

149. Bergen, "Challenging Uniqueness," 131.

150. Timothy Snyder, "The Fatal Fact of the Nazi-Soviet Pact," *The Guardian*, October 5, 2010, http://www.theguardian.com/commentisfree/cifamerica/2010/oct/05/holocaust-secondworldwar, accessed June 9, 2015.

151. Oren Baruch Stier, *Committed to Memory: Cultural Mediations of the Holocaust* (Amherst: University of Massachusetts Press, 2009); Noah Shenker, *Reframing Holocaust Testimony* (Bloomington: Indiana University Press, 2015).

152. Jeffrey Goldberg, "Is It Time for the Jews to Leave Europe?," *The Atlantic*, April 2015, http://www.theatlantic.com/features/archive/2015/03/is-it-time-for-the-jews-to-leave-europe/386279/, accessed March 25, 2015; Jeffrey Goldberg and Steve Inskeep, "After Attacks, Is Europe Still Safe for Jews?" podcast audio, *NPR Morning Edition*, MP3, 7:17, http://www.npr.org/2015/03/16/393284673/after-attacks-is-europe-still-safe-for-jews, accessed March 17, 2015.

Index

2Gs. *See* children of survivors
92nd Street Y, 67–68, 100

activists, 65, 67, 69, 72–75, 80–81, 86, 133, 148
Adenauer, Konrad, 44, 111, 122
Africa, 124, 133, 149–150
African Americans, 1, 34, 40, 60, 62–63, 66, 72, 74, 87–89, 132–133, 143, 169n45
Albright, Madeleine, 128–129, 149
Alexander, Jeffrey, 40, 150
Allies (World War II), 9–10, 19–20, 44, 46–47, 56, 83, 97, 111, 117–119, 124, 160n57
Alter, Robert, 39, 77, 79, 100, 114
American Academy of Jewish Research, 115
American Civil Liberties Union (ACLU), 90–91
American Jewish Committee, 54, 94
American Nazis. *See* neo-Nazis
American popular culture: effect of scholarship on, 140; Holocaust in, 2–5, 31–45, 57–61, 119, 136, 139
America's Holocaust narrative, 4–5, 26, 30–45, 57–58, 61, 82–83, 98, 101–102, 108, 113, 151
Anschluss, 112
antisemitism: American, 60–61, 73, 88, 93, 97, 110, 114, 133, 137, 140, 146; of American soldiers, 31–32; in Austria, 11; Christian, 11–12, 56–57, 68–70, 86; and Eichmann trial, 49–51, 55–56; European, 59, 104, 152–1532; in film, 34–35, 42; in literature, 31–34, 60–61; in Nazi Germany, 16, 33, 75–76, 82, 94, 102–104, 129–130, 136, 152; in Poland, 15; in postwar Germany, 44; in the Soviet Union, 79–80, 98–99; stereotyping in, 4, 88–89, 94, 131
Arabs, 24, 76, 78, 80, 89, 99
Arafat, Yasser, 90
Arendt, Hannah, 14, 27, 36, 46–56, 58–59, 61, 75, 85, 107
Argentina, 46, 50–51
assimilation, 27, 33, 40, 48, 55, 62, 64, 72, 129, 138

Atkinson, Brooks, 38
Aufbau, 48
Auschwitz-Birkenau, 19, 41, 46, 75, 77, 82, 130–131, 133, 135, 191n131; effect on theology, 64–71; in film, 42; in literature, 19, 58; memorials, 106–107; survivor testimonies, 15, 19, 30, 68; tourism, 143–144
Austria, 19, 66, 110–112, 123–124, 127

Babi Yar, 106
baby boom generation, 64, 71–76, 81, 116, 140
Bais Yaakov seminary, 145–146, 191n128
Baldwin, James, 88–89
banality of evil, 48, 50–51, 75
Bandy, Nellie, 6–7
Baraka, Amiri, 89
Barnes, Harry Elmer, 20
Barnett, Victoria, 69
Baron, Lawrence, 40, 94–95
Baron, Salo, 7–8, 10, 14–15, 49, 64, 115–116
Barraclough, Geoffrey, 44
Battle of the Bulge, 119
Bauer, Yehuda, 18, 112, 134–135, 183n16, 191n126
Beard, Charles, 20
Begin, Menachem, 42
Belgium, 106, 119, 152
Belsen. *See* Bergen-Belsen
Ben-Gurion, David, 9, 155n9
Benzaquin, Paul, 12
Berenbaum, Michael, 142–143, 182n5
Bergen, Doris, 141, 151
Bergen-Belsen, 19, 39, 58, 121–122, 133
Berlin, 2, 44, 56, 127, 166n157
Berman, Jakub, 112–113
Bettelheim, Bruno, 24–25, 28, 52–54, 58, 85
Bible, 9, 11, 65, 70
Birkenau. *See* Auschwitz-Birkenau
Bitburg controversy, 117–123, 125, 129–130
Black Power movement, 63, 88
blacks. *See* African Americans
Boder, David, 6
Bolsheviks, 129
Book of the Month Club, 32, 43

Bosnia, 124, 148–149

Boys, Mary, 67–68, 70

Brandt, Willy, 122

Broadway theater, 19–20, 25, 35, 56

Brooklyn College, 18, 116

Brown, Robert McAfee, 67–69

Browning, Christopher, 51, 75–76, 140–141, 147

Brown v. Board of Education of Topeka, Kansas, 62

Buchenwald, 6, 19, 25, 32, 82, 158n37

bureaucracy, Nazi, 18, 20–21, 50–51, 55, 75–76

bystanders, 57, 81, 83, 126

Capitol Rotunda (Washington, DC), 2, 4–5, 109

Captain Hook (fictional character), 1, 12

Cargas, James, 67, 140

Carson, Clayborne, 90

Carter, Jimmy, 98–102, 104–105, 107–110, 180n213, 182n3

Catholics, 46, 56–57, 62, 65–70, 92, 126, 128, 150

Catholic Theological Union, 115, 150

Central Historical Commission (postwar Germany), 14

Cesarani, David, 151

Chamberlin, William Henry, 20

children of survivors, 28, 62, 85–86, 124, 127–128

Christian Broadcasting Network, 133

Christian Century, 56, 87

Christian-Jewish relations, 67–69, 86–87, 121–122

Christopher, Warren, 149

Churchill, Ward, 137, 189n103

civil rights movement, 62–67, 74–75, 79, 87–91, 140, 146

Clergy and Laity Concerned with Vietnam, 65

Clinton, William "Bill" J., 107, 125, 128, 149, 153, 186n56

Cocoanut Grove fire, 12

Cohen, Beth, 26

Cold War, 45, 74, 81, 111

Cole, Tim, 40, 142–146, 191nn125–126

collaborators, 22–23, 28, 51–52, 98–99, 104, 109

Collins, Frank, 91

colonialism, 149–150

Columbia University, 7, 12, 15, 18, 22, 66, 72, 115

Commager, Henry Steele, 19–20

commemoration of the Holocaust: in Europe, 106, 117–123, 144; opposition to,
2–3, 113–117, 138, 147; religious services, 30; in the U.S., 2–5, 85, 94, 101–102, 109, 125, 140, 154

Commentary, 8, 23–24, 54, 77, 137

communism, 15, 40, 44, 49, 79, 104–108, 113, 117–118, 126, 166n157

compliance with Nazis, 15–16, 21–25, 28, 42, 53, 58, 85, 94

concentration camps, 6–7, 13–15, 19–21, 27–30, 53–55, 58, 82, 95, 101–102, 118–121, 124, 127, 133, 143–144, 170n53; in popular culture, 36–42, 59–60. See also names of individual camps

Conference on Jewish Relations, 14

Congressional Gold Medal, 120

Congress, U.S., 4, 26, 40, 73, 75–76, 99, 101, 120–121, 125

Connor, Bull, 74

Conservative Jews, 72, 81

Convention on the Prevention and Punishment of the Crime of Genocide, 44, 101

corporations' role in Holocaust, 74, 126–127

crimes against humanity, 7, 16, 33, 55, 102, 107–108, 121, 150

Cuddihy, John Murray, 134

Cultural Revolution (China), 1–2

Cuomo, Mario, 64

Czechoslovakia, 13, 41, 50, 128–129, 142, 159n45

Dachau, 19, 25, 31–32, 58, 82, 89, 91, 118, 133, 170n53

Dawidowicz, Lucy, 77, 84, 134, 160n61

death camps, 6–7, 15, 46, 49, 58–59, 84, 101, 119, 124, 126, 154, 161n73; in Bosnia, 148. See also names of individual camps

de-Judaization of the Holocaust, 102–108. See also universalization of the Holocaust

Democratic Party, U.S., 98

denial of Holocaust, 20, 90, 113, 129–132, 142, 146–147, 154

Denmark, 106, 152

deportation of Jews, 13, 16, 24, 40–41, 46, 51, 123–124, 154

de Sola Pool, David, 3

Des Pres, Terrence, 83–85

detention camps, 48–49, 53, 124

Deutscher, Isaac, 107

Diary of Anne Frank, The (book, Broadway play, and/or film), 19–20, 25, 35–41, 61, 94

diaspora, 8–9, 22–25, 53, 161n74

Diner, Hasia, 2, 30–31, 140

disabled. See handicapped, Nazi treatment of

displaced persons (DPs), 10, 14, 27, 82–86
documentation of Holocaust, 47–48, 83–84,
    95, 113–114, 123–124, 127–128, 131–132, 147; by
    Allies, 20, 158n37; by Germans, 7, 17, 20–22,
    76, 176n142; by Jews, 13–15, 17
Donat, Alexander, 52
Doneson, Judith, 94
Dorpalen, Andreas, 23
DPs. *See* displaced persons
Dubnow, Simon, 13–14

Eastern Europe, 8, 16, 20, 104–107
East Germany (German Democratic
    Republic), 44, 106. *See also* Germany
Eckardt, Alice, 67–70, 87, 134, 140
Eckardt, Roy, 66–67, 87, 134, 140, 177n153
Edwards, Ralph, 41
Egypt, 76, 79, 99
Eichmann, Adolf, 8–9, 23, 46–57, 59, 61, 74–75,
    82, 110–111
*Eichmann in Jerusalem: A Report on the
    Banality of Evil* (Arendt), 48, 107
Eisenhower, Dwight D., 7
Eisner, Jack, 96
Eizenstat, Stuart, 99–100
Eliach, Yaffa, 116
Elkins, Stanley, 57–58
Emerson, Ralph Waldo, 122
Emory University, xi, 115
Engel, David, 55, 115–116
Ericksen, Robert, 75
Esh, Saul, 24
Esquire, 90
ethnic cleansing, 124
ethnicity, 7, 47, 53, 61–64, 86, 106–107, 110, 124,
    126, 139, 141
Evans, Richard, 147
Exodus (book and/or film), 41–43, 61, 139,
    165n147, 191n131

Fackenheim, Emil, 64, 70–71, 116, 134, 140
Farrakhan, Louis, 133
Feingold, Henry, 73, 97
feminism, 58, 63–64, 72, 86, 89, 116, 169n48
Final Solution, 25, 99, 127–128; antisemitism
    in, 33, 75, 104–105; definitions, 1, 102; denial
    of, 131, 147; in Eichmann trial, 46–47, 56; in
    historical context, 15, 43; parallels with other
    situations, 74–76, 124, 137, 154; in popular
    culture, 45, 94–95; scholarship about, 15–23,
    52; uniqueness of, 7, 129–130
Fisher, Eugene, 67
Fleischner, Eva, 66–67, 70, 140
forced labor, 24, 58, 126–128, 134, 170n53

Ford, Henry, 122
Ford, Henry II, 64
foreign policy, U.S., 123–126, 149–150
former Yugoslavia, 125–126, 149, 153. *See also*
    Yugoslavia
France, 7, 18–19, 30, 35, 48–49, 53–54, 56, 78,
    100–101, 119, 126–128, 152
Frank, Anne, 19–20, 25, 35–41, 160n56. See
    also *Diary of Anne Frank, The*
Frank, Margot, 39
Frank, Otto, 25, 37–39
Frankl, Viktor, 68
Friedan, Betty, 57–58, 61, 169n48
Friedlander, Saul, 134, 141
Friedman, Philip, 13–18, 21–22, 30, 52–53, 84,
    115

Garrett, Leah, 31
gas chambers, 25, 27, 42, 78, 103, 105, 154
gay rights movement, 63–64, 133–134
Gellhorn, Martha, 31–32
gender studies, 136–137
genocide: antisemitism as motive for, 68, 74,
    77–78, 136; denial of, 20, 131–132; of Jews
    by Nazis, 4–5, 97–98, 102–103, 105, 134; in
    Library of Congress classification, 1; of
    other groups, 124–126, 134–135, 137–138, 145,
    147–151, 154
Genocide Treaty. *See* Convention on the
    Prevention and Punishment of the Crime
    of Genocide
Gentiles, 9, 43, 79, 144–145; Catholics,
    46, 56–57, 62, 65–70, 92, 126, 128, 150;
    Protestants, 13, 56–57, 68–69, 74–75, 87, 96,
    141; theologians, 10–12, 56–57, 65–71, 74–75,
    115, 140, 150
German Christians, 66, 69–70, 75, 141
German Foreign Office, 46, 75–76
Germany: American zone, 10, 14; history,
    18–19, 43, 136; post–World War II, 44–45,
    117–124, 127, 130–132; reaction to *Holocaust*
    miniseries, 95; reparations paid by, 122, 131,
    150, 155n9. *See also* East Germany; Nazi
    Germany; West Germany
Gesellschaft für deutsche Sprache, 95
ghettoes, Jewish, 8–9, 16, 21, 24, 42, 52–53,
    104, 110, 126, 143, 145; American urban, 60;
    Kovno, 13; Lodz, 66; Riga, 13; Terezin, 128;
    Warsaw, 13, 15, 24, 32–33, 52–53, 104, 113, 122
Glauber, R. H., 56
Glazer, Nathan, 2
God, post-Holocaust: in Christian theology,
    57, 65–70; in Jewish theology, 64–65, 70–71
Goldberg, Arthur, 96

Goldhagen, Daniel John, 136
Goldstein, Ellen, 99
Goodrich, Frances, 38
Gordis, Robert, 88
Gore, Al, 133
Gouri, Haim, 47
Grail (Catholic ecumenical organization), 66
Graver, Lawrence, 37
Great Britain. *See* United Kingdom
Greece, 46, 123–124
Greenberg, Irving "Yitz," 4, 30, 64, 71, 107, 140
Greenspan, Henry, 29, 83
griner (greenhorn), 26, 85
Gurs camp (France), 48–49, 53–54
Gutman, Israel, 112
Gutman, Roy, 125, 148
Gypsies. *See* Roma

Hackett, Albert, 38
Haganah, 24
handicapped, Nazi treatment of, 40, 45, 82, 103, 168n28
Haredim, 145–146, 191n128
Harper's Bazaar, 32
Harper's Magazine, 24–25
Hartman, Geoffrey, 47, 85, 94
Harvard University, 66, 117, 136
Hasidic Jews, 79, 116
Hausner, Gideon, 47, 50–53
Hayes, Peter, 14, 74, 140–141
Hebrew language, ix, 8–9, 11, 52, 157n12
Hebrew Scripture, 9, 11, 65, 70
Hebrew Union College, 72
Heidelberg, University of, 48
Herberg, Will, 62
heroism, Jewish, 14, 16, 22–23, 28, 33, 53, 85
Hersey, John, 32–33
Heschel, Abraham Joshua, 64–65, 78, 140
Heym, Stefan, 31
Hilberg, Raul, 2, 17–25, 28, 30, 48, 52–54, 75, 82–85, 120, 134
Himmelfarb, Milton, 77, 87
Himmler, Heinrich, 20, 25, 46
Hiroshima, 32, 83, 100–101
Hispanics, 60, 63
historicization of the Holocaust, 129–131, 139
historiography, 20, 53, 73, 102, 129, 140
Hitler, Adolf: and antisemitism, 68–71, 84, 88–89, 105, 130–131, 136, 151; era, 9, 122; military actions, 87, 112; regime, 17, 20, 75; subordinates, 25, 46–57
Hobson, Laura, 33–34
Hochhuth, Rolf, 56
Holland. *See* Netherlands, the

Hollywood, 19, 35, 42, 45, 94, 110
Holocaust: capitalization of word, 2, 10–12, 56, 138; definitions, 1–2, 50, 56, 102–103; denial, 20, 90, 113, 129–132, 142, 146–147, 154; effect on American Jews, 2–3, 64–65, 70–74, 76–82, 96–98; etymology (as burnt offering), 11; in film, 2, 19, 34–35, 37, 40–45, 60–61, 94–95, 110, 143–144, 183n9; in literature, 1, 31–37, 41–42, 95, 110; narrative, 4–5, 26, 30–45, 57–58, 61, 82–83, 98, 101–102, 108, 113, 151; other names for, 8–11, 30, 95, 102; studies, 2–5, 13–25, 48, 68, 74–75, 84, 102, 114–115, 135–137, 142, 145–147, 151; in television, 2, 45, 47, 93–95, 100, 143, 155n7; in theater, 25, 35–41, 56–57, 60–61, 94–95, 169n43; use of word in context of Nazi Final Solution, 1–13, 56, 169n43; use of word in other contexts, 1–2, 12
Holocaust (TV miniseries), 93–95, 100
Holocaust analogies, 78, 132–134, 148–154
"Holocaust and Heroism," 11, 22
Holocaust Council. *See* President's Commission on the Holocaust (later United States Holocaust Memorial Council)
Holocaust denial, 20, 90, 113, 129–132, 142, 146–147, 154
Holocaust Memorial Day, 2, 4, 109
Holocaust memorials, 1–2, 4, 99, 113–114; at Auschwitz, 106–107; in Berlin, 2; in Israel, 10, 15; in New Haven, CT, 142; in New York City, 2–3, 102; in the 1950s and 1960s, 2–4, 10, 14; in the Soviet Union, 106; at the Warsaw ghetto, 122; in Washington, DC, 1–2, 4, 98–105, 109. *See also* United States Holocaust Memorial Museum (USHMM)
Holocaust museums, 1–2, 4, 113; in Illinois, 150; in Israel, 15. *See also* United States Holocaust Memorial Museum (USHMM)
Holocaust narrative, American, 4–5, 26, 30–45, 57–58, 61, 82–83, 98, 101–102, 108, 113, 151
Holocaust, overemphasis on, 113–117, 121–122, 139–140, 148, 150
Holocaust studies, 2–5, 13–25, 48, 68, 74–75, 84, 102, 114–115, 135–137, 142, 145–147, 151
Holocaust survivors: and accountability of WWII institutions, 126–128; documentation by, 13–14; encounters with Christian theologians, 66, 71; and Holocaust commemoration, 2–3, 102–105, 125–126; and Holocaust deniers, 132, 147; interviews with, 6, 15, 17, 26, 28–29, 83–85, 101, 143, 176nn141–142, 190n119; in Israel, 3,

143; memoirs, 6, 17, 29–30, 48, 68, 83–84; non-Jewish, 2, 102–103; in popular culture, 32–33, 41–43, 60, 143; reaction to Bitburg controversy, 121; reaction to Hannah Arendt, 53–56; prominent, 94, 96, 100, 110, 112, 116, 125; silencing of, 28–30, 83, 85; testimonies of, 14, 17, 21, 26, 47–48, 82–86, 135, 144, 160n61, 162n101, 176n142; in the U.S., 2–3, 25–31, 90–93

Holocaust, uniqueness of, 14, 50, 102–108, 129, 132–138, 147–151, 181n230

homosexuals. *See* gay rights movement

Horowitz, Sara, 35, 42

House Un-American Activities Committee, 40

Hungary, 19, 46, 104, 106, 180n217

Hyman, Paula, 114

Iacocca, Lee, 64

identity politics, 61–64, 79, 97, 100

immigration of Jews: to Israel, 3, 41, 80, 143; to Palestine, 41–42; to U.S., 8, 26–27, 30, 73, 96–97

incomprehensibility of the Holocaust, 47, 134–135

International Committee of the Red Cross, 126–128

International Scholars Conference on the German Church Struggle and the Holocaust, 66

interviews with Holocaust survivors, 6, 15, 17, 26, 28–29, 83–85, 101, 143, 176nn141–142, 190n119. *See also* oral histories; testimonies of Holocaust survivors

Iraq, 76

Irving, David, 146–147

Isaac, Jules, 68

isolationism, 73, 97–98

Israel: Holocaust commemoration in, 56; Holocaust survivors in, 3; immigration to, 3, 41, 80, 143; independence, 9, 24, 42, 99; political policies, 153–154; reparations to, 150; significance for Jews, 86–87, 116, 137; Six Day War, 65, 69, 74, 76–80, 86–88, 100, 138–139; and the United Nations, 90; and U.S. policy, 98–99, 101–102, 137; and war crimes trials, 9, 46–57, 111

Israel Defense Forces, 24

Israeli Declaration of Independence, 10

Italian Americans, 63–64

Italy, 19, 30, 46

Jackson, Robert H., 47, 182n3

Jacobs, Paul, 56

Jaldati, Lin, 39

Jaspers, Karl, 107

Jerusalem, 8–9, 14, 23, 46–50, 54–56, 116

Jewish-Christian relations, 67–69, 86–87, 121–122

Jewish community, 61, 100, 107, 137; and African Americans, 87–90; and Carter, 98–100; diplomatic efforts, 73, 80, 95–98, 128; leaders, 3, 40, 72–73, 81, 86–87, 91–93, 95–100, 116, 128, 153; in New Haven, CT, 142; in New York, 2–3, 62–63; in Palestine, 9; revitalization, 64, 72, 116, 140; and the Six Day War, 77–79; in the Soviet Union, 79–81; spiritual leaders, 64–65; support for Holocaust commemoration, 3–4, 102, 113–117, 138–140

Jewish Councils. *See Judenräte*

Jewish Cultural Reconstruction, 49

Jewish Currents, 43

Jewish Film Advisory Committee, 40

Jewish history, 8, 11–12, 17, 19, 23, 79, 89; academic study of, 7–8, 70, 114–115

Jewish identity, 19–20, 35, 39–41, 65, 77–80, 89, 106, 116, 126, 130, 153

Jewish languages, ix, 8–9, 11, 13, 26, 33, 52, 157n12

Jewish leadership: in Europe, 16, 21–23, 51–53, 152; in the U.S., 3, 40, 72–73, 81, 86–87, 91–93, 95–100, 116, 128, 153

Jewishness. *See* Jewish identity

Jewish organizations, American, 26, 30, 72, 92, 96–98, 116–117, 121, 128, 138–141. *See also names of individual organizations*

Jewish Quarterly, 23

Jewish ritual, 64, 72, 116

Jewish Social Studies, 115

Jewish soldiers, 31–32, 34, 163n105

Jewish studies, 64, 72, 113–116, 139, 142

Jewish Theological Seminary, 72, 77, 100

Jews Against Genocide (JAG), 148

John XXIII (pope), 68

John Paul II (pope), 107, 128

Johnson, Lyndon B., 75

Jones, LeRoi. *See* Baraka, Amiri

Jordan, 76

Journal of Ecumenical Studies, 66

Journal of Historical Review, 131

Journal of Modern History, 19, 23

Journal of the History of Ideas, 19

Judaism (journal), 52, 70, 100

Judenräte, 16, 21, 23, 51–53

Kaes, Anton, 95

Kanin, Garson, 37–39

Katz, Steven, 135–136
Kazan, Elia, 34
Kennedy, John F., 62, 75
Kennedy, Joseph P., Sr., 62
Kerr, Walter, 38
Khmer Rouge, 1
Khurbn (utter destruction), 8, 10, 30, 102
Kindertransport, 66
King, Martin Luther, Jr., 65, 75; Papers
    Project, 90
kippot, 72, 152
Kluger, Ruth, 29
Kohl, Helmut, 117–118, 121–123
Kohner, Hannah, 41
Kohut, George, 12
Korczak, Janusz, 15–16
Kosovo, 149
Kremlin. *See* Soviet Union
Kristallnacht, 68, 130, 133
Kubrick, Stanley, 57, 59–61
Kushner, Tony, 72–73

labor camps, 127, 170n53
Landsmanschaftn, 30
Lang, Berel, 148
Langer, Lawrence, 28, 94
languages: Greek, 11; Hebrew, ix, 8–9, 11, 52,
    157n12; Ladino, ix, 11; Yiddish, ix, 8–9, 11,
    13, 26, 33, 52
Latvia, 104
Latvian Americans, 104
Lawson, Tom, 57
Lend-Lease program, 97
Lester, Julius, 88–89
Levi, Primo, 29–30
Levy's Real Jewish Rye, 62–63, 170n62
libel, 146–147, 191nn130–131
liberation of camps, 6–7, 14, 29, 31–32, 39,
    82–83, 101–102, 107, 143, 149, 158n37, 190n119.
    See also names of individual camps
Library of Congress (LOC) subject
    classification, 1, 81–82
Lieberman, Saul H., 77
Lifton, Robert Jay, 83–84, 100–101
Linz camp, 19. *See also* Mauthausen-Gusen
Lithuania, 13
Lithuanian Americans, 104
Littell, Franklin, 10, 66–67, 140
liturgies: Catholic, 57, 65; Jewish, 114
Locke, Hubert, 66–67, 70, 140
London Conference on Nazi Gold, 128
Longerich, Peter, 147
Los Angeles Times, 12, 43
Lottman, Herbert, 101

Lubetkin-Zuckerman, Zvia, 53
Lublin / Majdanek camp, 19, 104
Lumet, Sidney, 57, 60–61

Maier, Charles, 117, 121–122, 130
Mailer, Norman, 31
Malmedy, Belgium, 119
Mann, Abby, 45
Marquette University, 66, 115
Marrus, Michael, 49, 97, 107, 134
martyrdom, 22–23, 71, 106, 114
Matthäus, Jürgen, 151
Mauriac, François, 30, 100
Mauthausen-Gusen (near Linz, Austria), 41.
    See also Linz
Mazuri, Ali, 133
McCarthy, Joseph, 40
memoirs of survivors, 6, 17, 29–30, 48, 68,
    83–84
memorials to Holocaust victims. *See*
    Holocaust memorials
memory, 4, 14, 43, 52, 61, 107, 138,
    153–154; "boom," 124–129; collective,
    65; historical, 94, 117, 121–122, 147, 151;
    social, 94. *See also* remembrance of the
    Holocaust
methodology for Holocaust research, 14–17,
    83–84
Middle East, 76–79, 98–99, 154
Milgram, Stanley, 57–59, 61
Miller, Arthur, 57, 60–61
Miller, Merle, 31–32
Mineo, Sal, 42
Mitchum, Robert, 34
Mondale, Walter, 109
Monroe, Marilyn, 60
Morgenthau, Henry, 96
Morison, Samuel Eliot, 19–20
Morrison, Toni, 133
Morrow, Lance, 122
Morse, Arthur, 72–73, 95, 97, 101–102
Moses, A. Dirk, 147
Muslims, 133, 152
My Lai massacre, 59, 74

names for survivors, 26–27
Nasser, Gamal Abdel, 76
National Association for the Advancement
    of Colored People (NAACP), 89
National Broadcasting Company (NBC), 1,
    93, 100
National Conference of Catholic Bishops,
    U.S.A., 67
National Conference on New Politics, 87

National Council of Churches (NCC), 87
National Socialism (Nazism), 18, 43–44, 76, 102, 127, 131. *See also* Nazi Germany
Nation, The, 44
Native Americans, 62–63, 137
NATO (North Atlantic Treaty Organization), 149
Nazi Germany: attempted genocide of Jews, 1–2, 9–11, 14, 19–20, 25, 51, 56, 97–99, 102, 107–109, 129–130, 134–136, 154; bureaucracy, 18, 20–21, 50–51, 75–76; and Christian churches, 56, 66–67; concentration camps, 13–14, 27–28, 58; crimes against humanity, 16, 107–108, 124; death camps, 15, 19, 58–59; era, 7, 60–61, 152–153; ghetto life, 13, 145–146; *Judenräte*, 16, 51–52; persecution of non-Jewish groups, 23, 102–103, 105, 109–110, 137; in popular culture, 31–45, 60–61, 93–95; SS (Schutzstaffel), 20, 23, 25, 46, 74–75, 104, 119–121; totalitarianism, 49–50, 151; war crimes, 12–13, 20, 55, 110–111, 132 *See also* National Socialism (Nazism)
Nazi Party (National Socialist German Workers' Party), 76, 102
Neier, Aryeh, 91
neo-Nazis, 90–93, 99, 131
Netherlands, the, 12, 19, 35–40, 46, 56
Neumann, Franz, 18
Neusner, Jacob, 114
New Haven, CT, 142
Newman, Paul, 42
New School for Social Research, 14
New York Daily News, 38
New Yorker, 32, 48, 54, 56, 85
New York Herald Tribune, 38
New York Post, 38
New York Times, 2, 72, 89, 122; advertisement, 121; arts and culture coverage, 37–38, 57, 60, 63, 101; best-seller list, 31–32, 136; columns, 99, 129; letters, 3, 87; *Magazine*, 88, 106–107; use of word "Holocaust," 10, 12, 56
New York World-Telegram and Sun, 38
Nigeria, 149–150
Night (Wiesel), 30, 67, 100
Nixon, Richard M., 76
Nobel Prize, 12–13, 100, 149–150
Nolte, Ernst, 129–130
Nora, Pierre, 126
normalization of the Holocaust, 129–131
Normandy landing (D-Day), 117
Novick, Peter, 109, 133, 138–148
numbers of Holocaust victims, 3, 9, 19, 51–52, 78, 100–107, 109–113, 133, 141, 182nn3–5, 183n18

Nuremberg trials, 1, 7, 15, 17, 45–47, 50, 55, 61, 122–123, 182n3

obedience studies, 57–59, 170n54
Obrecht, Peggy, 68–69
Ofer, Dalia, 136–137
olah (sacrifice), 11
Olivier, Laurence, 110, 183n9
opposition to Holocaust commemoration, 2–3
optimistic portrayal of the Holocaust, 32, 37–41
Oradour-sur-Glane, France, 119
oral histories, 17, 84–85. *See also* interviews with Holocaust survivors; testimonies of Holocaust survivors
Organization of African Unity, 150
Orthodox Jews, 3, 15, 71, 145–146, 191n128
overemphasis on Holocaust, 113–117, 121–122, 139–140, 148, 150
Oyneg Shabbes, 13, 52
Ozick, Cynthia, 38, 90

Palestine, 8–9, 24, 39, 41–43, 76–77, 89, 98, 131, 153–154
Palestine Liberation Organization (PLO), 76–77, 90, 98
Palestine Post, 12
"paper walls," 73, 97
particularism, Jewish, 39, 107, 112
passivity ascribed to European Jews, 15–16, 21–25, 28, 42, 53, 78–79, 85, 96, 104–105
Pawlikowski, John, 69, 71, 107, 150
Peck, Gregory, 34
People for the Ethical Treatment of Animals (PETA), 1, 133
perpetrators, Nazi, 6, 70, 84, 111, 117–127, 151; documentation of, 15, 21; in Eichmann trial, 46–47; interaction with victims, 16, 21–22, 28; and *Judenräte*, 16, 21, 23, 51–53; SS (Schutzstaffel), 20, 23, 25, 46, 74–75, 104, 119–121
Peter Pan (televised stage production), 1, 12
Pick-Goslar, Hannah Elisabeth, 39
Pius XII (pope), 56–57, 69
Plath, Sylvia, 57–58, 61, 169n46
Poland: 1944 revolt, 24, 181n230; antisemitism in, 15; documentary sources, 52; government, 105–107, 112–113; Jews, 7, 9, 13, 15, 32, 52–53,106–107, 113; non-Jews, 104–105, 107, 109–110, 112–113, 134, 181n230; war crimes trials, 50; war memorials, 106–107, 122; Warsaw ghetto uprising, 15, 24, 32–33, 53, 113

Polish American Congress, 104
Polish Americans, 104, 107
political aspects of Holocaust
    commemoration, 98–108, 117–125
Power, Samantha, 132, 149
POWs. *See* prisoners of war
Prell, Riv-Ellen 65
Preminger, Otto, 41
President's Commission on the Holocaust
    (later United States Holocaust Memorial
    Council), 100–107, 109–110, 180n213, 182n3,
    186n56. *See also* United States Holocaust
    Memorial Museum (USHMM)
prisoners of war (POWs), 19, 24, 46, 83,
    109–110, 119–120, 124, 137
Protestants, 13, 56–57, 68–69, 74–75, 87,
    96, 141
protest movements, 61–67, 71–77, 79–81,
    86–93, 120–121, 140, 146, 148
Pulitzer Prize, 32, 35, 132, 148

rabbis, 2–4, 9–10, 12, 30, 64, 71–72, 77, 81,
    86–88, 92, 114, 116, 142
Rabinowitz, Dorothy, 47, 93–94
Ravensbrück, 32, 170n53
Reagan, Ronald, 107, 117–122, 125, 133, 185n43
Red Cross, 126–128
Reform Jews, 72, 87
refugees, 27, 34, 41–42, 48, 73, 85, 121, 125, 129
refusniks, 80
remembrance of the Holocaust, 4, 109, 117,
    126, 138
reparations, 122, 127, 131, 147, 149–150, 155n9
rescue of Jews, 41–43, 72–74, 139, 144
resistance by Jews, 10, 15–16, 21–25, 29, 42,
    52–54, 94, 113, 145–146
response of Americans to the Holocaust,
    72–74, 78, 95–98, 102, 186n56
revisionism, 20, 131
Rich, Frank, 94, 129
Ringelblum, Emanuel, 13, 15, 52
Ringelheim, Joan, 136
Rittner, Carol, 68–69, 140
Roback, A. A., 23
Robertson, Pat, 133
Roma (Gypsies), 2, 16, 19, 103–105, 119, 137
Roman Catholics. *See* Catholics
Roosevelt, Eleanor, 35
Roosevelt, Franklin D., 73–74, 95–97, 173n101
Rosenberg, Alfred, 181n221
Rosenberg, Ethel and Julius, 40
Rosenberg, Hans, 18–19
Rosenfeld, Alvin, 38, 94
Rosenfeld, Gavriel, 150

Roth, John, 67, 70, 74, 115, 140
Roth, Philip, 43
Rubenstein, Richard, 64–65, 74, 140
Ruether, Rosemary Radford, 67
Russia, 12, 24, 110. *See also* Soviet Union
Rwanda, 124

sacrifice, 11–12
Safire, William, 99
Saint John the Divine, Cathedral of,
    70–71
Saudi Arabia, 76, 90, 99
Schindler's List (film), 138, 143–144, 148
Schlesinger, Arthur M., Jr., 117
Schleunes, Karl, 75, 140
Schneerson, Isaac, 14
Schoenfeld, Gabriel, 137
Scholem, Gershom, 7, 49, 54
Schorsch, Ismar, 81, 94, 114, 135–136
Schwarzschild, Steven, 100
Second Vatican Council. *See* Vatican II
Segev, Tom, 111–112, 183n15
Sellers, Peter, 59–60
Semprun, Jorge, 6
Shanker, Albert, 88
Sharett, Moshe, 9
Shaw, Irwin, 31–32
Shenker, Noah, 151
Shirer, William, 43–45, 166n157
Shoah, 9, 11, 66–67, 102, 126
Shoat Yehudei Polin (booklet), 9
Shukeiri, Ahmad, 76–77
Siegel, Mark, 99
silencing: of Holocaust survivors, 28–30, 83,
    85; of Soviet Jews, 79–81
Sinai, 76, 79
Singer, Isaac Bashevis, 101
Sinti (Roma), 2, 102–103, 137
Six Day War, 65, 69, 74, 76–80, 86–88, 100,
    138–139
Sklare, Marshall, 78–79
Skokie, IL, 90–93, 99
slave labor (in Europe). *See* forced labor
slavery (of Africans and African Americans),
    1, 57–58, 133, 143, 149
Slavs, 110, 137
slogans, 80–81, 153
Smith, Elwin, 66
Snyder, Timothy, 112–113, 151
social ethics, 69, 71
Sontag, Susan, 47
Soviet Jewry, 79–82, 116
Soviet Union, 20, 24, 44–45, 59, 78–81, 98–99,
    105–110, 19–130, 137

Soyinka, Wole, 149–150
Spielberg, Steven, 138, 143–144
SS (Schutzstaffel), 20, 23, 25, 46, 74–75, 104,
  119–121
Stalin, Joseph, 12, 20, 104, 113
Stalinism, 49, 51, 112–113, 151
Stannard, David, 137–138
State Department, U.S., 73, 96–97, 149–150
Steiner, George, 70
Steinweis, Alan, 149
stereotypes of Jews, 4, 88–89, 94, 131
Stier, Oren, 151
Stone, John, 40
Student Nonviolent Coordinating
  Committee (SNCC), 89
supersessionism, 11
Supreme Court, U.S., 62, 91, 96, 191n130
survivors. *See* Holocaust survivors
Switzerland, 126–127
synagogues, 3, 8, 35, 72, 80, 114, 152
Syria, 76, 79

T-4 program, 103
Talmud, 77, 144
Taubman, Howard, 60
Taylor, Telford, 7
television, 2, 41, 45, 47, 93–95, 100, 120, 143,
  148, 155n7, 165n147
Temple (Jerusalem), 8, 156n10
Terezin (Czechoslovakia), 13, 128, 142, 159n45
testimonies of Holocaust survivors, 14,
  17, 21, 26, 47–48, 82–86, 135, 144, 160n61,
  162n101, 176n142. *See also* interviews with
  Holocaust survivors
textbooks, 19–20, 84
theologians, 2, 48, 86–87, 134–135, 172n90;
  Christian, 10–12, 56–57, 65–71, 74–75, 115,
  140, 150; Jewish, 64–71
Third Reich: administration, 75–76,
  122–123; genocide of Jews, 13, 18–19, 25,
  103–104, 112, 136; and the handicapped,
  82, 103; historians' approach to, 141; and
  Holocaust deniers, 131; in popular culture,
  43, 61, 93–94; supporters of, 66, 120. *See also*
  Hitler, Adolf; Nazi Germany
Time, 94, 122
Torpey, John, 132, 149
totalitarianism, 4, 49–50, 52, 55, 151
translation, 10–12, 47
trauma, 2, 7, 40, 77, 83–86, 138, 145, 163n105
Treblinka, 82, 112–113
Trevor-Roper, Hugh, 23, 48
trivialization of the Holocaust, 94–95, 116,
  121, 129–133, 137, 142–144

Truman, Harry S., 47
Twentieth Century–Fox, 34

Ukrainian Americans, 104
Ukrainian Anti-Defamation League, 104
Ultra-Orthodox Jews, 145–146, 191n128
unaffiliated Jews, 77–78
Union of Soviet Socialist Republics (USSR).
  See Soviet Union
Union Theological Seminary, 67–69, 87
uniqueness of the Holocaust, 14, 50, 102–108,
  129, 132–138, 147–151, 181n230
United Aid Committee for the Jews of
  Poland, 9
United Jewish Appeal, 41, 77, 96, 165n142
United Kingdom, 78, 97, 128, 146
United Nations (UN), 76, 79–80, 90, 123, 128,
  149
United States Army, 6–7, 18, 32, 34
United States Holocaust Memorial Council.
  See President's Commission on the
  Holocaust (later United States Holocaust
  Memorial Council)
United States Holocaust Memorial Museum
  (USHMM), 1–2, 4, 125, 142, 150, 186n57,
  190n119; and Carter, 98–102, 104–105,
  107–110, 180n213, 182n3; and Clinton, 125,
  186n56; critique of, 138, 142–145, 191n125;
  interfaith programs, 68–69; number of
  visitors, 1; and Reagan, 118, 125
universalization of the Holocaust, 3, 33,
  37–43, 45, 112, 135, 144, 150. *See also* de-
  Judaization of the Holocaust
Uris, Leon, 41–44, 139, 191n131

van Pelt, Robert Jan, 147
Vatican, 56–57, 126, 128
Vatican II, 56–57, 65, 68–69, 72, 86
veterans, American, 118–121
victims of the Holocaust: blaming, 66,
  84, 104–105; definitions, 109–113, 119–120;
  in Eichmann trial, 47–53; interactions
  with perpetrators, 16, 21–22, 28; label
  for survivors, 26–28, 85; non-Jews, 2, 16,
  102–113; numbers of, 3, 52, 105–113; in
  popular culture, 31–45; prominent, 100;
  restitution for, 126–128; strengths of, 83, 85;
  as witnesses, 13, 17
Vietnam War, 3, 59, 63–65, 74–75, 81, 86, 101,
  140
Vonnegut, Kurt, 57–58, 61

Waffen SS, 119–120
Waldheim, Kurt, 123–124

Wallant, Edward Lewis, 60
Wall Street Journal, 47, 93–94
Walser, Martin, 130
Wannsee Conference, 111
Warburg, Felix, 96
war crimes trials, 19, 95, 132, 147; Eichmann, 8–9, 12–13, 23, 46–56, 61, 82; Nuremberg, 1, 7, 15, 17, 45–47, 50, 55, 61, 122–123, 182n3
war criminals, 45, 50, 55, 75–76, 104, 110–111, 117–124, 170n53
Warsaw ghetto uprising, 15, 24, 32–33, 53, 113
Washington Post, 12, 93, 129, 185n43
Watergate, 75, 117, 140
Wayne State University, 66, 115
Weitzman, Lenore, 136–137
Weizmann, Chaim, 9, 130–131
Weizsäcker, Richard von, 122–123
Westerbork camp, 36
West Germany (Federal Republic of Germany), 44, 55, 111, 118, 122–123. *See also* Germany
White Citizens Councils, 146
White House, U.S., 73, 76, 96–105, 108–110, 117–121, 182n3, 182n5
Wiesel, Elie, 12–13, 64, 67–70, 74, 100–103, 116, 134–135, 141, 149; books, 30, 67, 80–81, 100–101; and Carter, 110, 180n213; and Clinton, 125–126, 149, 153; Elie Wiesel Foundation for Humanity, 68; Presidential Commission on the Holocaust (later United States Holocaust Memorial Council), 100–101, 105–107, 110; and Reagan, 120–121, 185n43; spokesperson for survivors, 27, 94, 100–103, 110, 125; and Wiesenthal, 100–101, 112, 183n15

Wiesenthal, Simon, 100, 110–113, 141, 183n9
Winter, Jay, 126
witnesses: in Eichmann trial, 47–48, 53, 82–83; in Lipstadt trial, 147; in Nuremberg tribunal, 17
witnessing. *See* testimonies of Holocaust survivors
Wolf, Arnold, 142
Wolfert, Ira, 31
women's movement, 58, 63–64, 72, 86, 89, 116, 169n48
World Jewish Congress, 10
World Zionist Organization, 9
Wright, Gordon, 24
Wyman, David, 73, 95–96

Yad Vashem, 10–11, 15, 22–24, 53, 68, 133
Yad Vashem Bulletin, 52
Yad Vashem Studies, 10
Yale University, 47, 58, 74, 136, 142
Yerushalmi, Yosef Hayim, 186n58
Yeshiva University, 3–4, 71
Yiddish, ix, 8–9, 11, 13, 26, 33, 52
YIVO Institute for Jewish Research, 14
Yom HaShoah, 30, 56
Yom Kippur, 78, 114
Yom Kippur War, 79, 90
Young, James, 3, 61, 101, 151
Young, Robert, 34
Yugoslavia, 106, 123–124; former Yugoslavia, 125–126, 149, 153

Zionists, 8–9, 22, 39, 48, 87, 89–90, 98–99, 113, 130, 137
Zuckerman, Yitzhak, 53

About the Author

DEBORAH LIPSTADT is Dorot Professor of Modern Jewish History and Holocaust Studies at Emory University. She is the author of *Beyond Belief: The American Press and the Coming of the Holocaust, 1933–1945*; *Denying the Holocaust: The Growing Assault on Truth and Memory*; *History on Trial: My Day in Court with a Holocaust Denier*; and *The Eichmann Trial*.

CPSIA information can be obtained
at www.ICGtesting.com
Printed in the USA
LVHW051933020919
629654LV00014B/1092/P

9 780813 564760